ELEPHANT'S LEG II: CREATIVITY IN ACTION

CRAIG HIGHT AND MARIO MINICHIELLO

COMMON GROUND

First published in 2025
as part of the **Design Principles and Practices Book Imprint**

Common Ground Research Networks
2001 South First Street, Suite 202
University of Illinois Research Park
Champaign, IL
61820

Library of Congress Cataloging-in-Publication Data

Names: Hight, Craig, editor. | Minichiello, Mario, editor.
Title: The Elephant's Leg II: Creativity in Action / edited by Craig Hight, Mario Minichiello.
Description: Champaign, IL : Common Ground Research Networks, 2025. | Includes bibliographical references and index. | Summary: "This book is a response to the question asked by incoming students of the Creative Industries sector: 'what can I do in the Creative Industries'. This volume is designed to provide a source of inspiration to readers in imagining their own futures within fields such as musical performance, media production, drawing and illustration, journalism, public relations, filmmaking, design, documentary, dramatic performance, virtual reality and others covered in these chapters"-- Provided by publisher.
Identifiers: LCCN 2021014172 (print) | LCCN 2021014173 (ebook) | ISBN 9781966214809(hardback) | ISBN 9781966214823 (paperback) | ISBN 9781966214816 (adobe pdf)
Subjects: LCSH: Cultural industries--Vocational guidance. | Cultural industries--Study and teaching (Higher)--Australia--Newcastle (N.S.W.) | University of Newcastle. School of Creative Industries.
Classification: LCC HD9999.C9472 E44 2021 (print) | LCC HD9999.C9472 (ebook) | DDC 384.023--dc23
LC record available at https://lccn.loc.gov/2021014172
LC ebook record available at https://lccn.loc.gov/2021014173

ISBN: 978-1-966214-80-9 (HBK)
ISBN: 978-1-966214-82-3 (PBK)
ISBN: 978-1-966214-81-6 (PDF)
DOI: 10.18848/978-1-966214-81-6/CGP

CONTENTS

Introduction:
Creativity in Action

Craig Hight and Mario Minichiello

The first book in this series, *The Elephant's Leg: Adventures in the Creative Industries* (2021), focused on people. It collected largely autobiographical accounts of individuals' journeys and drives into becoming part of the creative industries. The agenda of this first volume was to encourage readers to consider the diversity of pathways they might choose toward discovering their own true vocations.

This second volume focuses on practice; it presents creative research projects and collaborators reporting and reflecting on their experience of creative research, defined very broadly. These projects offer a snapshot of creative research affiliated with The Future Arts, Science and Technology Laboratory (FASTlab) a collaborative research hub at the University of Newcastle. This brings together leading thinkers, creatives, and industry partners to explore innovative solutions for real-world challenges by merging human emotion, creativity, and technology. FASTlab aims to drive change through creative methodologies and nontraditional collaboration. In the words of its director, Paul Egglestone,

> we explore the potential of human emotion, happiness, and play; open doors for non-traditional collaborators; and commercialize lateral thinking. As a translational research hub, FASTlab provides opportunities for community and industry partners to participate in research projects that provide tangible outcomes and solutions to real-world problems quickly. … The team has focused on building a vibrant culture of 'learning by doing,' creating several pathways for organizations, researchers, and creatives to engage with the lab and each other. Working with external research partners using a proprietary blended learning model, FASTlab has developed a low-cost series of concentrated learning events that enable students and researchers to see the positive impact that they are making through research and development, ensuring they are part of a process of change as well as developing their learning and experience. (Egglestone 2022)

The core imperative of this research entity has been to engage in complex, real-world "wicked problems" particularly through transdisciplinary and multi-disciplinary paradigms, a commitment especially to rapid prototyping to develop and work through potential solutions, and experimental responses to real-world prompts. Some of these projects engage directly with smart city initiatives which have been a feature of Australian urban planning in the last fifteen years. The projects collected here demonstrate the application of teams of staff (academic and technical) and students (higher degrees by research [HDRs] and PhDs), creative technologists, small-to-medium enterprises (SMEs), freelancers, and NGOs working together to address a range of research and development needs, often not met by other disciplines.

The broader context for these projects is a vibrant creative industries sector throughout the Hunter region within New South Wales.[1] FASTlab leans into the creative cultural precinct in the center of Newcastle where it is located but also leverages proximity to a variety of key areas of creative and cultural activity, such as the Clyde Street Precinct (Egglestone 2022; Egglestone et al. 2022).[2]

The projects within this collection cover a range of perspectives and experiences on aspects such as the application of research methodologies, the specifics of practice, the advantages and challenges of engaging in practice-based research, relationships with external partners, what it means to work in multidisciplinary teams, the value of bringing different knowledge domains together, and the broader possibilities of the contribution of innovative research. Collectively they highlight that creative practice and research are often one of the same or co-dependent processes that ensure novel and impactful outcomes.

The infographic (by FASTLab designer Carl Morgan) in the following pages offers a snapshot of methodologies deployed through FASTlab projects since its inception in 2018. Many of these are showcased in the creative research projects collated in this volume.

This volume is organized into five sections, showcasing different parts of a broader agenda focused on creativity and innovation, directed toward real-world problems, all encompassed under the FASTlab banner. The first section covers examples of collaborative problem-solving with external partners, projects

---

[1.] See Hunter Creative Industries — Final Report, available at https://hciss.newcastle.edu.au/hci/wp-content/uploads/sites/291/2019/03/Hunter-Creative-Industries-Final-ReportV5-1.pdf and McIntyre et al. (2023).

[2.] Located in Hamilton North, this is an industrial warehouse complex repurposed as artist-run spaces and a cluster of start-up businesses. See https://www.youtube.com/watch?v=2VHyW475CYo and https://www.50clydestart.com.au/about.

CREATIVE METHODS
with FASTlab Examples

1. Participatory + Collaborative Methods

Participatory Action Research (PAR)
Collaborative Inquiry
Co-Design and Co-Creation
Sandpit Workshops

2. Visual + Creative Expression

PhotoVoice
Digital Storytelling
Art-Based Research
Visual Methods

---

1. PARTICIPATORY + COLLABORATIVE METHODS

Participatory Action Research (PAR):
Engaging stakeholders in all phases of the research process.

Collaborative Inquiry:
Participants collaboratively explore and investigate issues of interest.
Sustainnovation Challenge

Co-Design and Co-Creation:
Stakeholders are actively involved in the design process. The House We Build, Safer Spaces for Women and Girls

Sandpit Workshops:
Intensive, interdisciplinary workshops aimed at generating innovative solutions. RAPID

2. VISUAL + CREATIVE EXPRESSION

PhotoVoice:
Using photography to document and discuss community issues.

Digital Storytelling:
Combining storytelling with digital media

Art-Based Research:
Using artistic methods to explore research questions.

Visual Methods:
Utilizing visual techniques like drawing, mapping, and video analysis.

3. Narrative + Storytelling
Narrative Inquiry
Appreciative Inquiry (AI)
Creative Writing and Poetry

4. Experiential + Immersive Approaches
Walk Shops
Walking Interviews
Ethnography
Performance-Based Research
Pop-Up Labs

5. Game-Based + Playful Techniques
Gamification and Serious Games
LEGO® SERIOUS PLAY®

3. NARRATIVE + STORYTELLING

Narrative Inquiry: Exploring personal stories and experiences.

Appreciative Inquiry (AI): Focusing on strengths and positive aspects.

Creative Writing and Poetry: Using writing and poetry as research tools.

4. EXPERIENTIAL + IMMERSIVE APPROACHES

Walk Shops: Conducting workshops while walking.

Ethnography: Immersing in the culture and environment of the study subjects.

Performance-Based Research: Using performance arts to explore research questions.

Pop-Up Labs: Temporary setups for real-world experiments and engagements.

5. GAME-BASED + PLAYFUL TECHNIQUES

Gamification and Serious Games: Applying game design elements in non-game contexts. The House We Build

LEGO® SERIOUS PLAY®: Using LEGO bricks to facilitate creative thinking and problem-solving.

6. Future-Oriented + Strategic Planning
Futures Workshops
Scenario Planning
Backcasting

7. Hands-On + Maker-Centered Methods
Design Thinking
Prototyping

8. Reflective + Sensemaking Practices
Sensemaking Sessions
Reflective Journaling
Heuristic Inquiry

6. FUTURE-ORIENTED + STRATEGIC PLANNING

Futures Workshops:
Exploring potential futures through creative methods.

Scenario Planning:
Developing and analyzing potential future scenarios.

Backcasting:
Planning backwards from a desired future to the present.

7. HANDS-ON + MAKER-CENTERED METHODS

Design Thinking:
A structured, human-centered approach to innovation.

Prototyping:
Creating physical or digital models to test ideas. (several of the RAPID projects)

8. REFLECTIVE + SENSEMAKING PRACTICES

Sensemaking Sessions:
Collaborative interpretation of complex data and situations.

Reflective Journaling:
Using personal journals to reflect on experiences.

Heuristic Inquiry:
Immersive and self-reflective exploration of research questions.

CREATIVE METHODS
with FASTlab Examples

9. Digital + Technological Methods
Digital Ethnography
Online Surveys
Social Media Analysis

10. Structured Dialogue + Facilitation
World Café
Open Space Technology (OST)
Focus Groups

9. DIGITAL + TECHNOLOGICAL METHODS

Digital Ethnography:
Studying cultures and communities through digital means.

Online Surveys:
Collecting data through structured online questionnaires.

Social Media Analysis: Analyzing content and interactions on social media platforms.

10. STRUCTURED DIALOGUE + FACILITATION

World Café:
Structured conversational processes for knowledge sharing.

Open Space Technology (OST):
Self-organizing group discussions on a central theme.

Focus Groups:
Guided discussions with selected participants to gather diverse perspectives.

which entail researchers working to address the R&D needs of industry, broadly defined. The second section reports on the first period of projects initiated under an internal funding program focused on encouraging research teams to work with industry partners to develop rapid prototype solutions to a diverse range of problems. The third and fourth sections cover projects engaged in, respectively, creative probes into cultural sectors and experimental research. The final section considers the implications of artificial intelligence for creative research practices.

REFERENCES

Egglestone, Paul. 2022. "Applied Chaos: The Future Arts, Science and Technology Laboratory." *Design Principles and Practices: An International Journal—Annual Review* 16 (1): 19–30. https://doi.org/10.18848/1833-1874/CGP/v16i01/19-30.

Egglestone, Paul, Mario Minichiello, Leicha Stewart, Braddon Snape, Michele Oshan, and Jennifer Milam. 2022. "The Clyde Street Precinct: A Case Study Exploring a Distributed Model of Arts Education Within a Community-Based Creative Ecosystem." Presented at the Peer Review Proceedings of the 16th International Conference of Design Principles and Practices, Newcastle, January 19–21, 2022.

McIntyre, Phillip, Susan Kerrigan, Janet Fulton, Evelyn King, and Claire Williams. 2023. *Creativity and Creative Industries in Regional Australia: Interconnected Networks, Shared Knowledge and Choice Making Agents*. Springer Nature.

Finding Solutions to Real-World Problems

Introduction

This first section of the book presents case studies in collaborations with stakeholders within the innovation economy, with creative researchers particularly working on R&D priorities developed in negotiation with industry-based collaborators.

In the first chapter (Chapter 1), Ben Matthews discusses the concept of transdisciplinarity, outlining the possibilities and challenges inherent to creative research involving multiple disciplines within the academy, before briefly discussing this in relation to two ongoing projects. Matthew's chapter provides a touchstone for other chapters in this volume, with multiple projects collected here engaging in transdisciplinary practice across diverse sectors.

The next three chapters (Chapters 2, 3, and 4) center on localized art-based projects that were developed under smart city agendas. These are all place-making initiatives developed in collaboration with New South Wales (NSW) city councils. Craig Hight and Andrea Cassin (Chapter 2) outline the development of an innovative intervention into urban design, centered on a multisite multimedia installation project designed to shift local community perceptions and use of inner-city locations in the City of Newcastle. These were installations developed using Crime Prevention Through Environmental Design (CPTED) principles but looking to extend the potential of this framework.

In Chapter 3, Paul Egglestone, Leicha Stewart, and Kristefan Minski provide an overview of four small place-making projects developed within the NSW town of Singleton, each staging distinctive forms of engagement and interaction for local community members. Designed to be short-term, focused site-specific installations, they collectively sought to spark conversations with the broader community about how to reimagine the central city.

In Chapter 4, Ralph Kenke and Elmar Trefz discuss one of these Singleton projects in detail, providing a detailed photo-essay walk-through of the design complexities inherent to a smart city installation. Their documentation of the problem-solving required to realize an interactive balloon lighting experience offers a textbook case of the challenges of implementing smart-tech innovation.

The final chapter (Chapter 5) is from Justin Dean, managing director of Envent, who is undertaking doctoral research as a structured form of R&D for his company. In the chapter, he outlines his personal and professional motivations for returning to the academy, and some initial reflections on the opportunities and challenges of developing a project on trust in artificial intelligence avatars while managing a company.

CHAPTER 1

Transdisciplinarity and the Role of Creative Industries in Science and Technology Research Teams

Benjamin James Matthews, Evan Gibbs, Amy Cain, Karl Hassan, and Christopher Lean

Introduction

The purpose of this chapter is to explore the role of transdisciplinarity and creative industries in science and technology research teams. By examining the background, significance, and growing importance of these concepts along with two recent case studies of primary research by the authors conducted in an Australian university setting, this chapter aims to shed light on their potential for fostering innovation, addressing complex challenges, and promoting interdisciplinary collaboration.

Transdisciplinarity plays a crucial role in addressing complex challenges that require collaboration among diverse disciplines. By transcending disciplinary boundaries, transdisciplinary research teams integrate knowledge, methodologies, and perspectives from multiple fields to develop holistic solutions (Lang et al. 2012). The significance of transdisciplinarity lies in its ability to go beyond traditional disciplinary approaches, fostering innovation and enhancing the understanding of complex problems through interdisciplinary collaboration.

Creative industries are increasingly recognized for their valuable contributions to science and technology domains. These industries, including design, arts, media, and cultural sectors, bring unique perspectives, methodologies, and ways of thinking to research teams (Hesmondhalgh 2013). They contribute to innovation by generating novel ideas, implementing user-centered design approaches and effectively communicating research findings to diverse audiences.

An example highlighting the significance of transdisciplinarity is the collaboration between the Australian Research Council Centre of Excellence in Synthetic Biology (CoESB), the Bacterial Regulation and Transport Laboratory (BRaTlab), and local craft brewers in the Wild Yeast Discovery and Brewing Project, otherwise known as the "Wild Yeast Zoo." This project brings together synthetic biologists, bioethicists, and creative industries scholars and students to discover native wild yeasts for brewing purposes. By merging scientific expertise, ethical considerations, and creative approaches, this transdisciplinary collaboration aims to advance the understanding of native yeast species while integrating aesthetic and artistic principles into the brewing industry.

The case study of the DeNovocastrians' iGEM 2020 project further exemplifies the growing importance of creative industries in science and technology. The collaboration between synthetic biology and creative industries scholars and students resulted in the development of a technique for microorganisms to monitor and clean up ecosystems polluted with hydrocarbons. Through the integration of design, branding, posters, videos, and other creative media, the team effectively communicated their research and engaged with broader audiences, highlighting the vital role of creative industries in scientific advancements.

Defining Transdisciplinarity

Transdisciplinarity refers to an approach that transcends the boundaries of individual disciplines and integrates diverse knowledge, methodologies, and perspectives to address complex problems. It goes beyond multidisciplinarity, which involves combining knowledge from multiple disciplines, by actively seeking to create new knowledge and frameworks that bridge disciplinary gaps (Jantsch 1970). Transdisciplinary research teams aim to foster collaboration and mutual learning among experts from different fields, integrating their insights and expertise to generate holistic and innovative solutions (Lang et al. 2012).

Key characteristics of transdisciplinarity include (Bammer 2005; Lang et al. 2012):

1. Integration and Mutual Learning: Transdisciplinary research teams emphasize the integration of diverse disciplinary knowledge and perspectives.

This integration requires active dialogue, mutual understanding, and the willingness to challenge disciplinary boundaries.

2. Problem-Oriented Approach: Transdisciplinarity focuses on addressing real-world problems that often transcend the scope of a single discipline. The research is driven by the need to find practical solutions and address societal challenges.

3. Stakeholder Involvement: Transdisciplinary research teams recognize the importance of engaging stakeholders from various sectors, including industry, government, civil society, and affected communities. Stakeholders' knowledge and experiences are valued and incorporated into the research process.

4. Reflexivity and Critical Reflection: Transdisciplinarity involves ongoing reflection on the assumptions, values, and power dynamics within the research process. Researchers critically examine their own biases and the potential impacts of their work on different stakeholders.

Case Study 1: Wild Yeast Zoo

Project Description and Objectives

The Wild Yeast Discovery and Brewing Project[1] is a unique collaboration between the Australian Research Council Centre of Excellence in Synthetic Biology (CoESB) and the Bacterial Regulation and Transport Laboratory (BRaTlab). The project aims to combine citizen science and commercial translation to discover native wild yeasts in the Hunter region of Australia, while ensuring compliance with the Nagoya Protocol, an international framework for protecting the intellectual property (IP) of First Nations.

In the first phase of the project, the team sent kits to participants in the Hunter region, to gather wild yeast samples from native flora. The participants refine and genotype the yeast, database it, and share the story of the flora, its location, and significance. Over time, the project seeks to build a comprehensive "zoo" of these yeasts—a database that can be accessed and used.

The project's objectives are:

a) To discover and characterize native wild yeasts in the Hunter region through a citizen science approach, engaging participants in yeast collection, refinement, and genotyping.

---

[1] See https://www.wildyeastzoo.com/.

b) To comply with the Nagoya Protocol by ensuring the protection of the intellectual property of native title holders and respecting their rights and contributions.

c) To establish a comprehensive yeast database that can be utilized by brewing industry stakeholders for the development of unique and region-specific brewing products.

Methodologies Employed and Outcomes Achieved

The transdisciplinary team from the CoESB and BRaTlab employs a range of methodologies to achieve the project's objectives. Initially, probe kits are sent to participants, who gather yeast samples from native flora in the Hunter region. The collected samples, along with the accompanying flora stories and location data, are sent back to the research team.

The team then conducts genetic sequencing and characterization of the yeast samples to understand their unique brewing characteristics. By analyzing the genetic information, the team identifies potential flavors, fermentation properties, and other traits that can contribute to the brewing process. These findings are documented and incorporated into the yeast database.

The outcomes of the project include the establishment of a comprehensive yeast database, showcasing the rich diversity of native wild yeasts in the Hunter region. This database becomes a valuable resource for the brewing industry, providing access to unique yeast strains that can contribute to the development of distinct and regionally influenced brewing products.

Lessons Learned and Impact on the Industry

The Wild Yeast Discovery and Brewing Project has yielded valuable lessons and made a significant impact on the industry. First, the project demonstrates the potential of citizen science approaches in engaging the public and promoting their active participation in scientific research. By involving participants in the yeast collection and refinement process, the project fosters a sense of ownership and community engagement, promoting a greater appreciation for the region's biodiversity.

Second, the project highlights the importance of complying with international frameworks such as the Nagoya Protocol to protect the intellectual property rights of native title holders. By incorporating compliance measures into the project's design, the team ensures that the rights and contributions of the landowners are respected and that the project operates ethically and legally.

The project's impact extends beyond the research team, with potential commercial translation opportunities for the brewing industry. The yeast database developed through the project offers unique and region-specific yeast strains that can be purchased and utilized by brewers. This fosters innovation, promotes the development of distinct brewing products, and contributes to the growth of the brewing industry in the Hunter region and beyond.

The success of the project is evidenced by its participation in programs such as the CSIRO ON Prime[2] and invitation to apply for the CSIRO ON Accelerate program. The project has also attracted media coverage, secured in-kind support from the Woodford Folk Festival, and received funding from various sources, including the ARC CoESB, Inspiring NSW and Inspiring QLD, Australia' Economic Accelerator (AEA) grant program, The University of Newcastle, the Integrated Innovation Network (I2N), The Genome Foundry and Hunter Biological Solutions Pty Ltd.

The Wild Yeast Discovery and Brewing Project serves as a model for transdisciplinary collaborations, citizen science initiatives, and industry partnerships, showcasing the potential of combining scientific research, community engagement, and commercial translation for mutual benefit and innovation.

Case Study 2: iGEM 2020 – The DeNovocastrians

Project Overview and Research Goals

The DeNovocastrians, a transdisciplinary student team from the University of Newcastle, Australia, participated in the iGEM International Science Competition 2020.[3] The team consisted of researchers, RHD (research higher degree) candidates, and undergraduate students from Design, Biology, and Information Technology disciplines. The project aimed to address the environmental challenge

---

[2] https://www.csiro.au/en/work-with-us/funding-programs/Innovation-programs/ON-Prime.

[3] https://competition.igem.org/

of hydrocarbons pollution commonly found in Newcastle, Australia, by utilizing synthetic biology and creative communication strategies.

Both synthetic biology as a discipline, and the iGEM competition are trans-disciplinary by nature (Diep et al., 2021). Prizes are awarded according to both the quality of the project completed, along with how clearly it is presented, communicated and its impacts on stakeholders both within and beyond the project team (Judging/Rubric - 2020.igem.org. n.d.).

The research goals of the DeNovocastrians were:

a) To develop a technique using synthetic biology to engineer microorganisms capable of monitoring and cleaning up ecosystems polluted with hydrocarbons, a petrochemical compound known for its harmful effects on the environment and human health.

b) To create effective communication strategies, including branding, posters, videos, website design, and pitch presentations, to raise awareness about hydrocarbons pollution, the team's innovative solution, and the importance of sustainable environmental practices.

Collaborative Processes and Methodologies Utilized

The DeNovocastrians employed a collaborative and transdisciplinary approach throughout the project. The team members from Design, Biology, and Information Technology disciplines worked together to integrate their expertise and perspectives, ensuring a holistic approach to problem-solving and innovation.

In the laboratory, the biology team focused on synthetic biology techniques to engineer microorganisms capable of detecting and degrading hydrocarbons. They employed genetic engineering methods, such as DNA manipulation and gene expression control, to create microorganisms with enhanced hydrocarbons-sensing abilities and efficient degradation pathways.

Simultaneously, the design and information technology team developed creative communication strategies to effectively convey the project's message and engage with the target audience. They collaborated on branding elements, including logo design and visual identity, to create a cohesive and impactful visual presence. The team also created informative posters, engaging videos, an interactive website, and a compelling pitch presentation to educate and inspire others about the project's objectives and potential impact.

Regular team meetings, workshops, and brainstorming sessions facilitated effective communication and integration of ideas between the different disciplines. The collaborative processes allowed for the exploration of creative solutions, the alignment of project goals, and the integration of scientific and design principles.

Key Findings, Innovations, and Societal Impact

The DeNovocastrians' project resulted in several key findings, innovations, and potential societal impacts. Their research demonstrated the successful engineering of microorganisms with improved capabilities to detect and degrade hydrocarbons, offering a promising solution for hydrocarbons pollution in ecosystems. The team's synthetic biology techniques and genetic engineering strategies showcased the potential of biotechnology in addressing environmental challenges.

The team's creative communication strategies played a vital role in raising awareness and engaging the public. The branding elements, informative posters, engaging videos, interactive website, and compelling pitch presentation effectively communicated the project's objectives, innovative solutions, and the urgency of addressing hydrocarbons pollution.[4] The DeNovocastrians' efforts contributed to increasing public awareness of the environmental impact of hydrocarbons pollution and the potential of synthetic biology in mitigating such issues.

As winners of a silver medal at the iGEM International Science Competition 2020, the DeNovocastrians gained recognition for their transdisciplinary collaboration, innovative research, and impactful communication strategies. Their success in the competition highlighted the importance of integrating diverse disciplines, such as synthetic biology and creative industries, to tackle complex environmental challenges.

The DeNovocastrians' project not only provided a potential solution for hydrocarbons pollution but also inspired future research, collaborations, and public engagement in the field of synthetic biology and environmental sustainability. The team's efforts showcased the power of interdisciplinary collaboration, innovative thinking, and effective communication in addressing environmental issues and fostering positive societal change.

---

[4] See https://2022.igem.wiki/denovocastrians/.

Challenges and Potential Solutions (Case Study Version)

Communication and Language Barriers Between Disciplines

Transdisciplinary collaborations, as observed in both the Wild Yeast Discovery and Brewing Project and The DeNovocastrians' iGEM project, face communication and language barriers between disciplines. Each discipline possesses its own specialized terminology, methodologies, and ways of thinking, which can impede effective collaboration (Nowotny et al. 2003).

To overcome these challenges, several strategies can be employed. First, fostering a culture of open and respectful communication is crucial. Creating spaces for dialogue, such as regular interdisciplinary meetings and workshops, promotes understanding and appreciation of diverse perspectives (Lang et al. 2012). These platforms provide opportunities for team members to share knowledge, align objectives, and bridge disciplinary gaps.

Second, the use of boundary objects and shared language can facilitate communication across disciplines. For instance, in the Wild Yeast Discovery and Brewing Project, the integration of creative industries scholars and students enabled the development of visual communication tools such as branding, posters, videos, and websites to effectively convey complex scientific concepts to broader audiences. Such boundary objects act as common references, fostering mutual understanding and facilitating collaboration (Star and Griesemer 1989).

Additionally, appointing boundary spanners or facilitators, as observed in The DeNovocastrians' iGEM project, can help overcome communication barriers. These individuals possess deep understanding and expertise in multiple disciplines, acting as intermediaries and translators to bridge disciplinary gaps, facilitate understanding, and foster collaboration (Bammer 2012).

Institutional and Funding Constraints

Both case studies highlight institutional and funding constraints as significant challenges in transdisciplinary collaborations. Many academic institutions and funding agencies prioritize *disciplinary* research, creating barriers to funding and recognition for transdisciplinary projects (Lang et al. 2012).

To address these constraints, advocacy for policy changes at institutional and funding agency levels is essential. This includes the establishment of dedicated funding programs specifically designed for transdisciplinary research, as observed in the Wild Yeast Discovery and Brewing Project. Such programs provide necessary resources and support for transdisciplinary projects (Bammer 2005). Furthermore, promoting evaluation frameworks that recognize and value the contributions of transdisciplinary research incentivizes researchers and institutions to engage in collaborative efforts (Nowotny et al. 2003).

Creating institutional structures, such as research centers or institutes, that foster transdisciplinary collaboration can also help overcome institutional constraints. These structures provide a supportive environment, facilitate interdisciplinary networking, and offer resources for transdisciplinary research (Bammer 2012). Collaboration across departments, faculties, or universities, as seen in both case studies, enables pooling of resources and expertise, creating a stronger foundation for transdisciplinary projects.

Strategies for Fostering Transdisciplinary Collaborations in Research Teams

Both case studies provide insights into effective strategies for fostering transdisciplinary collaborations in research teams.

1. Early Involvement: Engaging researchers from different disciplines early in the research process promotes a sense of ownership and commitment to the collaborative endeavor. Involving diverse perspectives from the outset allows for the co-development of research questions, methodologies, and goals (Lang et al. 2012). This approach was observed in both the Wild Yeast Discovery and Brewing Project and the DeNovocastrians' iGEM project.
2. Interdisciplinary Training and Education: Providing interdisciplinary training and education to researchers enhances their ability to engage in transdisciplinary collaborations. Gaining an understanding of other disciplines' theories, methodologies, and epistemologies enables effective communication and bridges disciplinary gaps (Frodeman et al. 2010). The incorporation of design, biology, and information technology disciplines in the DeNovocastrians' project exemplifies the value of interdisciplinary training.
3. Building Trust and Fostering Relationships: Building trust and cultivating strong relationships among team members are vital for successful transdisciplinary collaborations. Trust encourages open communication, mutual respect, and effective teamwork (Stokols et al. 2008). Developing personal connections and engaging in team-building activities, as observed in the Wild Yeast Discovery and Brewing Project, contributes to a supportive and collaborative atmosphere.

4. Recognizing and Valuing Contributions: Recognizing and valuing the contributions of all team members, regardless of their disciplinary backgrounds, is crucial. Acknowledging and celebrating diverse expertise and perspectives encourages active participation, boosts team morale, and promotes a sense of shared ownership (Lang et al. 2012). Both case studies demonstrate the importance of recognizing and valuing interdisciplinary contributions.

5. Reflexivity and Learning: Emphasizing reflexivity and learning throughout the research process allows researchers to critically reflect on assumptions, biases, and power dynamics (Bammer 2005). Regular evaluation, feedback sessions, and opportunities for reflection enable researchers to continuously improve and adapt their collaborative practices. The incorporation of iterative feedback and reflection processes in both case studies highlights the significance of reflexivity.

By incorporating these strategies, research teams can foster successful transdisciplinary collaborations, overcome challenges, and leverage the diverse expertise and perspectives to address complex research questions effectively.

Future Directions and Recommendations

Importance of Interdisciplinary Education and Training

Both case studies, the Wild Yeast Discovery and Brewing Project and the DeNovocastrians' iGEM project, highlight the significance of interdisciplinary education and training for fostering successful transdisciplinary collaborations.

To further advance transdisciplinary research, it is crucial to prioritize interdisciplinary education and training for researchers. Interdisciplinary education equips researchers with the knowledge, skills, and mindset necessary for effective collaboration across disciplines (Frodeman et al. 2010). The incorporation of diverse disciplines, such as synthetic biology, bioethics, design, and information technology, in these case studies exemplifies the value of interdisciplinary training.

Universities and academic institutions should develop interdisciplinary coursework and training programs that promote cross-disciplinary understanding and collaboration (Lang et al. 2012). These programs can expose researchers to different disciplinary perspectives, methodologies, and ways of thinking, fostering a transdisciplinary mindset. Additionally, mentorship and experiential learning opportunities, as demonstrated in the iGEM project, can provide hands-on experience in transdisciplinary research and enhance interdisciplinary skills (Frodeman et al. 2010).

Promoting Cross-Sector Partnerships and Knowledge Exchange

The case studies emphasize the importance of cross-sector partnerships and knowledge exchange in transdisciplinary research.

To facilitate knowledge exchange between academia, industry, and the broader society, it is crucial to promote cross-sector partnerships. Collaborations with industry, nongovernmental organizations, and community stakeholders can provide valuable insights, resources, and real-world contexts for research projects (Bammer 2012). The collaboration between the CoESB and BRaTlab in the Wild Yeast Discovery and Brewing Project demonstrates the benefits of such partnerships in bridging the gap between academia and industry.

Furthermore, fostering knowledge exchange platforms, such as workshops, conferences, and public engagement events, can facilitate the sharing of expertise, ideas, and best practices. These platforms provide opportunities for researchers, practitioners, and the public to come together, fostering mutual learning and promoting the co-production of knowledge (Lang et al. 2012). The engagement with the Woodford Folk Festival and Inspiring NSW in the Wild Yeast Discovery and Brewing Project exemplifies the use of such platforms to engage with the broader community.

Policy Implications and Support for Transdisciplinary Research

The case studies also highlight the need for policy implications and support for transdisciplinary research.

At the policy level, it is essential to recognize and value the contributions of transdisciplinary research. Policymakers should create funding mechanisms and evaluation frameworks that explicitly support and reward transdisciplinary endeavors (Nowotny et al. 2003). The success of the Wild Yeast Discovery and Brewing Project in securing funding from the Australian Research Council and matching funds from Hunter Biological Solutions Pty Ltd demonstrates the positive impact of policy support.

Furthermore, institutions and funding agencies should establish dedicated funding programs for transdisciplinary research to provide the necessary resources and support (Bammer 2005). These programs should emphasize the integration of multiple disciplines, public engagement, and societal impact in research proposals. The recognition and funding support received by the DeNovocastrians' iGEM project highlight the positive outcomes of dedicated funding programs for transdisciplinary initiatives.

Creating institutional structures, such as research centers or institutes, that prioritize transdisciplinary research can foster an environment conducive to collaboration and knowledge exchange (Bammer 2012). These structures should provide support, resources, and networking opportunities for researchers engaged in transdisciplinary endeavors.

By implementing these recommendations, policymakers, academic institutions, and funding agencies can create an enabling environment that supports and promotes transdisciplinary research, unlocking the full potential of interdisciplinary collaborations to tackle complex societal challenges.

Conclusion

In this chapter, we explored the role of transdisciplinarity and creative industries in science and technology research teams. We discussed the background and significance of transdisciplinarity in research teams, highlighting its ability to tackle complex problems by integrating diverse disciplinary perspectives. We also emphasized the growing importance of creative industries in scientific and technological advancements, showcasing their role in generating innovative ideas and applying design thinking approaches.

We examined the benefits of transdisciplinarity in research teams, including enhanced problem-solving and innovation, broader perspectives and interdisciplinary collaboration, and bridging the gap between academia and industry. We also explored the integration of creative industries in research teams, emphasizing their ability to contribute artistic and aesthetic principles to technology development.

We discussed the challenges and potential solutions in fostering transdisciplinary collaborations, such as communication and language barriers between disciplines, institutional and funding constraints, and strategies for fostering collaboration in research teams. We presented case studies, including the Wild Yeast Discovery and Brewing Project and the DeNovocastrians' iGEM project, to illustrate the application of transdisciplinary approaches in real-world contexts.

The integration of transdisciplinarity and creative industries in science and technology research teams has the potential to bring about significant advancements. By combining diverse disciplinary perspectives, researchers can develop innovative solutions to complex problems and foster a deeper understanding of the challenges they face. The incorporation of creative industries brings a unique set of skills and approaches that can enhance the design, communication, and societal impact of scientific and technological advancements.

Transdisciplinary collaborations also have the potential to accelerate the translation of research outcomes into practical applications. By bridging the gap between academia and industry, transdisciplinary teams can ensure that scientific discoveries and technological innovations are effectively translated into real-world solutions that address societal needs. This collaborative approach fosters the co-creation of knowledge, enhances the relevance and impact of research, and contributes to sustainable development.

We call upon researchers, policymakers, and stakeholders to embrace transdisciplinary approaches in research teams. Researchers should seek opportunities for collaboration, develop interdisciplinary skills through education and training, and engage in cross-sector partnerships to address complex challenges effectively.

Policymakers should recognize the value of transdisciplinary research and create supportive policy frameworks that incentivize and fund such collaborations. Institutions and funding agencies should establish dedicated funding programs, research centers, and evaluation frameworks that value transdisciplinary work and promote cross-disciplinary knowledge exchange.

Stakeholders, including industry partners, community organizations, and the public, should actively engage with transdisciplinary research teams, providing valuable perspectives and resources, and benefiting from the resulting innovations.

By embracing transdisciplinarity and harnessing the potential of creative industries in science and technology research teams, we can foster innovation, address complex challenges, and create a better future for society.

Acknowledgements:

The Wild Yeast Zoo project relied on EMCR Seed Funding from the CoESB for work described in this chapter. The authors would like to acknowledge the hard work of the students who were part of team DeNovocastrians and the support industry partner.

REFERENCES

Bammer, G. 2005. "Integration and Implementation Sciences: Building a New Specialization." *Ecology and Society* 10 (2): 6. https://doi.org/10.5751/ES-01469-100206.

Bammer, G. 2012. *Disciplining Interdisciplinarity: Integration and Implementation Sciences for Researching Complex Real-World Problems*. ANU Press.

Bardzell, S., and J. Bardzell, eds. 2013. "Toward a Critical HCI." In *Critical Theory and Interaction Design*. Bardzell. MIT Press.

Brown, T. 2008. "Design Thinking." *Harvard Business Review* 86 (6): 84–92.

Diep, P., Boucinha, A., Kell, B., Yeung, B. A., Chen, X., Tsyplenkov, D., Serra, D., Escobar, A., Gnanapragasam, A., Emond, C. A., Sajtovich, V. A., Mahadevan, R., Kilkenny, D. M., Gini-Newman, G., Kaern, M., & Ingalls, B. (2021). Advancing undergraduate synthetic biology education: Insights from a canadian igem student perspective. Canadian Journal of Microbiology, 67(10), 749–770. https://doi.org/10.1139/CJM-2020-0549/SUPPL_FILE/CJM-2020-0549SUPPLC.DOCX

Dorst, K. 2011. "The Core of 'Design Thinking' and Its Application." *Design Studies* 32 (6): 521–532.

Dunne, A., and F. Raby. 2013. *Speculative Everything: Design, Fiction, and Social Dreaming*. MIT Press.

Frodeman, R., J. T. Klein, and C. Mitcham. 2010. *The Oxford Handbook of Interdisciplinarity*. Oxford University Press.

Hesmondhalgh, D. 2013. *The Cultural Industries*. Sage Publications.

Jantsch, E. 1970. "Inter- and Transdisciplinary University: A Systems Approach to Education and Innovation." *Policy Sciences* 1 (4): 403–428. https://doi.org/10.1007/BF01405752.

Judging/Rubric - 2020.igem.org. (n.d.). Retrieved April 24, 2025, from https://2020.igem.org/Judging/Rubric

Kimbell, L. 2012. "Rethinking Design Thinking: Part I." *Design and Culture* 4 (3): 275–290.

Lang, D. J., A. Wiek, M. Bergmann, et al. 2012. "Transdisciplinary Research in Sustainability Science: Practice, Principles, and Challenges." *Sustainability Science* 7(suppl. 1): 25–43. https://doi.org/10.1007/s11625-011-0149-x.

Norman, D. A. 2004. *Emotional Design: Why We Love (or Hate) Everyday Things*. Basic Books.

Nowotny, H., P. Scott, and M. Gibbons. 2003. "Introduction: 'Mode 2' Revisited: The New Production of Knowledge." *Minerva* 41 (3): 179–194. https://doi.org/10.1023/A:1025505528250.

Sanders, E. B.-N., and P. J. Stappers. 2012. *Convivial Toolbox: Generative Research for the Front End of Design*. BIS Publishers.

Star, S. L., and J. R. Griesemer. 1989. "Institutional Ecology, 'Translations,' and Boundary Objects: Amateurs and Professionals in Berkeley's Museum of Vertebrate Zoology, 1907-39." *Social Studies of Science* 19 (3): 387–420.

Stokols, D., J. Fuqua, J. Gress, R. Harvey, K. Phillips, and L. Baezconde-Garbanati. 2003. "Evaluating Transdisciplinary Science." *Nicotine & Tobacco Research* 5 (suppl. 1): S21–S39. https://doi.org/10.1080/14622200310001625538.

Stokols, D., K. L. Hall, B. K. Taylor, and R. P. Moser. 2008. "The Science of Team Science: Overview of the Field and Introduction to the Supplement." *American Journal of Preventive Medicine* 35 (2): S77–S89. https://doi.org/10.1016/j.amepre.2008.05.002.

Tractinsky, N. 2004. "Aesthetics and Apparent Usability: Empirically Assessing Cultural and Methodological Issues." *ACM Transactions on Computer-Human Interaction* 11 (2): 215–241.

UNESCO. 2013. *Creative Economy Report 2013: Widening Local Development Pathways*. United Nations Development Programme. https://unctad.org/system/files/official-document/unctad_ditc_ted_2013d3_en.pdf.

CHAPTER 2

Newcastle Night Galleries:
Social Design, Crime Prevention,
and Creative Placemaking

Craig Hight and Andrea Cassin

Introduction

The principles of CPTED (Crime Prevention Through Environmental Design) are widely used throughout Australia, although, in practice, they tend to serve as a series of guidelines rather than providing clear templates or directives for urban planners. While these guidelines create challenges through their lack of specificity, they also provide a frame and opportunity for innovation. This chapter briefly outlines one such effort to deploy an innovative application of CPTED to questions of public space, based in the City of Newcastle (CN) in partnership with FASTlab and smart city stakeholders.

CPTED (Cozens 2016; Cozens et al. 2005; Ceccato 2020; Ceccato and Nalla 2020) is now embedded within city planning across Australia to address various public crime issues, with all Australian State and Territory governments now having publicly available CPTED guidelines (Clancey et al. 2016). Although widely used, this framework does not have a clear evidence base to help in assessing its effectiveness, as most such projects do not publish empirical data to demonstrate if their assumptions have been proven in specific contexts (Clancey et al. 2016). Clancey et al. (2012), for example, have critiqued the New South Wales (NSW) crime risk assessment guidelines, noting they are not clearly and precisely defined for urban planners, which provides scope for lots of uncertainty in how they might be implemented in different contexts.

Figure 1: Kuwumi Place Henges

Source: the authors

Perhaps not coincidentally, the range of design approaches applied in this area of planning has tended to be comparatively limited, leaning into more established urban design practices. McGuire et al. note measures such as "environmental design, street lighting, closed-circuit television (CCTV), pedestrian and traffic management, signage, transport links," together with initiatives in "alcohol/ gaming licences, hours of operation; police presence, patrols, contact points and availability" (McGuire et al. 2021, 28) are more common. As discussed below, this openness also provides license to adopt more innovative and creative possibilities under the CPTED banner.

The CPTED literature outlines a core set of principles within the field. The diagram included here (Figure 2) was offered by Cozens and Love in their 2015 review of CPTED to summarize its development since its inception in the 1960s.[1] Their "dynamic integrated model for CPTED" summarizes the gradual shift toward putting design principles into an increasingly wider social context. In brief, the more recent extensions of this framework are presented by the outer

---

[1] For the development of CPTED, see Jacobs (1961), Jeffery (1971), and Newman (1973).

Figure 2: A Dynamic Integrated Model for CPTED

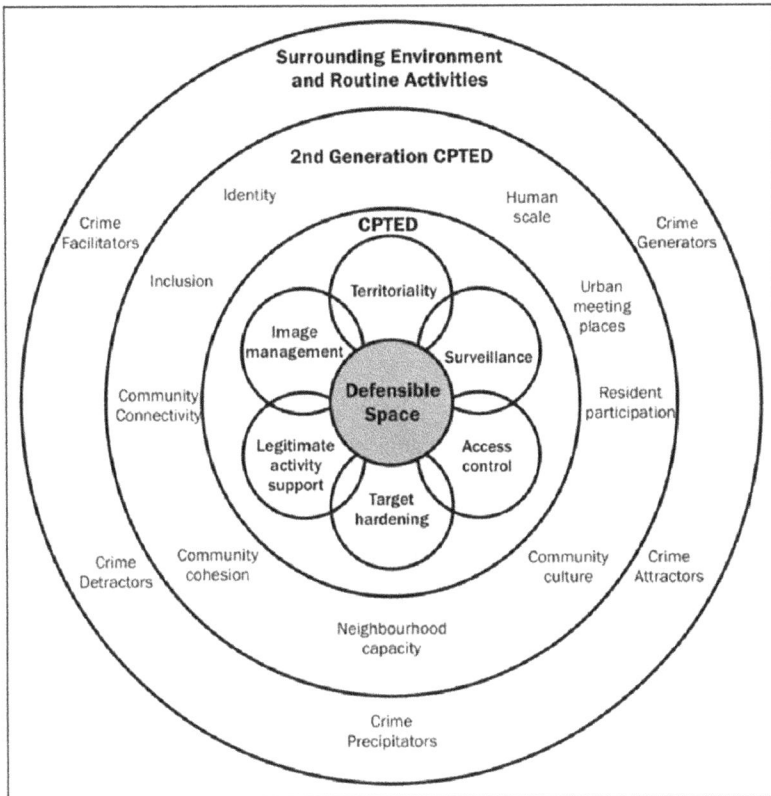

Source: Cozens and Love 2015, 6

concentric circles in this diagram, which have gradually added complexity to the social dimensions of spaces considered under a CPTED assessment.

As noted by Cozens et al. (2005, 328–356), what is now considered "first generation" CPTED largely focused on the factors included in the core circle grouped around a concept of "defensible space" in crime prevention. The core factors in the center of the diagram are well detailed in the literature.

- Territoriality: those initiatives aimed at increasing a sense of ownership from the local community and other stakeholders.
- Surveillance: which includes informal or natural surveillance by residents through more organised (e.g., security guards) and mechanical forms (e.g., increased lighting and the installation of CCTV systems).

- Access Control: such physical measures as fencing to limit unauthorized access.
- Target Hardening: essentially vandal proofing a space.
- Activity Support: a range of measures such as signage, pathways, amenities (water, power) to support activation of the space.
- Image Management: promoting the sense that a space is well tended and cared for.

In their 2015 review of CPTED, Cozens and Love note that underlying this framework are some basic, largely untested assumptions about the relationships between urban design, community activation of space, and criminal behavior (Cozens and Love 2015).

- That "eyes on the street" (referencing Jacobs 1961) always reduces crime.
- That "permeable streets" always reduce crime;
- That high densities of people always reduce crime;
- That mixed-use development always reduces crime;
- That CCTV always reduces crime; and
- That improved street lighting always reduces crime.

The so-called second generation CPTED has tended to focus more on social factors—looking increasingly toward the complexities of community demographics and their participation in a space (as suggested in the middle concentric circle in Figure 2). This extension of CPTED includes activities to build social cohesion, encouraging a diversity of use in spaces, building linkages with neighboring communities and localized services, and more specific anti-crime initiatives such as neighborhood watch. A key goal prioritized here is to support the "active guardianship" (Reynald 2011) of spaces by the local community.

More recently, some writers have argued that there is a "third generation" CPTED (Mihinjac and Saville 2019), which leans further into the complexities of human motivations and aspirations within a neighborhood. Here the focus is on concepts of "liveability," which means integrating the design of basic infrastructure and amenities, intended to enhance community members' personal aspirations and improve their quality of life. The distinction with so-called second generation CPTED is not always clear, but Mihinjac and Saville argue that the focus is more deliberately on fostering social cohesion over a longer period, inevitably incorporating more complex perceptions of "place" for different groups within that community. This drift toward more complex conceptions of CPTED includes community attributes which become increasingly harder to assess, measure, and test: What are the aspirations for different members of the community? How do they feel about specific places? And how do their perceptions of safety play into understandings of liveability?

Within our project we likewise drew on a "common sense" (i.e., untested) set of assumptions in addition to those noted above. These included assumptions that leaning into notions of creative placemaking would foster more active participation of spaces, that activation through public and interactive art would enhance liveability and naturally foster active guardianship of places. This is the frame for the Newcastle Night Galleries project. We drew upon (second and third generation) CPTED principles, and an agenda to showcase public art collections and leverage the potential of interactive technologies, bringing together smart city[2] stakeholders into the challenge of creating more liveable places.

In addition the Newcastle Night Galleries project also leaned into the concept of The Playable City (https://www.playablecity.com/) which emerged from the Watershed Pervasive Media Studio in Bristol (UK) in 2012, the basis for an annual design contest to foster innovative approaches toward the refashioning of urban spaces (Nijholt 2017, 2020). The original conception of a playable city explicitly critiqued smart city planning as overly preoccupied with a "vision of technology as a solution machine" (de Lange 2019) and with fostering efficiencies in city infrastructures and services (Innocent 2020).

A focus on creating places for play favors a "positive" interpretation of CPTED, in the sense of actively fostering social cohesion, by attracting broader parts of the community into spaces, encouraging their active guardianship, and fostering greater participation in a nighttime economy. This was designed in deliberate contrast to "negative" (punitive, disruptive) measures that might specifically target sections of the community seen as more responsible for antisocial activity and "undesirable" behavior. There was a clear understanding across the project collaborators that we were looking for a creative, playful set of design solutions in opposition to more established automated surveillance options such as CCTV.

The research team searched for test sites embedded within hotspots for different categories of crime data[3] and aligned with the City of Newcastle's nighttime economy strategy. In consultation conducted in September 2020

---

[2] There is not the space here to survey smart city initiatives, but they have their own historical development. See https://newcastle.nsw.gov.au/smarter-living-1 for the City of Newcastle's strategy.

[3] Collated by the NSW Bureau of Crime Statistics and Research, see https://www.bocsar.nsw.gov.au/.

a community survey had a total of 940 responses and included key insights relevant to this project). The survey sought to understand general community perceptions and attitudes regarding Newcastle after dark, and to inform a trial allowing low impact venues (such as small bars) to open later into the night. As part of the survey design several questions were asked that provided insight into perceptions of safety, and responses confirmed that while the community considers the city nightlife safe, a significant proportion of nightlife participants expressed negative perceptions of central city precincts. Among the possible measures suggested in the survey, there was a strong support for activating spaces, designing spaces for nighttime use and creative lighting solutions.[4]

A CPTED assessment of potential sites was performed through a detailed ground observation, tools such as Google Maps and Google Street View to consider proximity to entertainment precincts and transport routes, and their frequency of active transport (i.e., foot traffic, cycling, skateboard, etc.). Each site was the focus for the installation of interactive lightboxes hosting site-specific interactive media concepts developed and implemented through wider collaborations between the CON, FASTlab, the Newcastle Art Gallery, and local small-to-medium enterprises (SMEs) who provided industrial design and Internet of Things (IoT) expertise.

The broader goals of the project were to align with the City of Newcastle's strategy toward building "a smart, liveable, sustainable city," and a long-term effort to activate the nighttime economy. The primary functionality of the installations is focused on nighttime activation, with the solar-powered lightboxes expected to be "powering up" during the day and fully active from sunset to midnight. The eventual design solution focused on the development of a flexi-ble platform which could be adapted, evolved, and deployed in future sites—a platform which could be "tuned" to each place. A commitment to adhere as much as possible to sustainability principles entailed some global constraints, such as need to find locations that would not be too shaded, to allow effective solar powering. A hardened industrial design was decided early in the project and the design solution also needed to align with promoting augmented reality (AR) use (through the official CN app).

---

[4]. Other data reveals similar patterns and highlights the complexities in how different parts of the community perceive safety. See for example Transport for NSW, Safer Cities Survey Report: Perceptions of safety in pub-lic spaces and transport hubs across NSW, July 2023, available at https://www.transport.nsw.gov.au/industry/cities-and-active-transport/cities-revitalisation-and-place/festival-of-place-0.

The "Henge" Prototype

The prototype design developed for this project are 2-m-high interactive lightbox units, with multimedia installations providing layered forms of engagement. These units or "henges" (styled after Stonehenge) are designed to be moveable, to serve as temporary or semi-permanent parts of site infrastructure. Different components of these units are designed to be active at different times over a twenty-four-hour period, and these were grouped into clusters of five within each of the three Night Galleries sites.

Built from the ground up using materials such as recycled concrete, each key component in the modular design was developed separately within the workshops of the various SMEs involved in the project. Design Anthology, an industrial and product design studio, initiated the core industrial design and the manufacture of the prototype's concrete base and steel frame.[5] Design + Industry, a product design and development consultancy, took initial responsibility for the design and build of the electronic components of the henges,[6] then passed on final stages of design and implementation to SAPHI, a software and electronics development company.[7] Finally, XR (extended reality) and 3D animation studio VEARA implemented the design of a range of AR experiences linked to each set of henges and triggered by henge artworks.[8] The FASTlab team provided overall concept designs for the site-specific forms of play enabled by each set of five henges and worked with Newcastle-based music producer Huw Jones and sound designer Thomas Mitchell to develop soundscapes enabled across the three sites.

The sets of five henges offer layered forms of engagement. Users encounter digital and analogue forms of experience that take prominence at different times over a twenty-four-hour period. Displayed artworks, for example, are viewable throughout the day but are brightly backlit during the hours of powered operation. When proximity sensors are triggered by users, each unit "awakens" and is available for digital interaction.

For our three test sites (Figure 3), experimental interactive designs sought to leverage aspects of the immediate spaces to appeal to local community and commuters, while addressing the broader possibilities for the demonstration of

---

[5.] See https://designanthology.com/projects/newcastle-city-council-nightime-spaces/.

[6.] See https://www.design-industry.com.au/.

[7.] See https://saphi.engineering/portfolio/smart-henges-sensor-integration/.

[8.] See https://www.veara.com.au/.

Figure 3: Locations of the Three Test Sites for the Night Galleries in the Newcastle CBD

play. These sites were developed over 2021, with a development process lengthened and complicated by NSW COVID-19 lockdown protocols. Installation and launch of site 1 occurred in December 2021, while installation at sites 2 and 3 were delayed into 2022 due to concerns by CN over how to manage community caution over COVID-19 social distancing measures coming out of lockdown.

Site 1: Kuwumi Place

The concept experience for site 1 is focused on musical performance with users able to select from a set of looped sounds on each unit to play multiple combinations of beats and melodies. Set near each other, this set of Night Galleries functions as a dispersed dynamic music composition machine and features sound design from Newcastle-based music producer Huw Jones.

With a touch-sensitive button array mounted at the bottom of the artworks, the Night Galleries are accessible, intuitive to trial-and-error play. The site provides potential complexity in performance through multiple sound options on each unit. Some are themed with rhythm sound loops set to the same tempo, others with melody samples which can be played in a more improvisational way. With minimal experimentation, users recognize the capacity to play rhythm and melody to complement each other. An individual can easily move quickly between units to activate multiple sound files simultaneously, or the site facilitates multiple performers playing collaboratively.

Site 2: Market Street Steps

This site was disestablished after some weeks of onsite testing.[9] It showcased ten artworks curated around the theme of landscapes, reimagining the three

---

[9.] The project team belatedly recognized the site featured too much shade to allow for a full recharge of units during the day.

lawn levels as part of a natural landscape. Users passing by within 3 m of the Night Galleries trigger proximity sensors to activate one of a set of soundscapes conceptually aligned to each of the artworks, created by sound designer Thomas Mitchell. Multiple landscape sound files were loaded onto each unit, moving through a small, looped playlist of sound files that were kept shorter than other sites (less than twenty seconds). Soundscapes on unit henge directly referenced the displayed artwork and featured a mix of recorded sounds including bird or insect sounds, river/water noise, and incidental sound extracts such as farm equipment or children playing.

The AR "play" element of site 2 operated as an "Easter Egg" experience. Aimed particularly at children, the site rewarded explorative and persistent play. Users could access AR animations of four 3D modeled creatures triggered by an additional set of colored codes provided at the top level of the site (these "play" codes acted as a teaser for unlocking the hidden play aspects of the site). This AR experience was intended to reframe the landscape artworks as "habitats" for digital creatures, and the soundscapes as background sounds for the creatures themselves.

Site 3: Pacific Park

This site offers the most integrated multimedia art experience of the three test spaces, with all engagement layers tightly aligned to a set of abstract artworks, showcasing the potential for experimental, interactive art installations in public spaces (Figure 4). Pacific Park's multimedia experience centers on users selecting from a set of soundscapes on each unit (sound designs developed as creative responses to the site's abstract artworks by Thomas Mitchell), complemented by a set of experimental AR content which playfully extends the artistic experience of each artwork.

Two different types of proximity sensors operate across the site. An initial proximity sensor is triggered when users are within 3 m of each unit, hailing passers-by with a short (three seconds) extract of its featured soundscapes. A further distance sensor (triggered within 0.5 m, exclusive to the Night Galleries at Pacific Park) highlights the four-button array and invites exploration of the choices of soundscapes, each designed to complement and directly respond to the abstract artworks curated from the Newcastle Art Gallery collection.

The set of AR experiences is the most ambitious of the three sites, with each unit providing a distinctive "extension" of its featured abstract artworks. One artwork with fluid shapes appears (on users' mobile screens) to melt and flow

Figure 4: Pacific Park Night Galleries

Source: authors

beyond the frame of the unit. Another's geometric shapes are transformed (on their smartphone) into a 3D space with the Night Galleries at its center which users can navigate by using their mobile screen as a guide. An abstract artwork featuring a collective of bold, intersecting lines comes to life and explodes away from the frame of the henge display. Another artwork appears to emerge and wash up and over the user like a wave, as they view the piece on their phone.

Lessons Learned

This project drew upon CPTED guidelines for inspiration but also looked to experiment with possibilities for site-specific forms of play by building a platform for layered interactive media installations. The key outcome of the project, outside of the implementation of the "henges" themselves, was the development of working relationships within the smart city ecosystem. The project team fostered invaluable planning sessions on design possibilities involving diverse stakeholders from city administration, cultural and research institutions, and small-to-medium enterprises. The project generated awareness and respect of each other's capabilities that have fostered further initiatives. It reinforced an appreciation of the technical complexities of working within smart city space and more specifically demonstrated the potential for interactive art in public space. An overlap with COVID-19 lockdown protocols delayed the project,

Figure 5: Creatives and Technologists from CN, FASTlab, Newcastle Art Gallery, Design Anthology, SAPHI, and VEARA Involved in Final Testing of the Prototype in the Design Anthology Workshop

Source: Authors

dispersing the team at key points. This demonstrated the broader challenge of how to engage community members to foster interactive experiences relevant for residents and commuters, to retain their salience for the community over time, and especially to inspire and foster a sense of ownership which could reinforce a sense of "place" in line with CPTED principles. As of this writing, the henge prototype is being used within a Sydney-based Safer Cities project, and plans are in place for commercialization of the platform.

Acknowledgments

The Night-Time Spaces: Safety through Activation project was supported by funding from the NSW Department of Justice and Police Community Safety Fund.

REFERENCES

Ceccato, Vania, and Mahesh K. Nalla. 2020. *Crime and Fear in Public Places: Towards Safe, Inclusive and Sustainable Cities*. Taylor & Francis.

Clancey, Garner, Daren Fisher, and Natalie Yeung. 2016. "A Recent History of Australian Crime Prevention." *Crime Prevention and Community Safety* 18: 309–328.

Clancey, Garner, Murray Lee, and Daren Fisher. 2012. "Crime Prevention Through Environmental Design (CPTED) and the New South Wales Crime Risk Assessment Guidelines: A Critical Review." *Crime Prevention and Community Safety* 14: 1–15.

Cozens, Paul, and Terence Love. 2015. "A Review and Current Status of Crime Prevention Through Environmental Design (CPTED)." *Journal of Planning Literature* 30 (4): 393–412.

Cozens, Paul Michael, Greg Savile, and David Hillier. 2005. "Crime Prevention Through Environmental Design (CPTED): A Review and Modern Bibliography." *Property Management* 23 (5): 328–356.

de Lange, Michiel. 2019. "18: The Playful City—Citizens Making the Smart City." In *The Playful Citizen*, edited by René Glas, Sybille Lammes, Michiel de Lange, Joost Raessens, and Imar de Vries. Amsterdam University Press.

Hight, Craig, M. Minichiello, P. Egglestone, et al. 2022. "The Playable City: Refashioning Spaces Within Urban Social Design." Presented at the Peer Review Proceedings of the 16th International Conference of Design Principles and Practices, Newcastle, January 19–21, 2022.

Hight, Craig, Mario Minichiello, Paul Egglestone, et al. 2023. "The Playable City: Collaborative Workflows for Innovative Urban Social Design." *Design Principles and Practices: An International Journal—Annual Review* 16 (1): 97–107. https://doi.org/10.18848/1833-1874/CGP/v16i01/97-107.

Innocent, Troy. 2020. "Citizens of Play: Revisiting the Relationship Between Playable and Smart Cities." In *Making Smart Cities More Playable*, edited by Anton Nijholt. Springer.

Jacobs, Jane. 1961. *The Death and Life of Great American Cities*. Random House.

Jeffery, C. Ray. 1971. *Crime Prevention Through Environmental Design, Beverly Hills Calif.* Sage Publications.

Mews, Gregor H. 2022. *Transforming Public Space Through Play*. Routledge.

Mihinjac, Mateja, and Gregory Saville. 2019. "Third-Generation Crime Prevention Through Environmental Design (CPTED)." *Social Sciences* 8 (6): 182.

Newman, Oscar. 1973. *Defensible Space: Crime Prevention Through Urban Design*. Collier Books.

Nijholt, Anton. 2017. *Playable Cities, the City as a Digital Playground*. Springer.

Nijholt, Anton. 2020. *Making Smart Cities More Playable: Exploring Playable Cities*. Springer.

Stevens, Quentin. 2007. *The Ludic City: Exploring the Potential of Public Spaces*. Routledge.

CHAPTER 3

A Sense of Place: Fostering Civic Engagement Through Art and Technology

Paul Egglestone, Leicha Stewart and Kristefan Minski

Introduction

In 2020 University of Newcastle and the School of Creative Industries Future Arts, Science and Technology Laboratory (FASTlab) partnered with Singleton Shire Council to undertake a collaborative research and development endeavor and deliver four community arts installations as part of the Singleton Living Laneways project. The project aimed to revitalise the town through a curated series of public art experiences. It sought to foster new models of collaboration between citizens and council, encourage local spending, and bring people back into the township following the disruption caused by COVID-19. By integrating art and technology, the project also aimed to shift perceptions of public art in a regional setting and strengthen community engagement in a rural context. Four laneways were targeted for activation with one installation per laneway to be delivered one after the other to allow for reflection of the levels of engagement and UX (user experience) comfort zoning. The artworks included Shadowgram, Acoustic Alley, Media Orbs, and Oribotics. Shadowgram, Acoustic Alley, and Media Orbs went ahead throughout 2021; however, Oribotics was disrupted by COVID-19 limitations and was postponed indefinitely. The nature of these installations, the interactions citizens had with them, and what these interactions can tell us about ideas of place, placemaking, and community engagement are all valuable contributions to the emerging body of knowledge which considers the crucial role and benefits of the arts in communities and geo-social and geopolitical aspects of urban planning.

It is prudent at this point to set out the contextual details of the Singleton Living Laneways project. As this study is primarily interested in how individuals engage with community arts projects and how their perceptions of place are formed and mediated, the specific combination of social, temporal, and geopolitical conditions which define Singleton and its position relational to other Australian town and cities, particularly its relationship to Sydney and Newcastle, is a necessary consideration of this exploration. Singleton is a regional town of around 16,000 people, on the banks of the Hunter River in New South Wales (NSW), Australia. It sits on the traditional lands of the Wonnarua people and is located roughly 200 km north-north-west of Sydney and 70 km north-west of Newcastle. While Sydney is arguably Australia's most iconic city, well known for its harbor, Opera House, beaches, culture, and food and wine scene, and Newcastle has been undergoing a decades-long transformation from a heavily industrial "steel city" in the 1980s to a vibrant beachside city with a thriving arts and hospitality culture, Singleton has retained its reputation as a predominantly coal mining town despite being rich in historical and agricultural tourism opportunities as well as award-winning wineries and restaurants.

There are around seventeen active coal mines in Singleton, collectively employing 24% of the population (ABS). Along with other key regional NSW towns Muswellbrook and Cessnock, Singleton is part of the Hunter electorate, which at the time of the project was represented by member for Hunter the Hon Joel Fitzgibbon MP. Mr. Fitzgibbon, a Labor MP, held the Hunter seat (or its equivalent title) since 1996 and is well known as an advocate of the mining industry as an economic driver and provider of regional jobs and for his views on climate change policy, which are at odds with those of his party. (In September 2021 Mr. Fitzgibbon announced he would retire from Federal politics at the 2022 election). Given the primary industry and the town's reliance on coal mining for employment, Singleton may face significant challenges in the near future as Australia works toward net zero emissions in 2050. The Singleton Living Laneways project was conceived as a way to invite people to look at and think about their town in fresh ways and consider how they might like it to look in the future. In other words, it was conceived as a placemaking activity, a vehicle for exploring what other kinds of ways of imagining Singleton were possible.

Literature Review

The focus of this study is an exploration of what can be achieved with effective placemaking activities that engage citizens and invite them to reflect on their relationship with a particular place. We will consider the role of four art installations commissioned by Singleton Shire Council in collaboration with University of Newcastle as part of the Singleton Living Laneways project, for the specific purpose of engaging with citizens and gathering their feedback: memories, perceptions, and evidence of embodied experiences which represent their particular relationship to Singleton, the place in which they live. A systematic discussion of placemaking processes necessitates a thorough engagement with models of placemaking scholarship and related conceptualizations (Aquilino et al. 2021; Brownett and Evans 2020; Ellery and Ellery 2019; Lennon 2020; Lew 2017; Markusen and Nicodemus 2018). With increasing scholarly attention being paid to urban design which supports effective social policies and community well-being (Barton and Grant 2013; Ellery and Ellery 2019; Lennon 2020; Nijkamp and Mobach 2020), literature on placemaking, what it means and how to best achieve it, has likewise proliferated globally. The range of potential schemas for thinking about and discussing placemaking is extensive: health and safety considerations, mental health and community well-being, urban planning, tourism outcomes, educational, historical, architectural, psychological, economic, and political. For the purposes of this study and its relevant founding literature, the focal discussions of placemaking activities will primarily consider concepts that are related to the role of the arts, community arts and art installations as a means of facilitating citizen engagement and collecting community contributions. The literature outlined provides a strong theoretical foundation and conceptual context for how placemaking techniques which invite citizen participation and engagement can help city councils, community groups, and other stakeholders understand how community art projects can encourage citizens to reflect on their own perceptions and understandings of a particular place and, by extension, of themselves in relation to that place.

Many of the terms that are fundamental to a discussion of placemaking are broad and contested terms within a multidisciplinary field of theoretical work. Phrases such as community arts, civic engagement and public sphere, and, indeed, placemaking itself are not unproblematic labels to be used freely with an expectation of collective understanding. These terms refer to concepts that are deeply embedded in the human experience and as such are highly contingent on the context: individual, political, geographic, academic, or historical, for their meaning. Placemaking (or "place-making" or "place making") is often defined broadly in two ways, ways which tend to reflect either bottom-up, community-based generation of meanings, or top-down, professional planning efforts. The first emerges from a cultural geography tradition and considers "how a culture group imprints its values, perceptions, memories, and traditions on a landscape and gives meaning to geographic space (Lew 2017, 449). While the second involves professional design efforts to install particular understandings and perceptions of place, particularly for economic purposes such as encouraging tourism or investment (Lew 2017). While both approaches can be subsumed under the broad definition of "processes of creating spaces that are desirable to live, work and visit" (Lennon 2020, 449), here it may be beneficial to unpack what some of those various processes entail. To this end, Sweeney et al. (2018) suggest that the concept of assemblage, "the interconnectivity and flows between constituent parts…it is the flows of life, traffic, goods and money that give the street its intensity and its emergent sense of place" (573), can lead to a more nuanced understanding of placemaking and the role diverse initiatives can play in regenerating or, in the case of Singleton, NSW, reconceptualizing a city. Through an assemblage lens we can consider a combination of bottom-up and top-down activities in the process of placemaking.

The concept of civic engagement is also vital to this discussion, as analysis of the art installations and the community's interaction with them is underpinned by the assertion that individual's interactions with and contribution to these art installations constitutes the very actions that civic engagement requires. A brief but useful definition of civic engagement as "individual and collective actions designed to identify and address issues of public concern" (Carpelli 2000). This formulation is distinctive from descriptions of *political* engagement in subtle but important ways, with political engagement referring to efforts to influence government or the election of government officials. Civic engagement is typically undertaken in nongovernmental settings and in cooperation with others. In the case of civic engagement through interaction with the arts, it may be helpful to forefront the *action* involved in the interaction rather than the specific individual intention. Community arts programs may not explicitly set out to improve social conditions or address public concerns, nor may the citizens involved, but both may contribute to such outcomes, nevertheless, as such any interaction can arguably constitute civic engagement, especially in the case of community arts festivals and installations.

Importantly for this chapter, the suggestion that placemaking is not a "one and done" process but an ongoing, open-ended process of negotiation and evolution is well supported by many theorists in the field (Sweeney et al. 2018).

> *We view placemaking as an ongoing achievement, never a finished product, where the labour of placemaking continues long after the initial project has been installed. This labour is sometimes iterative, sometimes ephemeral, and it is central to the way placemaking acts to revitalise urban locales. (2018, 72)*

Of the four art installations for this arts festival, three took place during 2021; however, one was postponed indefinitely due to changing conditions and limitations related to the COVID-19 pandemic. Despite the postponement of the final art installation, Oribotics, it is valuable to discuss and document the impact and results of the other projects and examine their contribution to the iterative process of engaging citizens in community-focused placemaking efforts. More important than having a "completed" set of art installations undertaken are the small insights gained at each step in the process, building relationships through collaboration, engaging citizens who would not normally participate in civic matters, and creating shared experiences and memories that support the health of the community and become part of the setting narrative and discourse of place.

Dominating the theoretical landscape at the nexus of place, identity, and citizens' engagement in the arts is the tension between theorists who argue that the materialities of place, i.e., architecture, built environment, and structure, generate relatively stable behavioral patterns; thus, geographic considerations should be given significant weight in the meaning making process, and those who prioritize discursive resources in the process of placemaking and regard place as one option of many in the process of individual identity building. Di Masso and Dixon (2015) refer to this tension as the discursive versus material duality. There is significant discussion in discursive theory about the importance of the role of place in shaping behavior. For example, Toolis argues that

> *behaviour settings are extra-individual, meaning that the patterns of behaviour in the environment have characteristics that are relatively stable regardless of the individual actors within it. The concept that behaviour is place-specific and that situations and places are equal if not better predictors of behaviour than individual characteristics lends strong theoretical support to placemaking as a process for catalyzing change. (2017, 186)*

While others consider that distinctive and discrete "places" emerge in the collective imagination through a combination of discursive resources, not only through the symbols linked to a particular place but also through the narratives ascribed to those symbols by citizens and visitors alike and the plurality of memories, meanings, and perceptions that constitute a particular place's ongoing discursive narrative. For example, in an analysis of the language and images used in tourism brochures for the U.S. city of Vermont, Derrien and Stokowski claim that "discourses emerge within particular settings to express social and cultural relationships and meanings. In the context of environmental interpretation, the language and images of brochures can be seen as intentional discourses produced by agencies and organizations to achieve specific effects in readers" (277). They explain that in linking different conceptions of the symbol of "forest"—productive, recreational, dependent, etc.—to the city of Vermont, the creators of those tourism brochures are discursively "directing the production of place" (277). While neither ends of the spectrum are likely to be comprehensive enough to fully render placemaking processes while accounting for a range of contributing factors, given the value of the individual contribution to these art installations and the emphasis placed on lived experience, this chapter tends to favor a discursive frame of action as a framework for the analysis.

While symbols used for tourism purposes can be limited and repetitive, there is a distinct schism in the literature between studies which focus on placemaking in the service of developing dominant discourses for tourism purposes and those that are more grounded in examining the perceptions and assumptions citizens have for the place they live. Lew's analysis of sixty-two examples of placemaking studies found that 43% of articles features tourism as a primary focus, these examples of planned placemaking tend to feature top-down approaches by councils or governments to shape the popular image of a place through image building and myth-making discursive techniques (Lew 2017). Sofield et al. similarly argue that "placemaking has...become an institutionalized industry often supported by multimillion-dollar budgets, but rarely are communities in control" (2017, 1). As symbols used for tourism and economic purposes are often geared toward selling particular experiences or products that a place is well known for, these top-down processes may not always function in the best interests or well-being of residents. This study therefore seeks to analyze and engage with a more nuanced range of symbols and perceptions that emerge from living in a place and experiencing its changes and developments in an intimate way which comes from living and experiencing the realities of a place day-to-day.

The aim of the Singleton Living Laneways project was to solicit citizens' reflections of their day-to-day reality within the Singleton Shire community. In order to do so, a catalyst for critical reflection was needed and can often be provided in the form of a "fresh perspective" of place. Foucault's concept of heterotopia offers us a unique way of thinking about a place, particularly a place transformed, by the addition of community arts initiatives. Brownett and Evans contend that:

> *Foucault's concept of the "heterotopia" can meaningfully be applied to the way local arts festivals can transform community space. He perceived heterotopia as sites contiguous with everyday spaces; connected to, and yet apart from, those spaces. These spaces facilitate transformation through the activities that they engender. (2020, 2)*

The transformative power of heterotopias lies in their potential to remake familiar spaces into something new and unknown, by changing our perceptions of everyday spaces it can help us see familiar things with a fresh perspective, challenge prejudices and assumptions and allow space for self-reflection and evaluation. This is exactly what community arts installations can and do achieve (Brownett and Evans 2020). Brownette and Evans's empirical research into eight different community arts festivals in Southeast England found that "arts festivals also provide an opportunity for conversations about how the community are perceived or perceive themselves.

Organizers talked about using small grants to fund consultative art works to help people get to know their local area…or to find out more about their local community, or how they felt about themselves" (2020, 4). The four Singleton art installations sought to achieve this same end, by rendering familiar spaces, in this case four specific laneways in the center of town, new or different and by engaging various senses to bring the invisible or unnoticed to the fore of the embodied experience and then asking participants to document and contribute their subsequent reflections.

An emphasis on difference and also the centrality of embodied or lived experience similarly echoes through the Arendtian concept of "worldliness." "Arendt conceived the 'world' as the commonality of the shared space between people that enables them to recognize, acknowledge and appreciate each other as similar but unique" (2020, 452). Arendt is of the view that "modern society has eroded opportunities for informed critique, careful debate and the mutually considerate interactions that emerge from relationships that recognize, support and value difference. For her, the 'world' is an experience constituted by bonds that create a sense of something shared concurrent to facilitating respect for the uniqueness of different viewpoints" (Lennon 2020, 452). Arendt's unique conception of worldliness and the ability to see each other for who, rather than what, we are is a particularly relevant way of thinking about community arts projects.

> *To live together in the world means essentially that a world of things is between those who have it in common, as a table is located between those who sit around it; the world, like every in-between, relates and separates men at the same time. (Arendt 1958, 52)*

Just like Arendt's table metaphor, the space which simultaneously separates and relates, community arts installations which invite participant contribution or engagement have the potential to constitute that space "in-between" which enables relations and interaction between participants while highlighting the uniqueness of our individual lived experiences. For example, Shadowgram encourages participants to locate a shadow portrait of themselves on a landscape of the town, quite literally asking them to position themselves in relation to other residents and then adding their own individual comments or thoughts.

Such a plurality of voices and experiences is a repetitive motif of placemaking literature. One of the notable features of all the artworks encompassed within the Singleton Laneways Activation project case study is that they all facilitate the collection of contributions from the community. The Acoustic Alley installation captured soundscapes of the local area through field recordings and community contributions, then reinterpreting these in the context of the laneway setting with interactive embedded speakers. Shadowgram is described as a method for social brainstorming; it combines a video camera, a human-scale lightbox, an image analysis software, and a digital cutting machine to create stickers of participant's shadow portraits which they place on a large-scale image of the town, along with a comment written in an accompanying speech bubble. The shadow and text unit creates a microstory that weaves into larger dialogues and groups, and eventually creates a large-scale landscape of bodies, voices, ideas, and questions.

Similarly, Aquilino et al. document the various key discourses used to discuss and promote the "World Alternative Games," held in the rural Welsh town of Llanwrtyd Wells. The rurality of the town and the "alternativeness" of the games being held, competitions that are made possible by the rural location of the host city, are key discourses used to promote the games and more general tourism in the area. The scenes of rolling green hills of the Welsh countryside are symbolic of the rurality of the remote town. Aquilino et al.'s claim that "rurality can be understood as a discourse through which a place is shaped through the development of symbolic meaningful connections mutually affecting rural space and people" (2021, 139) is of particular relevance to this discussion, as the subject of the study, Singleton, the host town of the community arts and placemaking project, is an Australian town characterized by its rurality, albeit a rurality indicated through geographic symbols vastly different from those of the Llanwrtyd Wells study. Dry, open plains or paddocks indicate the frequent and ongoing drought conditions experienced in rural NSW towns. A colonial architecture-style pub on the corner of a main street.

The engagement of citizens with arts festivals and art installations as a more accessible method of civic participation and contribution to policy and planning considerations is a growing area of scholarship and is of particular interest to this study. "Critical placemaking can serve as a tool for civic engagement by facilitating empowerment" (Toolis 2017, 189). Community arts events and festivals offer unique opportunities for citizens to become involved, contribute, reflect and have their voices heard in a manner that a formal town hall meeting, hearing or inquiry would be unlikely to facilitate. Maton defines empowerment as "a group-based, participatory, developmental process through which marginalized or oppressed individuals and groups gain greater control over their lives and environments, acquire valued resources and basic rights, and achieve important life goals and reduced societal marginalization" (2008, 5).

As many theorists note, placemaking can be a top-down or bottom-up process depending on the level of community participation involved. Ellery and Ellery (2019) note the value of co-production of community and council in the planning and design process, they advocate the use of Arnstein's ladder of citizen participation (Arnstein 2015) to increase the likelihood that "a sense of place within the host community will be developed as an outcome of the planning and design process" (237). In Arnstein's ladder there are eight levels of citizen participation which are categories based on the degree to which citizen participation impacts decision-making: manipulation, therapy, informing, consultation, placation, partnership, delegated power, and citizen control. Manipulation and therapy are characterized by non-participation of citizens; informing, consultation, and placation are efforts of tokenism; and partnership and delegated power offer citizens control over decision-making processes.

The discussion throughout this chapter frames how and why community arts installations can facilitate community engagement and by extension civic engagement and how these arts projects can aid in formal and informal placemaking processes by stimulating reflection and contemplation of their town and their own place embedded within their community. Ultimately, qualitative data are essential to capture the perceptions of citizens and the things, people, and places that they ascribe meaning to. Given the relatively small scale of this project, the following discussion is an initial exploration of the four Living Laneways projects, Shadowgram, Acoustic Alley, Media Orbs, and Oribotics, within the specific context of the rural NSW town of Singleton. While similar studies have documented the role of community arts projects in other places, both large cities and small towns (Aquilino et al. 2021; Derrien and Stokowski 2017; Di Masso and Dixon 2015; Thomas et al. 2015), this chapter offers unique insights into placemaking processes and community arts projects specifically within an Australian context and a rural setting. The feedback on this project is highly context and place dependent and as such are not generalizable beyond the parameters of the original study. Even the temporal position of the project, undertaken throughout 2020 and 2021, makes community engagement particularly specific to the upheaval and uncertainty caused by the COVID-19 pandemic.

The case study incorporates four art installations commissioned by the University of Newcastle in partnership with Singleton Shire Council. The installations occupied one "laneway" each with the goal of activating that particular laneway to achieve the following goals: explore new models of collaborative dialogue between citizens and governance, encourage citizens to support local businesses by buying local, bring people back into the township post-COVID-19 and change public perceptions of art in a regional Australian community. The projects chosen for participation include Shadowgram, which was developed by the Ars Electronica research team (Roland Haring, Matthew Gardiner, Christopher Lindinger, and Hideki Ogawa); Acoustic Alley, which was developed by Dr. Nicole Carroll and associate professor Jon Drummond, professor Paul Egglestone and Dr. Kristefan Minski; Media Orbs, which was developed by Ralph Kenke; and Oribotics, which was originally planned to be conducted by Professor Paul Egglestone, Dr. Simone O'Callaghan, and Dr. Kristefan Minski from the School of Creative Industries.

The Living Laneways Artworks

Four individual pieces of work were commissioned for the project. Each was proposed to a small peer group of FASTlab researchers led by the project chief investigator. After initial feedback from the team the concepts were presented to Singleton Council either by the artist themselves or by Minski, performing in the role as FASTlab's artist and producer for the Living Laneways series.

Across the four commissioned works, the original intention of the researchers was to engage and elicit ideas, thoughts, and reflections from Singleton's citizens about perceptions of their town using four different approaches, each responding to the selected location and allied to the individual artwork. Shadowgram's focus was to capture written expressions from individuals. Placing Ralph Kenke's substantial interactive "Burns Lane Cloud" installation, or "Media Orbs" as it was referred to by the Council, in Burns lane and capturing the community's reaction to it on video alongside a questionnaire provided the additional dimension of audiovisual data to accompany the written contributions. Media Orbs probed people's responses to a socially situated artwork that was highly novel and unusual in this context creating a framework for responses to arts and culture in the town. The Sounds of Singleton sought direct engagement from the community in the co-creation of a sound installation. The data collected through this piece envisioned by sound artists Nicole Carroll and Jon Drummond provided a useful reflection on people's appetite for and willingness to participate in a digital "crowd sourced" collaborative artwork designed to reflect their personal soundscapes of Singleton. With its perceived and real higher barriers to participation—requiring a mobile phone and the skills to record and upload audio content to a web server—Sounds of Singleton engaged a different community who seldom participate in formal consultation processes run along traditionally accepted lines. The final Living Laneways piece was also collaborative, though for this work community members participated in a physical workshop conducted at the newly opened Singleton Art Gallery. Oribitiks workshops implicitly exposed participants to alternative outlooks and possibilities through digital upskilling allied to traditional craft skills. The workshops were inherently collaborative and by their nature participatory.

Shadowgram – Bourke's Arcade

The first of the works to be selected through this process and formally commissioned by Singleton Council was titled Shadowgram. Developed by Ars Electronica Futurelab, the Shadowgram installation opened in Bourke's Arcade, Singleton, on Tuesday March 16 (2020). It was conceived as a method of social brainstorming through a creative catalyst methodology, a system that enables the audience to discover and contribute through their creativity. The term shadowgram refers to an analogue photographic technique of Photogenic Drawing, whereby an object placed on a sheet of photosensitized paper that through a light-activated chemical reaction creates a shadow image of the object on the paper. Shadowgram is a conceptual extension of this idea, combining a video camera, a human-scale light box, an image analysis software, and a digital cutting machine. Each personal shadow portrait acts as a start point for responding to the project provocation, the question "What is our tomorrow?" With each shadow is an associated text presented on a sticker. The shadow and text unit creates a microstory that weaves into larger dialogues and groups, and eventually creates a large-scale landscape of bodies, voices, ideas, and questions.

In the first two days of operation an average of twelve people participated in each two-hour session, and seventy shadowgrams were made. Participants generally spent

Figure 1: A Singleton Family Participates in the Shadowgram Installation Inside Bourke's Arcade

around five to ten minutes interacting with the work, while some conversations with information trainers went for much longer. Many participants said they would return with family or friends. A follow-up report of the project and its participants notes a number of highlights, including this interaction with an old Singleton resident:

> *This quite frail 89-year-old woman and her daughter were asked if they would like to make a shadow picture. The daughter said they were in a hurry but the 89-year-old showed interest. She was helped onto the platform (she walks with a stick) and made a shadowgram. She had a conversation about living here for most of her life and made a reference to now being over the hill. At our suggestion her shadow was stuck on top of the hill overlooking the town. She then sat with her daughter for 30 minutes looking at the work. We believe it was a profound reflective experience for both mother and daughter contemplating her life within this community.*

Figure 2: Tri Wall Artworks Created by Ari Chand

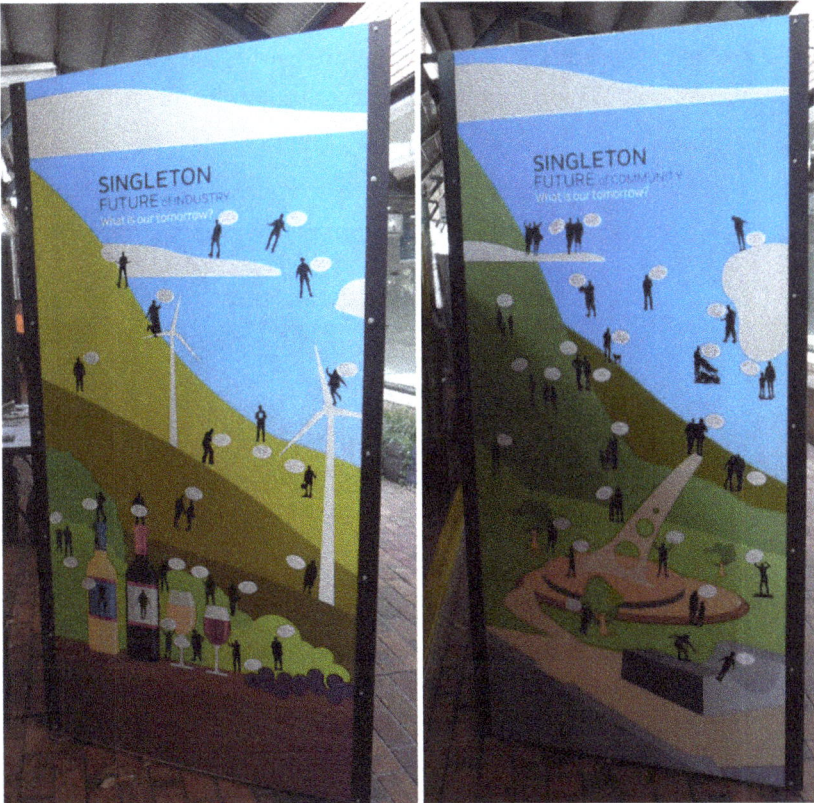

Other comments made on the text stickers included: "Such a thriving community if you get amongst it. We love Parkrun," "More arts and craft shops," "Local businesses run by locals. More things for young people," "I love all the disability access my community offers," and "A community where my family can grow."

Burns Lane Cloud — Burns Lane

Ralph Kenke is a FASTlab artist and researcher whose practice-based research investigates prototyping as the origins of innovation for speculative art and design concepts. For this piece, the second in the Living Laneways program of work, Singleton Council initiated a transformation of its city center to become more attractive for pedestrians. The city had decided to close Burns Lane, a narrow road connecting its old town center with its modern shopping center. However, blocking car traffic at Burns Lane polarized its citizens. A debate on the value of public spaces and the benefits of road accessibility split the community on the temporary closure of Burns Lane. Through a creative and interactive solution, Kenke's response prompts a reframing of the community's perception of loss — in this case the temporary loss of access — to the benefits of a newly gained and repurposed space, thereby prompting citizens to experience their city in a different light.

Figure 3: Initial Technical Plan and Final Installation

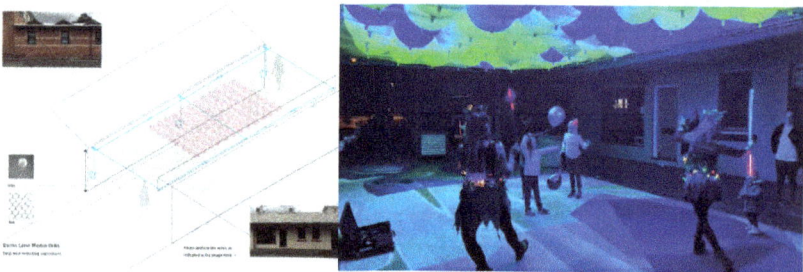

The work itself comprised 100 helium-filled latex balloons suspended 3 m above Burns Lane, creating an overhead canopy with a cloudlike appearance. Embedded within the large balloons, chosen to match the volume of the human body, a series of proximity sensors automatically switched the color of inbuilt LEDs in response to the movement of people beneath them. The balloons changed from vibrant green to blue, leaving visible traces of people's paths as meandering lines of temporarily ignited blue balloons. The "Burns Lane Cloud" installation, or "Media Orbs" as it was referred to by the Council, was subsequently awarded three Australian Graphic Design Association Awards (AGDA) in Multi-sensory installations, Spatial Design and Technological Innovation. (See the following chapter for a more detailed discussion of this work, later relabeled "Ballooino."[1])

Acoustic Alley – Tre Bella Lane

FASTlab's Nicole Carroll is a composer, performer, sound designer, and builder working with audio, video, and tangible objects. Her work spans installation, improvisation, and fixed media performance, across noise, soundscape, and acousmatic genres. Working with Jon Drummond, an academic, a composer, and a sound artist whose work explores interactive electroacoustics, robotics, sonification, and acoustic ecology, she created the third in the series of art installations for Singleton's laneways project. "Acoustic Alley" was a soundscape experience that invited people to record the sounds of Singleton on their smartphone and submit them to an online portal. Sounds recorded by citizens were combined with audio files captured by Carroll and Drummond who also created a series of "mix loop" files designed to connect people with the sonic heritage of Singleton. The team adapted three of Singleton Council's benches embedding motion sensors to trigger audio files played from technology mounted within the benches themselves.

Figure 4: Technical Diagram of Bench "Speaker"

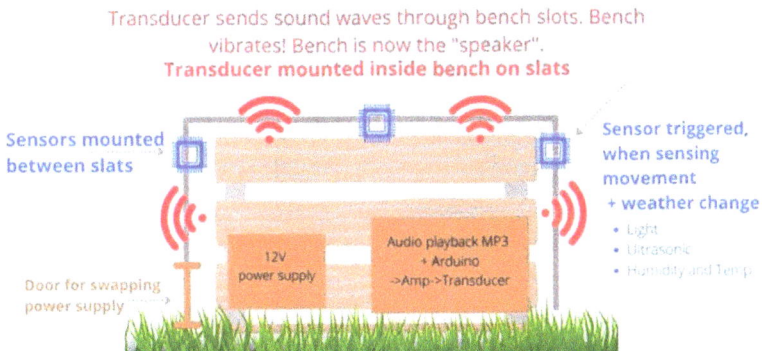

Singleton Laneway Audio Installation

Self-Contained: All equipment is housed inside benches

Transducer sends sound waves through bench slots. Bench vibrates! Bench is now the "speaker".
Transducer mounted inside bench on slats

Sensors mounted between slats

Sensor triggered, when sensing movement + weather change
• Light
• Ultrasonic
• Humidity and Temp

12V power supply

Audio playback MP3 + Arduino ->Amp->Transducer

Door for swapping power supply

---

[1] Media Orbs was the term the Singleton council referred to the project through implementation. The project's preferred term Ballooino refers to the primary circuit board (PCB) designs.

The benches were in Tre Bella Lane, a busy pedestrian thoroughfare connecting the carpark to the high street. Described by Vicki Brereton, Council's director of organization and community capacity, as "the perfect opportunity for people to get involved in a public art experiment while promoting greater engagement with the town centre," the Acoustic Alley offered a further channel for citizens to engage.

Figure 5: Acoustic Alley Audio Benches in Tre Bella Laneway with a Passer-By

Figure 6: Proposal Slide for Oribotics

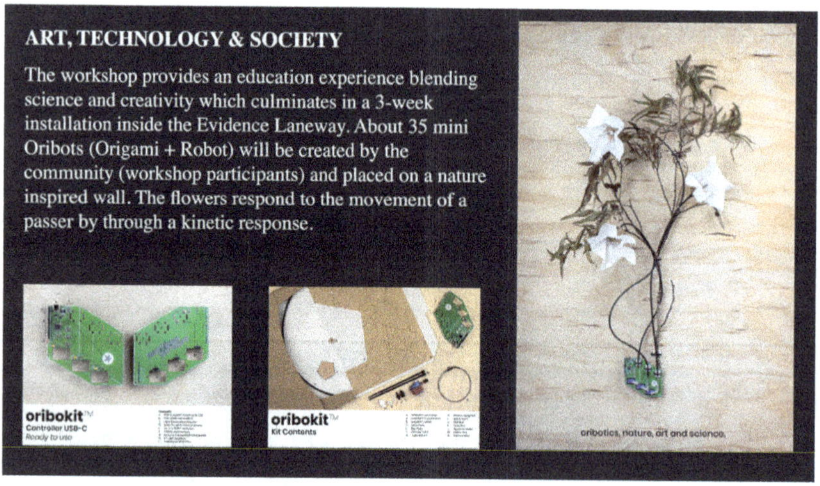

Oribotics – Evidence Lane

The final piece in the Singleton Living Laneways project introduced the Singleton community to Oribotics, Matthew Gardiner's ongoing art/science fusion of origami and technology, specifically "bot" technology, such as robots, or intelligent computer agents known as bots. Oribotics is a joining of two complex fields of study. Ori comes from the Japanese verb Oru, literally meaning "to fold." Origami, the Japanese word for paper folding, comes from the same root. Oribotics is origami that is controlled by robot technology: paper that will fold and unfold on command. During the workshops participants assembled one hundred oribotic "flowers" that were later wall mounted on a temporary public display in the Evidence Laneway. The flowers opened and closed in response to changing levels of light detected through a series of sensors which activated the inbuilt mechanical robotics manipulating the paper flowers.

Conclusion: Findings and Next Steps

These small installations in a regional town within NSW demonstrate the potential for site-specific experimentation within a (smart city) placemaking frame. Each of the laneways projects drew from a commitment toward co-design with local stakeholders (including but not limited to the "client" Singleton council) to determine the location and nature of the interactive experience to be developed by small, multidisciplinary design teams. Each installation provided a focus and a prompt for participatory engagement from members of the local community, and each offered a distinctive opportunity for them to surface their own voices within a reimagining of places using sophisticated and innovative technologies.

REFERENCES

Amineh, R. J., and H. D. Asl. 2015. "Review of Constructivism and Social Constructivism." *Journal of Social Sciences, Literature and Languages* 1 (1): 9–16.

Aquilino, L., J. Harris, and N. Wise. 2021. "A Sense of Rurality: Events, Placemaking and Community Participation in a Small Welsh Town." *Journal of Rural Studies* 83: 138–145.

Arnstein, S. 2015. "A Ladder of Citizen Participation." In *The City Reader*, edited by Richard T. LeGates and Frederic Stout. Routledge.

Barton, H., and M. Grant. 2013. "Urban Planning for Healthy Cities." *Journal of Urban Health* 90 (1): 129–141.

Brownett, T., and O. Evans. 2020. "Finding Common Ground: The Conception of Community Arts Festivals as Spaces for Placemaking." *Health & Place* 61: 102254.

Delli Carpini, M. X. 2000. "Gen.com: Youth, Civic Engagement, and the New Information Environment." *Political Communication* 17 (4): 341–349.

Derrien, M. M., and P. A. Stokowski. 2017. "Discourses of Place: Environmental Interpretation About Vermont Forests." *Environmental Communication* 11 (2): 276–287. https://doi.org/10.1080/17524032.2016.1211160.

Di Masso, A., and J. Dixon. 2015. "More Than Words: Place, Discourse and the Struggle over Public Space in Barcelona." *Qualitative Research in Psychology* 12 (1): 45–60.

Ellery, P. J., and J. Ellery. 2019. "Strengthening Community Sense of Place Through Placemaking." *Urban Planning* 4 (2): 237–248.

Lennon, M. 2020. "The Art of Inclusion: Phenomenology, Placemaking and the Role of the Arts." *Journal of Urban Design* 25 (4): 449–466.

Lew, A. A. 2017. "Tourism Planning and Place Making: Place-Making or Placemaking?" *Tourism Geographies* 19 (3): 448–466.

Markusen, A., and A. G. Nicodemus. 2018. "Creative Placemaking: Reflections on a 21st-Century American Arts Policy Initiative." In *Creative Placemaking*, edited by C. Courage and A. Mckeown. Routledge.

Nijkamp, J. E., and M. P. Mobach. 2020. "Developing Healthy Cities with Urban Facility Management." *Facilities* 38 (11/12): 819–833.

Sofield, T., J. Guia, and J. Specht. 2017. "Organic 'Folkloric' Community Driven Place-Making and Tourism." *Tourism Management* 61: 1–22.

Sweeney, J., K. Mee, P. McGuirk, and K. Ruming. 2018. "Assembling Placemaking: Making and Remaking Place in a Regenerating City." *Cultural Geographies* 25 (4): 571–587.

Thomas, E., S. Pate, and A. Ranson. 2015. "The Crosstown Initiative: Art, Community, and Placemaking in Memphis." *American Journal of Community Psychology* 55 (1–2): 74–88.

Toolis, E. E. 2017. "Theorizing Critical Placemaking as a Tool for Reclaiming Public Space." *American Journal of Community Psychology* 59 (1–2): 184–199.

CHAPTER 4

Ballooino Media Balloons: Floating Pixels for an Agile Design of Responsive Public Spaces in Smart Cities

Ralph Kenke and Elmar Trefz

Abstract

Public spaces provide a place for citizens to meet and interact. People tend to socialize through digital platforms rather than meeting serendipitously in urban settings. Smart cities, media architecture, and media facades are aimed at creating experiential public spaces. Issues such as technology integration, scalability, and affordances in the context of urban design and government management are at the center of the media architecture discourse. Critics are calling for fewer screen-based experiences as well as a move away from rigid architectural structures. This pictorial on Ballooino media balloons aims to explore how familiar objects combined with embedded systems design can lead to the creation of experiential public spaces that invite citizen engagement. We position this study as part of the TEI community's collective effort to thrive in the area of human–computer interaction, which places people at the center of the research and design process.

Introduction

Research and development of media facades is contributing to the growing demand for smart cities. Media balloon research is situated at the crossroads between media architecture and public interactive art installation research.

The components of smart cities bring both benefits and challenges. There is no "smart city in a box," despite this term being currently used in the discourse (Hemment and Townsend 2013). The notion of smart cities enables major capital cities, megacities, and small cities alike to prepare for more robust technological infrastructure and imagine an environment for their future citizens (Cardullo and Kitchin 2019; Gehl [1971] 1987). De Wall terms smart cities "urban imaginaries" (De Waal and Dignum 2017). We identify two views or imaginaries (Kitchin 2014) that aim for slightly different objectives. The first is driven by a focus on technological infrastructure, urban planning, investment policies and economic growth. The second has a different motivation—to create a "control room" (Breuer et al. 2014) that enables real-time regulation and governance, a smart city that can monitor activities, effectively control public utilities, and even use data to project scenarios for either safety reasons or future urban development.

Figure 1: Ballooino Launch

Source: all images by authors

Both imaginaries provide benefits. The first involves improved technological infrastructure, which will improve access to public services, reduce administrative tasks, and eliminate bureaucratic processes by digitizing government services. This version invites new skilled citizens and demonstrates the diversity and openness of a city. The second vision, real-time regulation and monitoring, may provide safer and more effective urban spaces. Responding quickly to the needs of citizens for urban spaces is promising. According to Rob Kitchin (2014):

> *Over the past 15 years, the concept of smart cities has gained traction amongst businesses, governments, the media and academia to refer to, on the one hand, the use of information and communication technologies (ICTs) to stimulate economic development and, on the other, the extensive embedding of software-enabled technologies into the fabric of cities to augment urban management. With respect to the first vision, a smart city is one whose economy is increasingly driven by technically inspired innovation, creativity and entrepreneurship, enacted by smart people. It is posited that smart policies and judicious investment in appropriate fiscal measures, human capital and technological infrastructures and programmes will attract businesses and jobs, create efficiencies and savings and raise the productivity and competitiveness of government and businesses. The second perspective envisages a smart city as one that can be monitored, managed and regulated in real-time using ICT infrastructure and ubiquitous computing.*

The challenge with the technocentric view is that it is focused on up-to-date technologies and value-for-money purchases rather than on human interactions. It is more concerned with transactional human interactions rather than a cultural shift that can transform cities into smart cities. In contrast, the control room perspective raises a moral concern: Are citizens comfortable with a panopticon city? It is questionable whether citizens benefit from real-time monitoring while sacrificing their privacy for the sake of safety.

Researchers have argued that theoretical and practical approaches to designing smart cities tend to be top down (Cardullo and Kitchin 2019). Media architecture aims to address the lack of engagement of citizens when shaping ideas for public places. The field of media facades, in particular, has made significant progress in recent years (Scully and Mayze 2018). The digital displays, projections, and bespoke electronics in media facades are part of a new wave of designing cities for a digital urban future: "A media facade is any external building surface with an integrated capacity to display dynamic graphics, images, texts, and spatial movement" (Heausler 2009). Media facades are different from urban screens or digital billboards, which are typically used for advertising. Sade (2014) argues that:

> *media facades hold the potential to tell, or embody, unfolding stories that have rich interconnections with practices, people and place — as opposed to projections of a globalized culture through a televisual aesthetic and advertising images,*

However, McCullough (2013) argues that despite the promising use of new technologies, most media facades result in a screen-based or billboard approach and "seldom as genuine extensions of architecture."

With their ability to turn large structures into interactive displays, media facades offer exciting possibilities for the future of smart cities. However, critics have pointed out that they are limited in the context of public spaces. For example, "in stressing the integration of a dynamic display with a building envelope, the media facade is a more restricted category than the urban screen" (Buckley 2019). Media facades are projected onto flat vertical building surfaces; therefore, their use in activating public places is limited in places without such structures.

Therefore, our research project focuses on the development of media balloons, with the aim of offering the opportunity to explore responsive public spaces that sit outside the media facade constraint. Media balloons are floating pixels that do not rely on a flat surface and can be placed away from buildings and their facades. Even the construction of a floating temporary built environment is possible.

Cost for Responsive Public Spaces

Apart from the fact that media facades have limited application to future smart cities, particularly in the development of responsive public places, given their reliance on vertical attachment to buildings, a second limitation is their operational expenses and building costs, which must be considered when designing a project. The high cost of media facades is including in the budgets of smart cities, which may lead to "sterile, overly planned, prohibitively expensive, and uniform and conformist results. Cities struggle to complete such projects within the predicted budgets and timeframe" (Conway 2013; Sennet 2013). For example, the project Living Connections, which will last ten years, has cost 39.5 million CAD (Paquin 2019). In total, 2,807 LED lights were installed on a bridge in Montreal, tinting the steel structure a different color each season—orange in summer, red in autumn, blue in winter, and green in spring.

The aim of media balloons is to reduce costs using a rapid probing method to facilitate the exploration of responsive public spaces. This pictorial demonstrates the flexibility, scalability, and versatility of media balloons.

Theoretical Position

This research project is situated at the intersection between smart city design, media architecture and media facades. Using a human-centered design approach, we contextualize our discoveries by documenting the process, methods and observations in this pictorial. An example of the successful implementation of human-centered media architecture in public spaces is Jeppe Hein's social benches.[1] This modification of existing park benches shows that media architecture need not be technocratically inspired but can make use of well-known existing objects. Focusing on human needs can create experiences that engage and excite the public. Similarly, a modification of an existing object of play — the balloon — led to the development of media balloons in this research. Media balloons address the limitations of media facades, which include their technological complexity, lengthy research and development phase and lack of flexibility in addressing site-specific constraints during implementation. Another feature of media balloons is their scalability for temporary use. Our study is linked to a commissioned responsive public space project. Thus, to address the core challenge faced by the city council, we proposed an urban plan to temporarily convert a road into a pedestrian zone, which had consequences for the city's infrastructure and mobility. In our proposed responsive public space installation, we developed a media balloon that enabled interaction with citizens while displaying a collaborative experience. To create the proposed responsive public space installation, we applied a rapid probing method and developed a range of media balloons for testing. In this chapter, we divide the process into three components:

1. Propose a site-specific responsive public space installation and collaborate with city client
2. Hardware and software design
3. Housing and structural design.

This is followed by a comparison of the two design modes for the media balloons (also described as inflatable pixels): touch-responsive and proximity-responsive public space installations.

---

[1] https://www.jeppehein.net/project_id.php?path=works&id=102.

Audit for a Site-Specific Responsive Public Space Installation

Burns Lane is located in a rural Australian city. The proposed initiative was to temporarily block motor vehicle traffic and convert the lane into a space where the public was invited to interact. We offered pedestrians a new perspective of their familiar terrain. The city representative informed us that citizens were divided on the blocking of motor vehicles; thus, our proposal was aimed at increasing foot traffic in Burns Lane. Jan Gehl suggests that a public space is both a place to linger and a link to somewhere else. Following our site observation, we identified the characteristics of the place, which connected the city's main road (John Street) with its newly built shopping mall parking lot.

Related Works

We derived the idea for media balloons from other media facade designs with consideration of the critique that media facades can be more than a display or projection of visual content. Therefore, we conceptualized a single unit that can respond to citizens' activities. We also wanted to ensure that the design was not technocentric nor intrusive in terms of collecting private data. Our focus was to invite citizens to engage with their public space (Figure 2) (Burns Lane) in

Figure 2: Burns Lane

Figure 3: Burns Lane Cloud

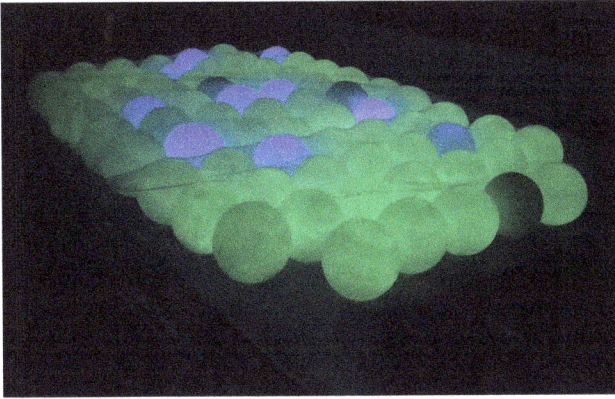

a playful way. We addressed this by designing what we called a media balloon, an object that was familiar and inclusive across a broad demographic. Based on the rapid probing method, media balloons are flexible, static, moving, and responsive installations that are scalable for temporary use. For our site-specific responsive installation, we designed what we termed the "Burns Lane Cloud" (Figure 3).

We intentionally aimed for a pixel aesthetic, despite being aware that such a format is limited in visualizing content because of its low resolution. Informed by other media architecture prototypes, we understood that "despite being a very simple and low-resolution LED matrix, it enables the creation of visual content and participatory interaction on many levels" (Cordeiro 2018). Similar to Chromapollination (Hespanhol and Tomitsch 2012), which was strongly informed by the site in which it was installed, Burns Lane Cloud hovers as a white cloud above pedestrians during the day and transforms into a vibrant light source at night.

Few projects have explored the use of balloons in responsive public spaces. The most important work was conducted by WHITEvoid, an interactive art and design studio in Berlin that has created Electric Moons, a kinetic balloon installation using LED light. The installation at St. Maria Church in Stuttgart, Germany, was powered with wires and responded to music at the church rather than to visitors, who were not able to engage with the balloons.[2]

---

[2] https://www.whitevoid.com/news/

Responsive Public Space Installation: Pitch for a City Client

Prior to commencing the project, we conducted an audit of the location and interviewed the client (Singleton Council). After interviewing council members, we were able to define the key challenge faced by the council and envision a concept for a site-specific responsive installation. In our proposal, we offered a range of ideas and solutions to turn Burns Lane, a temporarily blocked road, into a public space. Citizens were divided about the temporary closing of a road that connects the city's main road with its shopping center situated one block away.

The built environment surrounding Burns Lane inspired us to propose an elevated interactive element (Figure 4). Given the similar height of buildings on both sides of the road, we initially considered a floating sail or a similar construction. This idea resonated with most council members because the initial idea for a responsive public space had been based on a media facade approach in which graphics would be projected onto the buildings on both sides of the road.

Figure 4: Render of Burns Lane Cloud

[D] Render of Burns Lane Cloud

We received approval for our proposition to suspend floating pixels between the two roofs that would display various visuals (e.g., colored graphics showing a house, tree or beach) created by interactions with citizens, either individually or collectively. Within the limitations of pixel graphics, we explored the visuals that could be created by citizens interacting with and determining the individual colors of media balloons.

Figure 5: Burns Lane Cloud. Top View

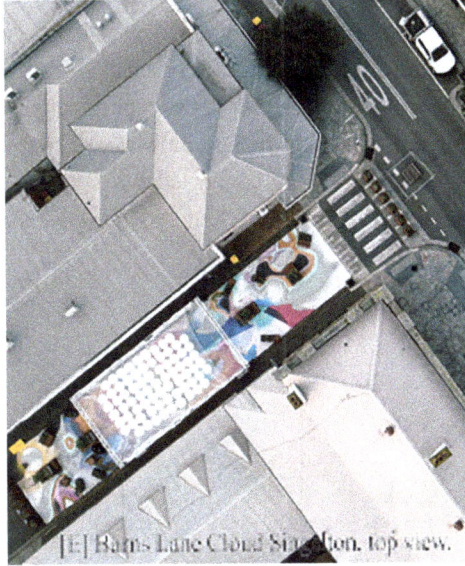

[E] Burns Lane Cloud Simulation. top view.

Figure 6: Three Examples of Colored Pixel Graphics

Figure 7: Three Examples of Colored Icons

We divided these potential graphics into six categories: color pixel graphics (Figure 6), color icons (Figure 7), dual-color icons (Figure 8), dual characters (Figure 9), colored heat map (Figure 10), and dual tracking map (Figure 11).

We decided to explore the idea of a responsive balloon, a single floating pixel that responded by changing color when a person physically interacted with the installation. The initial proposition (first mode) was to stay true to the balloon's nature by using a conductive "string" connected to a circuit and a red/green/blue (RGB) LED inside the floating helium balloons. However, given the client's

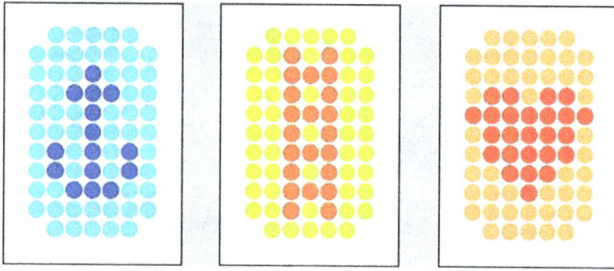

Figure 8: Three Examples of Dual-Colored Icons

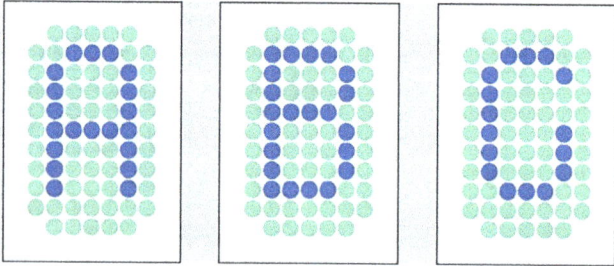

Figure 9: Three Dual-Colored Characters

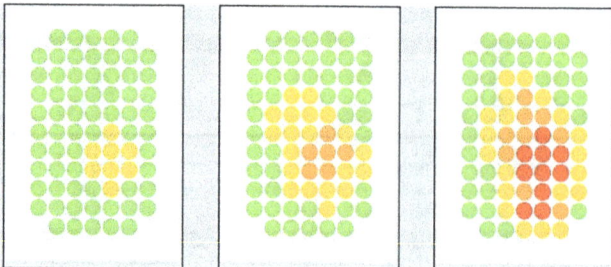

Figure 10: Sequence of Colored Heat Map

Figure 11: Sequence of Dual-Color Tracking Map

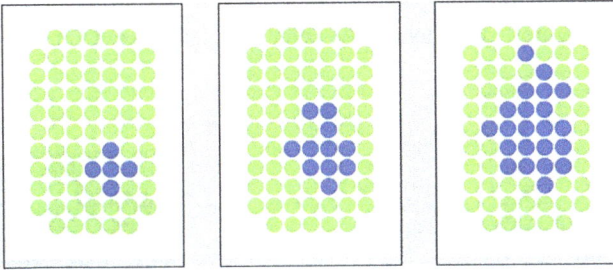

concern about balloons escaping and COVID-19 restrictions, we developed a second mode: a proximity sensor (Figure 5) that enabled interaction without physical contact.

Interactive Modes and Response

Before designing the media balloons, we created renders and drawings to communicate to the client the intention of the two different interaction modes. Both modes relied on a dark surrounding; consequently, the interaction took place after sunset. First mode: Using a conductive "string" connected to a circuit at the bottom of the balloon (Figure 12) that enabled intact and changed the color red/green/blue (RGB) value of the balloon. This mode enabled determining the color of the floating pixel and on a large-scale install display any colored graphic (Figures 6–11). Second mode: A ground-pointing proximity sensor attached to the

Figure 12: First Mode, Conductive String, Interactive Touch Sensor

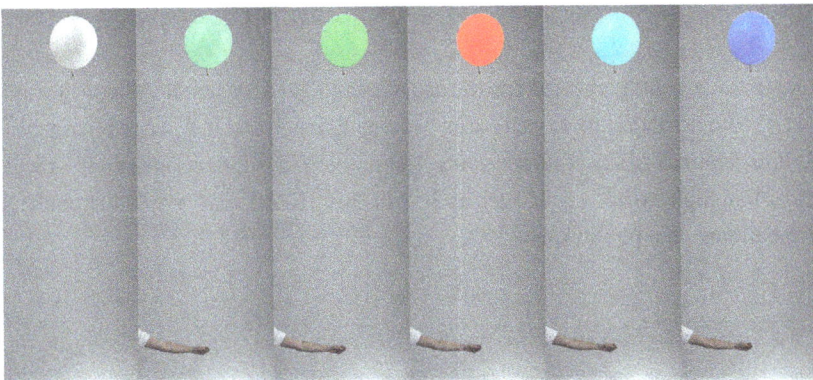

bottom of the balloon enabled interaction by a person positioning underneath it (Figure 13). To achieve an intuitive interactive response, a dual tracking map was displayed (Figure 11), switching the color between green and blue (Figure 14).

Figure 13: Second Mode: Interaction with Proximity Sensor

Figure 14: Prototype Control Units

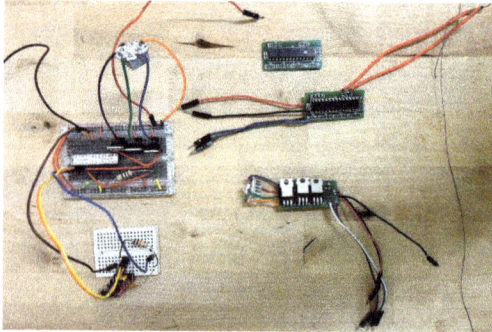

Ballooino Design and Development

Our initial research revealed that the use of common LEDs inside balloons would not be sufficiently bright to achieve an experiential look and feel in a public space.[3] While common LEDs provided some illumination in a dark environment, it was clear that high-power LEDs such as 3 W or 9 W RGB LEDs would be required for balloons in a public space.[4]

---

[3] https://core-electronics.com.au/led-mixed-bag-10mm-11921.html.

[4] https://core-electronics.com.au/3w-9w-rgb-led-common-anode.html.

However, common batteries were not capable of powering these LEDs; thus, we had to find rechargeable batteries with sufficient voltage and current to power them over a prolonged period. After further research, we identified the 18650 lithium-ion battery, which has a current of 2,600 mAh and a voltage of 3.7 V.[5]

To achieve an optimal balance between brightness and duration, we used the 3 W LED rather than the 9 W LED. The 3 W LED uses up to 350 mA, resulting in a minimum duration of 2,600 mAh/350 mA = 7.43 hours.[6]

The first proof of concept was developed by soldering a 18650 battery to the green pin of the 3 W LED and reusing the housing of a LED torch (Figure 15).[7] A heat sink needed to be attached to the back of the 3 W LED to dissipate heat (Figure 16).[8] The assembled unit, including housing, LED light, battery, and heat sink, was then dropped inside a deflated 90 cm Qualatex balloon (Figure 17)[9] with a string attached to the back of the unit. The balloon was then inflated with helium.[10] Once the balloon was inflated to its full size, the housing was pulled back into the neck of the balloon to center the LED and simultaneously seal the balloon. We chose a housing with a diameter that enabled us to create an airtight seal.

Figure 15: Housing LED Torch

[5] https://core-electronics.com.au/polymer-lithium-ion-battery-18650-cell-2600mah-solder-tab.html.

[6] https://core-electronics.com.au/3w-9w-rgb-led-common-anode.html.

[7] https://www.jaycar.com.au/handy-led-torch/p/ST3432

[8] https://core-electronics.com.au/al-heat-sink-with-adhesive-tape-13-13-7mm.html.

[9] https://www.spotlightstores.com/party/balloons/latex-balloons/qualatex-round-latex-balloon/BP80339039.

[10] https://www.spotlightstores.com/party/balloons/helium-tanks-balloon-kits/amscan-balloon-time-plus/BP80491532.

The illuminated helium balloon (Figure 18) with the string attached was then walked along the main street of Newcastle, New South Wales, to collect initial feedback from pedestrians. Pedestrians were fascinated by the unusual sight of a floating helium balloon illuminated in green, and many wanted to touch it.

Figure 16: Heat Sink

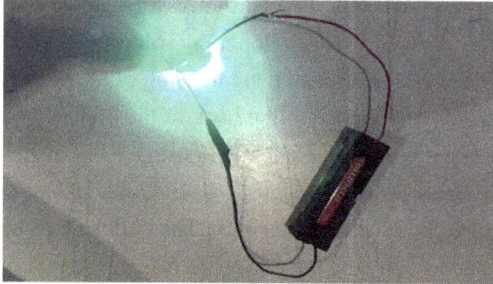

Figure 17: Qualatex Balloon

Figure 18: On the Streets of Newcastle

Based on the positive feedback received from the proof of concept, we proceeded with developing a prototype of nine balloons that would change color in response to sensory input. The initial aim was to use the Arduino platform to drive the 3 W RGB LEDs and receive sensory input. To minimize size, we decided to use a barebones Arduino setup.[11]

The first nine prototypes were designed to run off a through-hole primary circuit board (PCB).[12] The final units were designed (Figure 19) to run off a surface mount device PCB.[13] An unforeseen challenge was finding the right housing for the PCB, LED, sensor, and battery. While LED torch housings appeared ideal in terms of their shape,[14] they were too heavy to allow the helium balloons to float.

Further research led to polyethylene terephthalate (PET) preforms, which are used to make PET plastic bottles. In their basic form, they have the ideal shape to house the PCB, LED, sensor, and battery.[15] Finding the ideal size proved to be a challenge, but after testing multiple sizes (Figure 22), we identified an appropriate size that would seal the balloon, would be light enough to enable the helium balloon to float, and had sufficient space to fit all parts. The right size (Figure 19) was a 100 mL tube, 32.5 mm wide and 162 mm long.[16]

Figure 19: Final Control Units

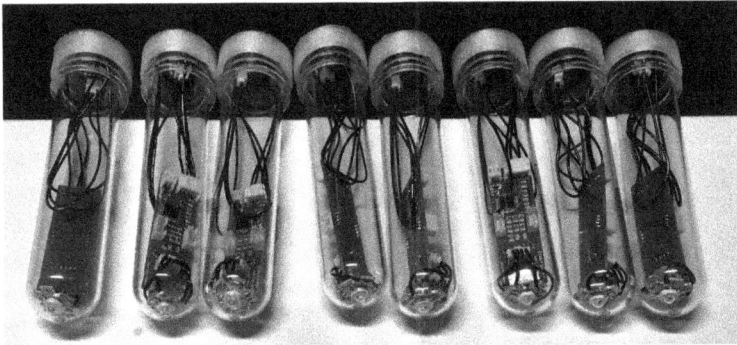

---

[11] https://hackaday.com/2013/07/10/build-a-bare-bones-arduino-clone-which-maximizes-its-use-of-real-estate/.

[12] https://oshwlab.com/SEMNON/burnspcbsocketboard2.

[13] https://oshwlab.com/SEMNON/ballooinov2.

[14] https://www.jaycar.com.au/outdoors-automotive/lighting/torches/c/0EA?sort=popularity-desc&q.

[15] https://www.alibaba.com/showroom/pet-preform.html

[16] https://ntoufeiya.en.alibaba.com/product/60656261900806852211/30ml_45ml_100ml_Clear_Plastic_tube_bottle_price.html?spm=a2700.shop_plgr.41413.21.2ac66677JgP7v9.

Figure 20: Touch Sensor

Figure 21: Presence Sensor

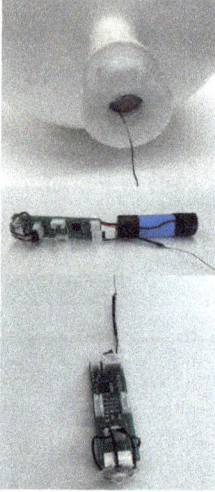

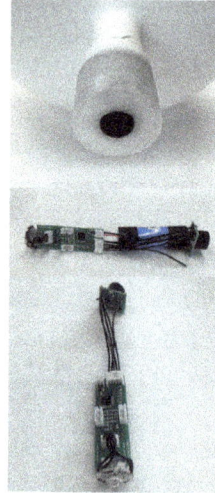

Figure 22: Test Housings

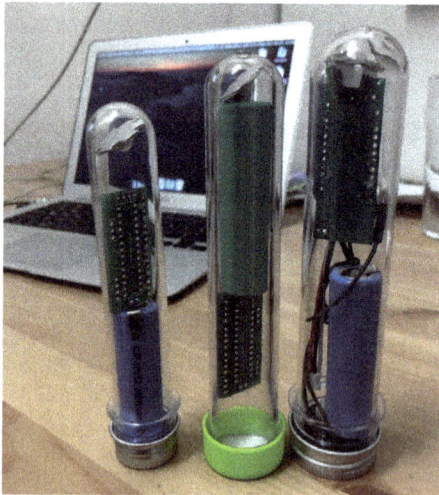

The next step was to test one touch sensor (Figure 20) and one presence sensor (Figure 21). For touch sensing, a conductive string was chosen that was connected to an input pin on the Arduino and would trigger an on or off signal.[17] To detect presence, the Devantech SRF02 ultrasonic sensor was

---

[17.] https://github.com/PaulStoffregen/CapacitiveSensor.

chosen,[18] which can sense whether someone is standing underneath the balloon or not. While ultrasonic sensors can theoretically sense objects, their reliability with humans is not sufficient. Ultrasonic sensors are primarily used to measure distances to and from flat surfaces. Therefore, we could only sense if someone was there or not; consequently, we had to use a binary value of on or off.

The first nine prototypes were built to cycle and loop through RGB values of 0 to 255 for each color (Figure 23) as well as a mix of all when touch or presence were detected (Figure 24). The barebones Arduino was designed to sit on a PCB designed using EasyEDA.[19] The key components were an ATmega328 chip[20] as well as three metal–oxide–semiconductor field-effect transistors (MOSFETs) to control each LED channel mounted on a fabricated PCB, first designed in Fritzing,[21] then in EasyEDA. Further, a conductive thread (Figure 20)[22] and the Devantech SRF02 ultrasonic sensor (Figure 21) were used.

Figure 23: Netting Mounting   Figure 24: Test for Touch Sensor

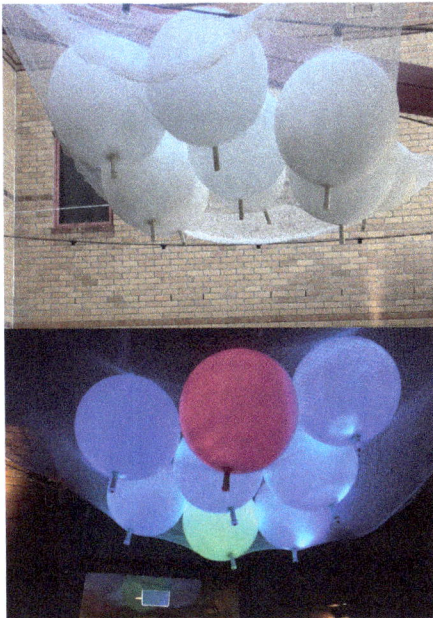

[18] https://www.robotgear.com.au/Product.aspx/Details/285-Devantech-SRF02-Ultrasonic-Sonar-Range-Finder.

[19] https://easyeda.com.

[20] https://www.microchip.com/en-us/product/ATmega328

[21] https://fritzing.org.

[22] https://oshwlab.com/SEMNON/burnspcbsocketboard2.

The testing setup for the prototype units was nine 90 cm Qualatex balloons inflated using an air compressor.[23] The balloons were mounted in a 3 × 3 grid, 2.5 m high (Figure 23) using bird netting.[24]

Both the touch sensor (Figure 24) and the presence sensor (Figure 25) successfully detected touch and pressure, respectively, and looped through the full range of RGB values. The setup was stress tested for five days in heavy rain and wind without failure. After five days, the balloons began to lose air. The batteries had to be recharged each day because the Arduino algorithm had not yet been optimized for longevity. We further tested the nine balloons indoors, with the balloons lasting up to fourteen days (Figure 26). Following the successful test, a further light sensor was included on the PCB to enable an automatic power on after sunset.[25] The units (Figure 26) were programmed to automatically turn on after sunset and stay on for four

Figure 25: Test for Presence Sensor

Figure 26: Balloon Test

Figure 27: Color Test

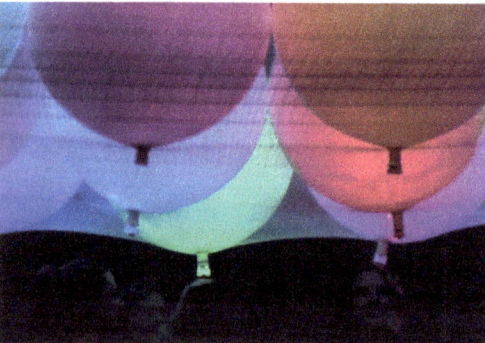

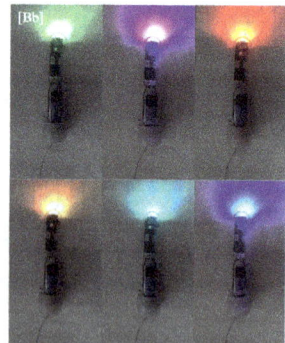

---

[23] https://www.4wdsupacentre.com.au/thumper-air-compressor-mkiii.html?gclid=Cj0KCQjw6ZOIBhDdARIsAM-f8YyFhyV5adOXtYjnQ5zG-fFK5hhYIeegjC3QZXWQK47pdPtmB-_Z7Zq4aAlNCEALw_wcB.

[24] https://www.bunnings.com.au/diamond-econetting-10m-x-10m-x-5mm-white-anti-bird-net_p3041129.

[25] https://core-electronics.com.au/adafruit-als-pt19-analog-light-sensor-breakout.html.

hours, after which they would switch off. They would then recalibrate at sunrise and switch on again at sunset, effectively implementing a circadian rhythm. This rhythm, including code optimization, would allow the units to run for four continuous days for four hours each day. The batteries would then require a four-hour recharge after day 4 and can be reused on day 5.

For the final units, a surface mount device PCB was designed (Figures 29–31) and developed to save space and weight. The Arduino Mini Pro

Figure 28: Caps

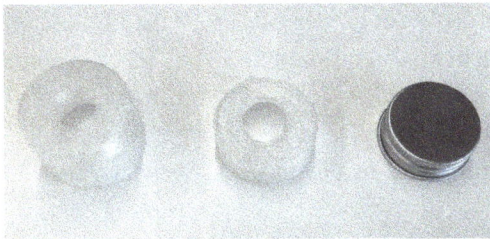

Figure 29: PCB 1

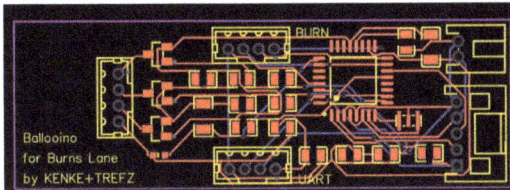

Figure 30: PCB 2

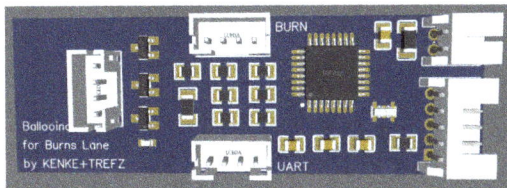

Figure 31: PCB 3

schematic[26] was used as a foundation. Added to the Arduino Mini Pro schematic were the light sensor, the three MOSFETs, the JTAG connectors for the 3 W LED, the battery, the touch and ultrasonic sensors, and a resistor and a capacitor to stabilize the circuit. The final design is licensed under the open-source GPL3 license.[27]

Cap Design

The cap design to hold the components inside the PET preform evolved from an aluminum cap to a 3D-printed cap that would fix the sensors in an optimal position. Cap size was further increased to enable the sinking of the ultrasonic sensor flush inside the cap. The added thickness also stabilized the direction of the sensor. When using an aluminum cap without a drilled hole (right-hand

Figure 32: Installing 1

Figure 33: Installing 2

[26.] https://www.arduino.cc/en/pmwiki.php?n=Main/ArduinoBoardProMini

[27.] https://oshwlab.com/SEMNON/ballooinov2.

Figure 34: Installing 3

Figure 35: Installing 4

cap in Figure 28) or the smaller 3D-printed cap (middle cap in Figure 28), the ultrasonic sensor tilted randomly, while with the thicker cap, the sensor remained straight (left-hand cap in Figure 28).

Burns Lane Cloud Installation

To test the second mode in the field, we set up a temporary rigging structure and populated the center of Burns Lane with seventy-four media balloons to create an interactive cloud elevated 3 m above the road (Figures 32-36). The balloons were first inflated using the compressor before being placed into bird netting, which was stretched across a 12 × 6 m rigging system. To optimally position the media balloons and Ballooino kit, we used cable ties and steel wire to minimize the movement of individual units.

King Street Window Installation

We also installed the media balloons in a King Street window (Figure 37). The aim of this installation was to test the use of the balloons in a future gallery space on the ground floor of University House. While the colorful media balloons attracted participants to play and explore the installation, there was little visual indication of what they aimed to do with this interaction. In contrast to the second mode, with its proximity sensors and dual-color design, the first mode appeared to provide too much interaction and color, causing participants to interact with a single balloon rather than many, as was the case at Burns Lane.

Figure 36: Burns Lane Installation

Figure 37: King Street Window

What was interesting to observe at both installations was that participants needed little to no instruction to interact with the installation. It was also observed that participants would watch others interact first and then step into the installation to explore their own interactions.

Conclusion

We learned many lessons in our design and installation of the Ballooino media balloons. The research and development of the media balloons has addressed some of the challenges of media facades. The flexibility and low cost of the media balloons in responsive public spaces indicate that they may contribute to the design of smart cities in the future. The use of both media balloon modes in two public spaces resulted in active engagement with citizens. The human-centered design approach in which a familiar object was transformed resonated with individuals from a range of demographics. This makes public installations less technocentric and improves citizen engagement. However, limitations included the charging cycle of batteries and the durability of latex balloons with both air and helium. In particular, the outdoor location and harsh weather exposure demonstrated the fragility of the media balloons. We also discovered that the interaction at Burns Lane was a more collective experience in public space than the installation at King Street. Due to the simplicity of walking underneath the media balloons, citizens were able to explore the intransitivity of the installation. Also, the use of the dual colors (green and blue) signaled immediately that the installation responded to the people entering Burns Lane Cloud. While the touch sensor set up at the King Street windows invited people to play with the media balloon as an object, its offering to change and determine the color of the media balloons using the conductive string resulted in individual-focused interactions. As we installed both modes of the Ballooino in two different environments, it is challenging to compare Burns Lane Cloud with the King Street window. We are convinced after observing both installations and designing the Ballooino unit that media balloons empower citizens to engage with responsive public spaces. The media balloons are economically attractive in comparison to the high costs of media facade. The media balloons shown in this pictorial offer an alternative to the media facade. The Ballooino media balloon is an innovative tool for smart cities to build responsive public spaces that invite citizens to explore their appetite for a smart future.

Acknowledgments

This research project was made possible with the support of the Singleton Council (New South Wales, Australia) in collaboration with the FASTlab research center at the University of Newcastle. In particular, we wish to express our gratitude to FASTlab's director, Paul Egglestone, and co-director, Mario Minichello, for the opportunity to conduct our study. In addition, our thanks go to Aaron Parker for his contributions to this research project. We would also like to thank Dr. Kristefan Minski and Christopher Saunders for their invitation to participate at the Singleton Laneway Art Festival in 2021.

REFERENCES

Breuer, Jonas, Nils Walravens, and Pieter Ballon. 2014. "Beyond Defining the Smart City: Meeting Top-Down and Bottom-Up Approaches in the Middle." *TeMA—Journal of Land Use, Mobility and Environment* June 2014: 153–164.

Buckley, Craig. 2019. "3: Face and Screen—Toward a Genealogy of the Media Façade." In *Screen Genealogies*, edited by C. Buckley, R. Campe, and F. Casetti. Amsterdam University Press.

Cardullo, Paolo, and Rob Kitchin. 2019. "Being a 'Citizen' in the Smart City: Up and Down the Scaffold of Smart Citizen Participation in Dublin, Ireland." *GeoJournal* 84 (1): 1–13.

Conway, R. 2013. "Are Smart Cities Just for Smart Arses?" *Sensemaking*, November 25. http://sensemakingblog.word-press.com/2013/11/25/are-smart-cities-just-for-smart-arses/.

Cordeiro, Artur Vasconcelos. 2018. "Building Pixels with Others: A Participatory Experience to Make a Low-Resolution LED Matrix." In *Proceedings of the 4th Media Architecture Biennale Conference*, edited by C. Zhigang. Association for Computing Machinery.

De Waal, Martijn, and Marloes Dignum. 2017. "The Citizen in the Smart City: How the Smart City Could Transform Citizenship." *IT-Information Technology* 59 (6): 263–273.

Gehl, J. (1971) 1987. *Life Between Buildings: Using Public Space*. Van Nostrand Reinhold.

Heausler, M. 2009. *Hank Media Facades: History, Technology, Content*. Avedition.

Hemment, D., and A. Townsend. 2013. "Here Come the Smart Citizens." In *Smart Citizens*, vol. 4, edited by D. Hemment and A. Townsend. Future Everything Publications.

Hespanhol, Luke, and Martin Tomitsch. 2012. "Designing for Collective Participation with Media Installations in Public Spaces." In *Proceedings of 4th Media Architecture Biennale Conference: Participation*, edited by C. Zhigang. Association for Computing Machinery.

Kitchin, R. 2014. "Making Sense of Smart Cities: Addressing Present Shortcomings." *Cambridge Journal of Regions, Economy and Society* October 2014: rsu027. https://doi.org/10.1093/cjres/rsu027.

McCullough, M. 2013. *Ambient Commons*. MIT Press.

Paquin, Alexandra Georgescu. 2019. "Public Data Art's Potential for Digital Placemaking." *Tourism and Heritage Journal* 1: 32–48.

Sade, Gavin. 2014. "Aesthetics of Urban Media Façades." In *Proceedings of the 2nd Media Architecture Biennale Conference: World Cities*, edited by M. Brynskov, P. Dalsgaard, and A. Fatah gen Schieck. Association for Computing Machinery.

Scully, Michael, and Samuel Mayze. 2018. "Media Façades: When Buildings Perform." In *Proceedings of the 4th Media Architecture Biennale Conference: Participation*, edited by C. Zhigang. Association for Computing Machinery.

Sennet, R. 2013. "No One Likes a City That Is Too Smart." *Guardian*, December 4. http://www.guardian.co.uk/comment-isfree/2012/dec/04/smart-city-rio-songdo-masdar.

CHAPTER 5

Immersed in R&D: Collaborating from Within Industry

Justin Dean

Introduction

I am in the early stages of a PhD journey in the field of artificial intelligence (AI), with a focus on elucidating the causal relationship between anthropomorphic avatars and their impact on human behavior, particularly in terms of trust. Leveraging my design perspectives and over two decades of industrial experience, which encompass practical research and development methodologies, I'm striving to uncover insights within the context of our design consultancy practice. The inherent benefits of conducting practice-based research lie in its real-world applications, yielding outcomes that offer immediate advantages to the public.

I have always wanted to do a PhD as I see this as the pinnacle of education in one's chosen field. I want to be recognized as an expert in my area of expertise and use these credentials and knowledge to help others in my field as well as the general public and add to the relevant academic literature.

I am using my design perspectives, including twenty-five years of industrial experience, on aspects including the application of practical research and industry development methodologies and moreover, the specifics of our own design consultancy practice policies and procedures regarding inclusive interactive design. The advantages of engaging in practice-based research stem from real-world applications and outcomes that have an immediate benefit for the public.

Envent is a professional industrial design consultancy specialising in providing intuitive digital navigation and wayfinding solutions. Our passion for innovation, research and delivering the latest technology leads us into new areas of discovery, ultimately arriving at improved solutions for our clients. We want to help clients reach their goals and expose them to the latest available technology that can improve their clients positive experience when engaging with their services.[1]

This collaboration with the University of Newcastle (UON) is helping me to align the long-term strategic goals of my company's technology development with community feedback and expectations in an ever-evolving technological landscape (Figure 1). This research includes, with the UON's guidance, the continual

Figure 1: Accessible Landscape Digital Wayfinding Directory

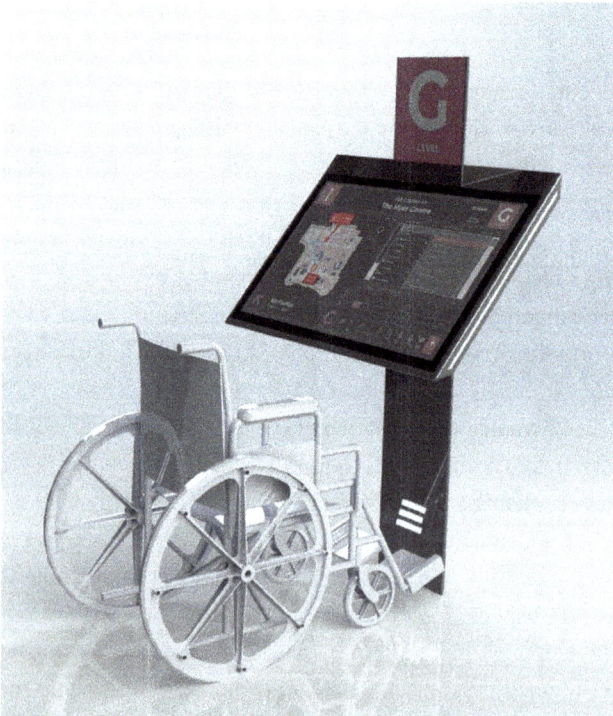

Source: Envent

---
[1] https://www.envent.com.au/about/.

iterative assessment of government ethical guidelines around AI development and the community's understanding and acceptance of AI technical developments.

AI has proliferated since the global pandemic and the COVID-19 (coronavirus disease 2019) crisis, with its profound social changes, served as an ideal scenario for the application of emerging technologies and sparked my interest due to the lack of transparency around the design and implementation of AI thermal facial recognition (AITFR). AI's potential in predicting consumer behavior faces ethical and technical challenges (Uysal et al. 2023). Addressing privacy concerns, ensuring data quality, overcoming technical challenges, maintaining privacy, and ensuring algorithm transparency are crucial. Businesses must navigate these challenges to harness AI's power responsibly.

AI-related technology stands out as a significant tool in the response to the COVID-19 crisis, aiding in slowing the virus's spread through surveillance and contact tracing (OECD 2020; Wang et al. 2015). AI and facial recognition technology (FRT) are widespread across many industries, but there is still a high level of mistrust that needs addressing (Shi et al. 2023). Involving the community will increase their trust and understanding regarding AI, in particular the integration of anthropomorphic avatars as moderators on trust when used with facial recognition and guided by ethical frameworks and inclusive design methodologies.

The community's involvement will help inform current and future company design strategies, and the factors that influence AI acceptance through the use of anthropomorphic avatars in facial recognition health protocols. In turn, the research aims to expand the literature on how, when, and where to involve the community in the design process. I want to ensure the technical outcomes align with insights gained from the community feedback in ways that usefully inform the design process.

The opportunity we, the UON and I, have is to facilitate these elements being mirrored in the human-to-machine relationship to improve engagement and development of meaningful ongoing discourse and to create loyalty, then conversely the machine-to-machine relationship to deliver empathic responses and exchanges between AI systems.

A key part of our collaboration is to apply the definition of human trust into AI. Trust is quantifiable, learnable, and observable. Trust can be defined as the firm confidence in an individual or entity's ability to act in a righteous and dependable manner, fulfilling commitments and maintaining consistency, irrespective of the situation. The firm belief in the reliability, truth, or ability of someone or something. The opportunity here is to unravel the reason for lingering mistrust of AI agents and tools: Is it the avatar design, is it the lack of general AI in the interaction, or is it the design process itself that has inherent flaws? Our research will uncover these elements through the help of close evaluation of existing literature.

Firstly, to substantiate the bolstered trust aspect, a comprehensive definition of trust in human-to-human interactions must be established. This will include the Eight Pillars of Trust (Horsager 2012): clarity, compassion, character, competence, commitment, connection, contribution, and consistency. This necessitates an exploration of the foundational elements of trust across moral, ethical, cultural, gender, legal, and social paradigms. Similarly, the factors contributing to distrust in these interactions must be comprehensively understood and defined. Armed with this knowledge, the objective is to incorporate these aspects into the AI model. This involves identifying key human cues and triggers of trust, as well as mitigating triggers of distrust, spanning facial expressions, verbal cues, non-verbal signals, speech patterns, and behavior. These features will be integrated into our AI model wherever feasible.

My study focuses on the contemporary technological advancements that intentionally shape human nature and behavior through deliberate design choices, manifesting across numerous facets. Because of this calculated behavior alteration, a subconscious sense of distrust toward AI emerges, especially in scenarios where human presence is absent during AI interactions. This unease is notably evident with the proliferation of facial recognition technology spanning various industries. This apprehension is further exacerbated by the dearth of enforceable governmental regulations, legal controls, ethical frameworks, or guiding principles to oversee and standardize AI development. Consequently, there exists a lack of benchmarks and references for assessing the ethical integrity of AI and providing transparency to users.

The wealth of insights gathered through our joint, multidisciplinary research with the UON will provide insights and pathways for future university/industry project collaborations. Outcomes will include studies, journals, surveys, interviews, and design workshops and product prototyping, to pave the way for the assimilation of newfound knowledge into the practical attributes that will reshape our prototype AI's "persona." Our belief rests on the premise that integrating these behavioral traits into the sentinel AI will effectively embody the human attributes of trust and elicit a positive cognitive and empathetic response from users. This, in turn, corroborates our hypothesis, indicating heightened user engagement and a reduction in distrust levels.

Collaboration with the Academy

I have been fortunate in my academic journey to have been given the opportunity to work with FASTlab, from the School of Humanities, Creative Industries, and Social Sciences as part of the UON. The relationship with the UON and FASTlab was to initially collaborate on a COVID-19 TechVoucher grant issued by the NSW government. The program provides support funding for technology-rich startups, scaleups, or small-to-medium enterprises (SMEs) to collaborate with Publicly Funded Research Organisations (PFROs) to conduct R&D projects that accelerate the commercialization of products and services that address the impact of COVID-19. As I had an undergraduate degree at the UON, I decided to contact the UON to initiate a discussion around working together to apply for the grant and was steered toward the FASTlab team who were excited about the opportunity. As a result, we partnered with a view to apply for the grant and subsequently my company was awarded funding in 2022 to develop COVID-19-related technology that would reduce the spread of future outbreaks of the virus. The TechVoucher program is designed to enable more NSW businesses to accelerate the commercialization of innovative R&D products and services that address the health and economic impacts of COVID-19. A TechVoucher can only be used to reimburse the business for paid PFRO invoices for delivered R&D contract services.

This is a research collaboration which has presented opportunities, challenges, deep reflection and a constant reevaluation and development for the "why" am I doing a PhD. Some of the challenges that have arisen in dealing with the UON include distance and online meetings, time management and scheduling, adjusting to an academic mindset and applying the newly acquired research tools I have learned. Distance can be seen as a challenge. Being a two-hour drive away from the UON makes it impractical for in-person meetings, necessitating most meetings to be conducted online. This can pose challenges in terms of communication, coordination, and building rapport.

Scheduling my study around work requires much discipline. Balancing regular scheduled meetings with the UON around a busy full-time work schedule can be difficult. Prioritizing and allocating time for meetings while ensuring productivity at work is a juggling act that requires careful planning and time management that I have so far been successful in maintaining to a high level.

Adjusting my mindset and transitioning from an entrepreneurial mindset to an academic one can be challenging. My everyday focus must be on helping people with revenue generation always in the back of my mind. In academia, there is

Figure 2: Envent Australia's Commercialization Process

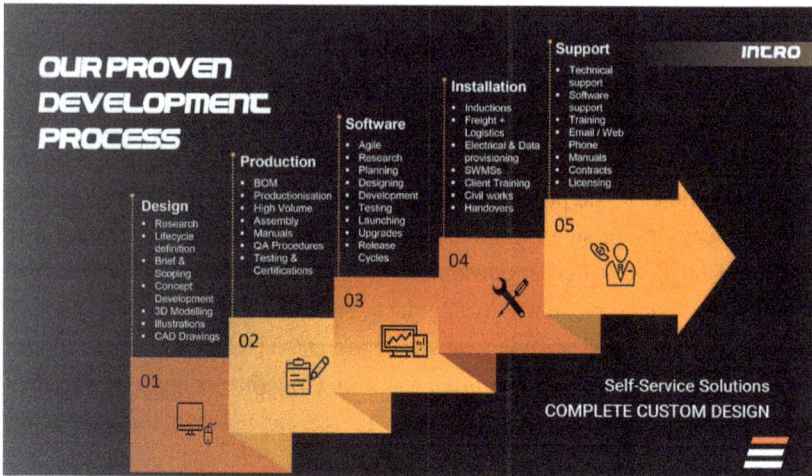

Source: Envent

often a focus on research, theory, and rigorous analysis, which may differ from the more pragmatic, immediate results-oriented approach of entrepreneurship and developing my company's, Envent Australia's, commercialization process. The symbiotic relationship between the two paradigms, I have found, is the best of both worlds and will lead to a better end result when applied theory meets experiential instinct.

Acquiring and applying the correct research skills has been a steep learning curve. Reacquainting myself with academic research methods and resources, such as Google Scholar and peer-reviewed journals, requires time and effort. Navigating through hundreds of articles and isolating relevant information to strengthen arguments demands a different set of skills compared to typical business research or design processes. It involves critical thinking, analytical skills, and the ability to synthesize information effectively.

Working with the UON is already providing a heightened sense of authority, credibility, and granularity to the research methodologies and outcomes. It is a positive collaboration and opportunity to work with the academy to harness global knowledge bases and proven research methodologies to underpin my own practical industry-based research methodologies. This will help refine my own tacit methodologies but also help the UON to see how an agile yet relatively stubborn business can adapt to working in multidisciplinary teams.

The value of bringing different knowledge domains together blends the fast-paced, practical development aspects for commercialization with the pragmatic university-based research and development methodology to ensure there is depth of knowledge. The endeavor of engaging in practice-based research is not without its challenges; for example, engaging in practice-based research includes condensing timescales to coincide with the university's structures while engaging with the institution's formal ethical and documentation protocols which gives a deeper, intensive view of the research.

This collaboration also has the potential to refine our methodologies while showcasing how agile businesses can seamlessly integrate into multidisciplinary teams. The amalgamation of the UON's diverse knowledge domains brings forth a blend of rapid-paced practical development for commercialization and the pragmatic approach of university-based research and development methodologies. This fusion ensures a robust depth of knowledge.

Partnerships between businesses like mine and universities like UON often involve different cultures. Dealing with these differences helps share ideas, new ways of thinking, and creative methods. It is a chance to learn from different points of view and change how things are done effectively. By engaging with the student body at UON, and actively seeking a broad response to our data gathering with end-users, we are taking a cross section of as many diverse cultures and tacit backgrounds as possible in order to promote diversity, inclusiveness and to generate unbiased innovation.

My company gains from having a diverse team, for example people with different backgrounds, experiences, and viewpoints. Working with academia brings in new talent, creativity, and thinking from various fields. This mix of diversity informs my research design process, including developing end-user engagement opportunities through surveys and workshops to gain feedback on our prototype will spark innovation and push forward the creation of fresh ideas.

Access to Knowledge Bases and Methodologies

Engaging in academic research will, and already has, given my company a competitive advantage. The knowledge gained from my research collaborations guides strategic choices, product creation, and market strategies. The knowledge gained from our in-depth workshops and focus groups will keep our solution at the cutting edge of the latest social trends of each, increasingly tech-savvy, generation. Keeping up with the latest progress guarantees adaptability and importance in a constantly changing business environment.

Access to expertise has facilitated working with supervising professors who possess extensive practical and theoretical knowledge, providing for invaluable insights. Their methodological experience can offer guidance and enhance the quality of the project's outcomes.

I have deepened my knowledge regarding AI ethical development considerations and governmental frameworks during the design process. Undertaking a formal ethics review within the university framework ensures adherence to strict policies and procedures. Embracing human-centered design principles fosters empathy and consideration for diverse perspectives, leading to more ethical and socially responsible outcomes. This process can be humbling, rewarding, and insightful, providing a framework for ethical decision-making throughout the project.

Reflecting on my collaboration with FASTlab, several key aspects have come to light, shaping my experience in profound ways. This journey has been both humbling and transformative, defining my professional and personal growth. My collaboration with the UON and my research journey has significantly deepened my understanding of the following objectives: elevating trust and engagement with AI, addressing fear and uncertainty, and the comparative analysis of engagement and trust levels.

Our study with the UON will also compare the engagement and perceived trust outcomes against AI with the same functionality with no anthropomorphic avatars applied. As part of my PhD study, I have developed a physical interactive "sentinel" technology with the aim of creating an anthropomorphic graphic user interface (GUI) to develop, test, and validate user engagement and to increase the level of trust in AI and human engagement. For the "sentinel" personality, we will initially develop a range of anthropomorphic "avatar" character options to review before selecting the best "avatar" to deliver the most perceived [trust experience] in the ensuing experimentation. These options will be tested, evaluated and surveyed and the most trusted option will be selected to implement into our design workshops, experiments, and hypothesis.

Addressing fear and uncertainty in the everyday use of AI has been a key focus of my collaborative work with UON. My research also underscores the significance of transparency, information accessibility, and openness in mitigating fear and uncertainty within human–AI engagements. By promoting transparency and providing accessible information about AI systems, we seek to instill a sense of trust and confidence among users. This proactive approach acknowledges and addresses common concerns surrounding the opacity and unpredictability of AI technologies.

Figure 3: A Simplified, Non-avatar Option for the Sentinel User Interface for COVID-19 Safety Protocols

Source: Envent

Moving Forward

Overall, my collaboration with the UON and our research endeavors have provided me with a comprehensive understanding of the multifaceted dynamics involved in enhancing trust, engagement, and transparency in human–AI interactions. By combining theoretical insights with empirical analysis, we strive to contribute to the advancement of AI technologies that are not only intelligent but also empathetic and trustworthy.

Envent's development team will coordinate our R&D activities with the UON's resources to achieve a collaborative approach to each development task in this project. Collaboration for the commercialization will occur across all tasks, ensuring transparent and verified inputs from both parties follow a streamlined methodology that is checked and approved prior to moving onto the next stage.

This will fast-track the development to enable us to be market ready at the end of 2025. This collaboration will involve splitting up the research and development tasks into specialized resources and teams to help facilitate the expedition of the research, prototyping and testing and final results to establish the final specifications for production and release.

We need to undertake further research and development with the UON to finalize the thermal and facial detection camera capabilities. The results and subsequent conclusions and refined actions will give us a bulletproof platform that has been tested many hundreds of times across all anthropometric data, including race, gender, skin tone, facial hair, and glasses to ensure our product is ethically designed, meeting the new stringent international standards.

We intend to reach our users by targeting the institutions and companies that will be procuring the technology. So, our marketing strategy would be a direct approach to hospitals, educational and retail organizations and institutions which will be covered by our ethics submission with the UON.

A second tiered approach would be to sell directly to smaller retailer organizations and clubs for general public access. This would be achieved via social media marketing and targeted specific industries using paid for Google advertising and procured databases to proactively contact each potential customer. We will be developing a marketing plan with the UON as the development progresses.

Envent is seeking development resources from the UON, along with commercialization expertise and validations, governance, research methodology framework, and intellectual capital review, to oversee and assist in the hypothesis generation, testing, results gathering, and conclusions at each stage. The UON will provide kind software developers, research facilitators, testers, and guidance on the above. This will provide additional resources to check and double-check the results generated and the conclusions made by the Envent development team. This will increase the quality of output of all aspects of the solution.

It is also envisaged in the future that the UON can help fast-track the sales and distribution of the technology. The UON has also indicated they can facilitate and expand distribution into the UK by establishing further development in that region. That would be an incredible contribution and add to the success of the commercialization effort. A possible partnership between the UON and Envent may result in the formation of a spinout company or joint venture, originating from academic research. This could play a vital role in boosting economic growth, generating employment opportunities, and enriching local communities. This income and revenue generation would serve as a connection between theoretical understanding and real-world implementation.

REFERENCES

Horsager, D. 2012. *The Trust Edge: How Top Leaders Gain Faster Results, Deeper Relationships, and a Stronger Bottom Line*. Simon & Schuster.

Shi, J., X. Hu, and X. Guo. 2023. "The Lesser of Two Evils: Assessing the Public Acceptance of AI Thermal Facial Recognition During the COVID-19 Crisis." *Risk Analysis* 44 (4): 958–971. https://onlinelibrary.wiley.com/doi/10.1111/risa.14198.

Uysal, E., S. Alavi, and V. Bezençon. 2023. "Anthropomorphism in Artificial Intelligence: A Review of Empirical Work Across Domains and Insights for Future Research." In *Artificial Intelligence in Marketing (Review of Marketing Research)*, vol. 20, edited by K. Sudhir and O. Toubia. Emerald Publishing.

Wang, S., S. O. Lilienfeld, and P. Rochat. 2015. "The Uncanny Valley: Existence and Explanations." *Review of General Psychology* 19 (4): 393–407. https://doi.org/10.1037/gpr0000056.

RAPID (Research and Project Innovation and Development) Prototyping

Introduction

The three chapters in this section focus on the Research and Project Innovation and Development (RAPID) prototyping program organized through UON's FASTlab. These are case studies in leveraging small-scale funding to develop academia–industry linkages, and test concepts through real-world prototyping.

"Rapid prototyping" is a widely used approach for implementing design solutions. In the context outlined in this section, however, this refers to a more open approach to fostering research innovation using short-term, trial-and-error practice. Usually small in scale but large in ambition, these projects leverage available technologies, infrastructures, and expertise to generate new knowledge through practice. This typically means intersecting existing ideas, practices, and/or technologies in novel ways, trialing combinations in open-ended laboratory settings (which might be in formal, institutional settings, or within a real-world "living lab").

Paul Egglestone, in the first chapter (Chapter 6), provides an overview of this RAPID program, which has instigated open competition for small-scale funding centered on transdisciplinary collaboration involving industry partners. As he outlines, this program fostered an eclectic range of projects, most of which achieved short-term goals but more importantly fostered crucial research collaborations, while a few projects evolved into or inspired larger-scale research programs.

Egglestone and Craig Hight then, in the second chapter (Chapter 7), provide more detailed overviews of five RAPID projects, highlighting some of their achievements and including key insights from research collaborators. These projects focus on environmental, sustainability, and cultural goals and reflect the broader playground of innovation fostered under the program.

The final chapter (Chapter 8) from Helena Bezzina covers a RAPID project which does not involve a laboratory or engaging with emerging technologies. Instead, it prompts a reimagining of an existing cultural/institutional space, with collaborators, in order to intervene in the well-being of young people. This is a project which was trialed using RAPID funding but has since evolved into a doctoral research project.

CHAPTER 6

RAPID: A Transdisciplinary Research Initiative That Creates Value and Impact

Paul Egglestone

Abstract

To address the many complex or "wicked" problems of our modern, networked, information-based, and technology-facilitated age, academic attention has turned toward transdisciplinary research approaches, i.e., the application of expertise from various schools of thought and knowledge backgrounds to arrive at creative and innovative solutions to environmental, health, cultural, economic, and social challenges. While there is a growing body of literature occupied with developing appropriate mechanisms for measuring such research, there are few papers available which document the actual process of initiating a faculty-based transdisciplinary research program which requires not only collaboration between disciplines within the university but also the contribution and collaboration with an industry partner. This chapter documents the principles and practices of a unique transdisciplinary initiative called RAPID (Research and Project Innovation and Development), along with the observable outcomes of several RAPID case studies. It provides insights and reflections from the program participants themselves and sets out both the benefits offered by such a program as well as the challenges of such a research environment.

Introduction and Methodology

This chapter explores the mechanics of transdisciplinary innovation by examining how seemingly disparate professional and community actors worked together to co-create value on a range of projects that aimed to explore complex social challenges. The study draws on case study data from 2017 to 2022 for a University of Newcastle (UON) research program called RAPID, a novel approach to fostering transdisciplinary collaboration and accelerate progress toward solving real-world, complex problems. While transdisciplinary research alludes to the potential of novel and wide-reaching discoveries, it brings with it unique challenges.

After briefly surveying the background literature, this discussion explains the principles of the RAPID program, sets out the transdisciplinary approaches adopted by RAPID research projects, and explores the benefits, outcomes, and challenges that emerged over six years of research practice. The five specific projects outlined in sections which follow this chapter reveal key challenges and critical success factors that the transdisciplinary teams experienced as they navigated a range of complexities and unique challenges, from problem identification and stakeholder management to communication, attitudes to risk-taking and failure, and tight deadlines. The chapter concludes with an outline of some qualitative participant reactions to the program and by discussing the relevance of the RAPID approach for transdisciplinary team-based research projects.

This study adopts data analysis and qualitative case study methodologies, assessing RAPID research project data from six years of operation (drawn from forty-two project applications), followed by snapshots of five case studies (all of which were successful applicants). Data sources include RAPID project guidelines and documentation, proposal documents, and pitch decks from submitting researchers, correspondence with external and internal stakeholders, and project evaluation information.

Background: Transdisciplinary Research

Transdisciplinary research is an approach that is growing in popularity for application to complex, real-world problems, also known as wicked problems. Writing in the *Technology Innovation Management Review* (2018), Kees Dorst points out that "over the last three decades, humanity has networked itself, to great advantage…but, in doing so, we have also inadvertently networked our problems, thereby creating complex tangled webs of relationships in which progress is difficult to achieve".

Wicked problems are defined as complex, involving multiple possible causes and internal dynamics that are not necessarily linear and may pose highly negative consequences if not dealt with effectively (Peters 2017). These are problems that challenge policymakers, academia, and industry by deviating from previous frameworks of understanding and thus being resistant to conventional models of policy analysis or traditional solutions.

Transdisciplinary research and innovation have been defined as distinct from previous conceptions of interdisciplinary research as approaches necessarily needed to evolve to better address the intricate nature of these problems. Whereas interdisciplinary research integrates tools, data, and theories from two or more disciplines to solve problems beyond the scope of a single area or research practice, transdisciplinarity involves "efforts conducted by actors from different disciplines working jointly to create new conceptual, theoretical, methodical, and translational innovations that integrate and move beyond discipline-specific approaches to address a common problem" (Zafeirakopoulos and van der Bijl-Brouwer 2018). In adopting a transdisciplinary approach, researchers and policymakers are better positioned to fully understand the complexity of a problem through viewing it through several frameworks and ideally developing innovative solutions that benefit society.

One of the consequences of this—and a particular challenge of transdisciplinary research—is the necessity of finding solutions to problems which sufficiently meet the needs of the multiple stakeholders involved. Often, this may involve negotiating several different motivations to produce a mutually beneficial outcome. Academics, scientists, industry leaders, policymakers, and funding agencies will likely all have specific expectations from a project and an anticipated outcome. Laura Schmidt and colleagues emphasize that clarifying the expectations of all stakeholders is the key to successful stakeholder engagement and involvement. "Not articulating objectives carries the danger of pursuing diverging intentions and expectations, leading to limited impact of transdisciplinary research and disappointments among those involved" (Schmidt et al. 2020).

There are two notable trends in the current literature on transdisciplinary research and innovation. The first is the particular focus on the use of this approach for solving challenges related to finding *sustainable* solutions to problems. Sustainability is built on three main pillars: (1) environment, (2) economy, and (3) society. Sustainable solutions are those that, according to Burton's early definition, "[have the] ability to meet the needs of the present without jeopardizing the ability of future generations to meet their needs" (1987). As actions to counteract climate change threats become more urgent, citizens are demanding more sustainable industry practices (Sachs et al. 2019). Thus, there is an increasing imperative for industries to develop manufacturing solutions which incorporate energy-efficient, waste-reducing processes and ethical labor practices. Balancing these features with continuing economic viability requires complex problem-solving skills to find innovative solutions, in other words, a transdisciplinary approach.

The other prominent trend, found in many recently published papers, is extensive theorizing concerned with identifying the most effective way to measure the impacts of transdisciplinary research and innovation. Hansson suggests that as the necessity of transdisciplinary research increases in line with the complexity of societal, economic, and environmental questions, finding ways to link the transdisciplinary research process to social change outcomes is the most pressing challenge. "Consequently, the field of transdisciplinary research is searching for ways of proving the value and providing evidence to support the effectiveness of such research" (Hansson and Polk 2018). While there is a clear imperative to continue to update ideas of what constitutes research output and how innovation metrics and markers of success should be conceptualized, there is a pressing need to examine accounts of how transdisciplinary research has been initiated, structured and funded by universities. Such an examination — as set out here — helps provide productive blueprints for other institutions to successfully implement similar programs and develop localized solutions and knowledge.

University – Industry Collaboration

University–industry (UI) collaboration is also a key subject of recent scholarly attention, with specific questions about the changing role of the university being highlighted by industry funded research projects. There is a broad range of studies documenting the increasing interaction between universities and industry globally, the findings of which are diverse. Some (Di Maria et al. 2019) assert the benefits for the firms involved far outweigh those for the researchers (this, it must be noted, was measured only by the number of publications generated), while many others (Harman 2010; Sjöö and Hellström 2019; Lubbe et al. 2021) cite a range of benefits.

To help conceptualize the delicate relationship between (broadly) universities, industry, and government, Loet Leydesdorff offers us the Triple Helix Model for innovation. Within this model, each sector is visualized as a circle (helix) with overlapping edges (Leydesdorff 2012). The overlapping edges represent the interactions between sectors. As interactions increase within this framework, each component evolves to adopt some characteristics of the other institution creating "hybrid institutions" whereby institutional spheres, in addition to performing their own traditional functions, "assume the roles of the others, with universities creating a industrial penumbra, or performing a quasi-governmental role as a regional or local innovation organiser" (Leydesdorff 1998). Managing these institutional relationships effectively is crucial to the development of innovative and inclusive public policy and a vibrant and modern cityscape which supports its inhabitants with economic and lifestyle opportunities. As Brem and Radziwon note, "collaboration between universities and their local stakeholders is becoming a key success factor for the growth of regional entrepreneurial ecosystems" (2017). While Yuzhuo Cai et al. (2019) discuss the lack of productive interactions between transnational corporations and transnational universities, this chapter will adopt a more localized focus in order to demonstrate how local industries or corporations and universities can benefit from collaboration to find innovative solutions for real-world problems within a specific set of regional influences and circumstances.

In Australia, there are sections of the academic community and major media that are of the view that "industry links and university commercialisation efforts threaten traditional research and scientific values, and accepted norms of academic life including academic freedom" (Harman 2010). While Harman's study of researchers participating in industry-linked research projects noted that participant's concerns included threats to research autonomy, the commercialization of knowledge, the low intellectual level of some work, and pressures on researchers to spend time on commercial activities, one of the key advantages of receiving industry research support was found to be that research teams tended to be better qualified, more senior, and more productive in their research than academics without such partnerships. Generally, respondents were aware of both the benefits and risks of industry funding: On the positive side, they identified the main benefits as the provision of additional resources, support and enhanced career opportunities for students, opportunities to apply basic research results to industrial problems, less red tape than with government funding, and enhanced university prestige. More recent studies suggest that emerging concepts such as academic entrepreneurship, the "third mission" and UI collaborations are developing at the nexus of science, technology and innovation policy studies (Sjöö and Hellström 2019). In performing a systematic analysis of forty papers focused on UI collaborations, the authors conclude that "the availability of resources (or lack thereof) ultimately separates the possible from the impossible" and that one of the strongest predictors of UI collaboration was prior experience. "Personal relations across the university–industry boundary creates familiarity and trust, build a shared history and facilitate an understanding of the parties' routines and expectations—all of which are found to be associated with the institutionalization of collaboration" (Sjöö and Hellström 2019, 281).

While the findings in this field of inquiry are varied, this chapter aims to contribute a pragmatic discussion of how transdisciplinary innovation has been managed within a structured grant program (RAPID) and offers reflections on researcher's participation in the program.

What Is RAPID?

RAPID (Research and Project Innovation and Development) is a small grant funded initiative to encourage cross-disciplinary research, innovation, and industry engagement on behalf of the School of Humanities, Creative Industries, and Social Sciences (HCISS) at the UON. The RAPID program is run through the Future Arts, Science and Technology Laboratory, FASTlab, the university's research, development, and innovation lab.

RAPID was established to provide opportunities for academic staff, industry partners, and communities to get involved in research projects that deliver tangible outcomes and responses to real-world problems quickly. For academic researchers, it gives them a chance to apply their creative problem-solving skills to help their partners approach a challenge differently. (Egglestone 2021)

The objectives of the RAPID program mirror the spirit of FASTlab with a focus on discovering problems that matter and finding value opportunities and alternative pathways to goals through playful innovation and experimentation. While current research and development literature espouses the "fail fast, fail often" approach, RAPID grants of up to AUD 10,000 (£5,000) encourage an experiment-and-iterate model for developing innovation. RAPID grants offer academics from the school the opportunity to partner with academics from other UON disciplines and an external partner (a government agency, community, business, or NGO) to develop innovative solutions to localized, real-world problems in a series of research "sprints" conducted over three to six months. This time frame, which is much shorter than traditional academic research, ensures that any solutions or products developed are industry relevant and fit-for-purpose at the time of their development. The grant offers approved projects a small budget as well as human and technological resources to enable partners to work together on user-driven, real-world problems. Acceptance into the program is based on an application process which includes a round of project proposals, followed by a "pitch" made to a panel of judges. The three-person judging panel consists of two external judges, recruited from industry, and one from within the UON, supported by a representative from the school to provide any further or contextual information to the panel. The judges provide formal feedback to the cohort, and informally to all participating teams, focused on how to move forward with their idea/pitch. In this way, unsuccessful teams may receive crucial feedback that enables them to begin a project and source funding rather than wait until the next round. The grants are awarded on the same day, immediately following the pitch presentations.

The promotion and communication of RAPID across the School, the industry, and the wider community focuses on the "spirit" of the program, in particular six principles intended to drive behavior:

- Discover problems that matter.
- Play, innovate, and experiment.
- Fail fast and move on.
- Build relationships between researchers and industry partners.
- Look for IP and value opportunities.
- Spot alternative pathways to the endgame

Formal "rules" for the program are kept to a minimum, but applications need to clearly state the research objectives and significance, outline the research design and methods, explain capability to deliver (resources and people), show plans for future external funding, and provide a budget. Applicants must include researchers from at least two different disciplines together with an external industry partner.

The plans for external funding can come from industry partners in advance or be outlined as a plan toward further funding in the future. This might involve an Australian Research Council (ARC) Linkage grant (that also encourages co-operation between academic institutions and industry), offering between AUD 50,000 and AUD 300,000 a year for two to five years with a requirement for obtaining matching funding from at least one Partner Organization.

Linkage promotes national and international research partnerships between researchers and business, industry, community organisations and other publicly funded research agencies. By supporting the development of partnerships, the ARC encourages the transfer of skills, knowledge, and ideas as a basis for securing commercial and other benefits of research. (Australian Research Council 2021)[1]

---

[1] See https://www.arc.gov.au/funding-research/funding-schemes/linkage-program/linkage-projects.

Other funding may be acquired through Cooperative Research Centre (CRC) funding. CRCs are an Australian Government initiative, designed to support Australian Industries' ability to compete and produce, and are offered to help companies partner with the research sector to overcome industry related challenges. These grants can be short term (up to three years) or medium to long term (up to ten years), are for industry-led projects, and can often include the provision of a PhD program. Therefore, there is an orientation that proposals should lead to ongoing commitment and are seeding future collaborations rather than being a project limited by the budgetary scope.

The RAPID program was supported by a small "Engagement" team from within the school. These academics planned the various events, coordinated marketing and support processes, and promoted the initiative through informal communication channels where needed.

RAPID Projects

Between 2017 and 2022 there have been eighteen RAPID projects approved for funding from forty-two proposals, giving a 43% success rate. Three grants are awarded each year and applications increased from five in the first year to nine in the most recent year (average seven a year), as knowledge of, and experience with, the program became more widespread with academics and potential partners.[2]

The transdisciplinary nature of the program is evident in the range of disciplines included in the forty-two proposals. These include Creative Industries, Design, Media Production, Sound Design, Interactive Design, Visual and Interactive Art, Communication, Creative Technology, Museums and Galleries, Music, Health, Biodiversity, Innovation, Information Technology, Psychology, Public Relations, Social Work, and User Experience Design. Generally, successful applications had higher rates of transdisciplinarity (2.6 different disciplines per project, compared to 2.3 for unsuccessful projects.)

Industry partners included State and Local government, arts and health organizations, community groups, specialist research organizations, private industry, and private technical specialists. More than half of listed industry partners over the six years were either private technical specialist organizations (e.g.,

---

[2.] A far greater number of projects were initiated, but many of these were not able to build collaborations toward a final submission within the compressed timeframe.

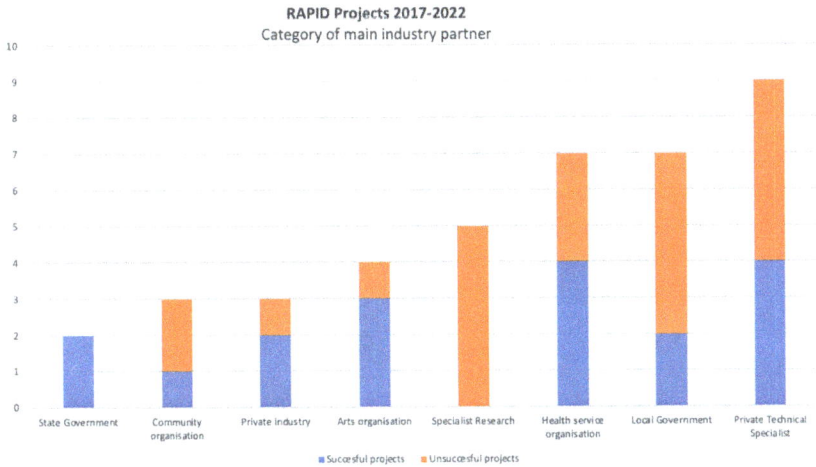

Figure 1: Number and Category of Main Industry Partner for RAPID Projects 2017–2022

IT developers, media production providers), health service organizations (e.g., disability care providers, psychology clinics, emergency rescue services), or local government (see Figure 1).

Transdisciplinary Success

A comparative analysis of successful and unsuccessful projects across six years shows that successful applicants increasingly pitched more complex problems (e.g., how to count koalas in the Australian bush, how to reduce waste in the fashion industry), that needed greater transdisciplinarity (e.g. one successful project involved researchers from the fields of creativity, plant ecology, visual arts, and public relations), and with intended outcomes that mattered more widely to the community (emergency rescue, species decline, stress management).

Judges reported that unsuccessful projects tended to have less complexity, required fewer research collaborators, and positioned industry partners as specialists needed to help provide researchers with missing skills. This compared to successful project industry partners who were invested directly in the "problem" and seen as genuine stakeholders in research design and execution.

The complex and transdisciplinary nature of projects often mean that RAPID teams develop solutions which can have benefits in multiple fields. Broadly speaking, the proposed projects fall into four main categories: solutions to support improved health outcomes (particularly mental health); solutions to support

Figure 2: Category of Wicked Problems for RAPID Projects 2017–2022

RAPID Projects 2107-2022
Category of "wicked problem"

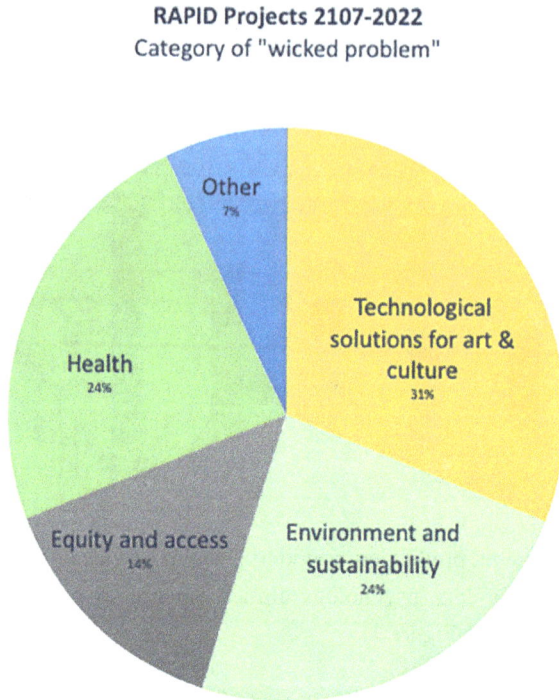

Figure 2: Category of Wicked Problems for RAPID Projects 2017–2022

environmental challenges; experiments to promote technological solutions for art and culture; and explorations into improving access and equity issues (see Figure 2).

Applications for projects that address health-related issues include the "Backyard Detectives" project, a venture designed to act as a community science project, using a fine grain sensor-based DIY kit that can assembled by children and their parents to read how much coal dust is dispersed into the atmosphere from uncovered coal train loads (see the summaries which follow this chapter). This project deployed Internet of Things (IoT) sensor-based technologies to enable crowdsourced data as a citizen science project. Other health-related projects include support for speech rehabilitation through mobile AI technology and the use of virtual reality and binaural music patterns to create a mindfulness app that veterans, athletes, and executives under pressure can use to optimize their brains to better cope with stress and to enhance problem-solving.

Proposed projects in the environmental and sustainability category include an app to help people identify which color bin (regular, recycling, or green waste) their household refuse should go in; the development of a living herbarium app to raise public awareness of Australian flora, using Newcastle and the Hunter Valley as a pilot location; and a project that addresses the development of low-waste fashion design practices. Known as the "Six Seasons" project, this is a partnership between Newcastle fashion label High Tea with Mrs Woo and UON School of Creative Industries academics with backgrounds in fabric and textiles, natural history illustration, and soft sculpture. This project developed a more sustainable way of creating and using textiles to manufacture clothing.

Projects using technology in the arts and culture domain include "This Land AR" a transmedia initiative, comprising an augmented reality (AR) Indigenous music, visual, and sound installation (Matthias et al. 2019). One project explored the use of an extended reality (XR) interactive approach to augment audible elements in the public exhibition "WARWAR: The Art of Torres Strait," an exhibition held at the Newcastle Art Gallery. Another exhibition project titled "Please Touch: a virtual engagement with Sodeisha sculptural ceramics" translated Japanese ceramic works into VR experiences (See Siang et al. 2019). In a similar vein, Entangled is a project that sought to update traditional notions of screen writing and linear storytelling for the application to VR technologies. With the user experience in mind collaborators Una Rey, Simon Weaving, and Andy Gallagher proposed to "develop a Newcastle-based capability for the creation of virtual reality (VR) content that engages users with a sophisticated understanding of the unique nature of the VR experience rather than the application of linear storytelling techniques adapted to, or forced upon, the medium (Weaving 2021).

Another arts and culture project aimed to better utilize the smart city technology being embedded throughout the Newcastle CBD to playfully show how a relatively "passive" element of the smart city's infrastructure ("smart poles") could potentially be activated to invite interaction from citizens. The proposal was for a small number of smart poles to be assigned conceptual "personalities," differentiated by their configuration of interactive, haptic, sensory, participatory technologies.[3]

In the category of equity and access, "Challenging stigma: Re-imagining Parenting Possibilities" used theater techniques as a tool for changing attitudes toward parents with intellectual disabilities (Irvine et al. 2021), while "The House We Build" was a project that used an urban planning game and interactive digital intervention to better engage local communities in complex planning decisions

---

[3] More detailed snapshots of a handful of projects follow this chapter.

that would directly impact their lives. Although the latter project was not selected by RAPID judges, "the FASTlab team took the decision to work with staff from the Urban Planning and Smart Cities teams at the Council to further refine the project and identify the resources required to deliver it" (Drummond et al. 2022).

> *The 'House We Build' project arose from an inclusive desire to create a safe space for participants to engage constructively in dialogue about urban planning in the city of Newcastle. The main objective of the 'House We Build' research process was the gamification of a public consultation process using a compelling online game, informative animation, aesthetic website, and eventually leading the public to a citizen survey where they could share their ideas for the future of the city. This was designed with the aim of enabling greater participation in the City of Newcastle planning process. The game gave each player the power to make realistic planning decisions. However, each decision had consequences, with potential advantages and disadvantages. Our practice-led research aimed to give the player a sense of their responsibilities to the greater community while balancing their own individual concerns. Therefore, the game was designed as a simple user participation and elicitation research tool, as part of the public consultation process. (Egglestone 2022)*

Another project unsuccessful in a RAPID round but which later gained traction was eventually retitled "Wild Yeast" (https://www.wildyeastzoo.com/) and is supported by supported the Australian Research Council Centre of Excellence in Synthetic Biology, and Inspiring Australia Through the Inspiring Qld and Inspiring NSW state networks (see Chapter 1 in Section I of this volume). HEAD2ART, a successful RAPID collaboration between UON researchers, headspace Newcastle, and the Museum of Art and Culture Lake Macquarie (MAC) to support young people to build social and emotional resilience, is also discussed in detail in a later chapter.

Discussion and Conclusion

Participants from the various RAPID program projects cited a similar range of benefits for themselves, the stakeholders, and/or the industry partners involved in their projects. For academics, a key benefit was the extension of their professional network, the requirement of transdisciplinarity connecting academics with people they would not have otherwise met either from other disciplines across the UON, or industry and the wider community. Developing "pitching" skills was acknowledged to be useful in accessing alternative forms of funding. Building CV's and supporting the development of Research Opportunity and Performance Evidence statements (ROPE) for future grant applications (these are specific to Australian researchers) was also a major incentive.

> *RAPID has been really useful in helping some academic colleagues and early career researchers kickstart their research careers. It's a staged approach to getting started with clear outcomes and equally clear pathways to develop further with the research team and industry partners already connected. (Egglestone 2021)*

Others cited the motivation and drive to achieve research outcomes in the short "sprint" format of the RAPID program, encouraging researchers to experiment, gather feedback, and apply feedback in a fast-paced, iterative process to develop the best possible solution. For example, throughout the development of the Sodeisha project "Please Touch," primary school students were offered the opportunity to interact with the VR exhibition; however, one child who suffered from epilepsy was not able to safely participate. The researchers took the VR prototype back to the design phase and developed an epilepsy friendly version of the VR experience. Not only does this offer significant benefits of increased levels of accessibility and inclusivity for the community, but these breakthroughs at the coalface of new and emerging technology can offer even more prospects for researchers to discuss their research at conferences and in peer reviewed journal articles.

Through partnership with industry, researchers gained access to technology that may not have been available to the university, while industry partners gained access to the advanced skills and technical expertise of the UON academics to help produce industry-led solutions to local challenges. One example of this beneficial resource mutuality is seen in the *Entangled* VR project, where the external partner was able to share with academics the highly advanced and rare 3D 360 VR camera required to film the action, and gained access to the screenwriting capability, studios, locations, student crew members, and post-production facilities of the university.

Judging consisted of a senior university researcher in addition to two senior industry and/or innovation leaders. Inclusion of the senior university leader provided awareness of RAPID at the faculty and chancellery level as well as guidance to early and mid-career researchers on how to leverage industry activities to impact and engagement metrics. Similarly, the two senior judges from the industry or the "start-up" community provided a degree of mentorship for projects and an increased opportunity for connectivity through introductions and experience. Feedback to the RAPID teams was specific and directed toward the opportunity and ideas for the next step or resubmission next year. Every team, regardless of they were successful in RAPID funding, benefited from bespoke feedback.

Many participants also cited the creative alchemy that occurs when collaborators of various backgrounds and specialties "bounce" ideas of one another and encourage innovative thinking to overcome challenges. Industry partners tended to be selected by researchers based on demonstrating similar interests and values but possessing diverse yet complementary skill sets and approaches. Brett McMahon from the "Six Seasons" project outlines the benefits of this creative collaboration:

> A harmonious team dynamic, with a lot of combined experience meant that there were always creative solutions on hand, and sometimes a problem was turned into an unexpected positive outcome… working with a group of similarly motivated colleagues who pushed and tested all elements presented, result[ed] in an outcome that exceeded our expectations.

Feedback from RAPID program participants suggested that so-called soft skills such as communication, time management, and teamwork were crucial to producing successful solutions or project outcomes. Weaving, who drew on his prior experience pitching ideas in the film industry, suggests that skills acquired from previous industry experience can also be valuable resources. He notes that industry expectations around deadlines, outcomes, and ROIs are generally more rigid than academic expectations of research output and some academics could be unfamiliar with this distinction.

Programs like RAPID inevitably pressure test traditional models of intellectual property (IP) ownership which potentially stifles ideation through collaboration. Commercial organizations fear value "leaking" through collaborating with external parties. The RAPID program places its focus on *creating* value rather than capturing it. However, adopting Henry Chesbrough's "open innovation" (Chesbrough 2003) co-creation approach to research and development required an assessment of several alternative intellectual property models that better reflected all parties' contribution to joint value creation while providing a route to exploiting new knowledge within a framework that recognized and rewarded contributors appropriately. The UON was proactive here in proposing a series of models ranging across exclusive licensing, shared revenue from negotiated commercialization and joint ownership of intellectual property as an alternative, or supplement to the standard provisions in its existing Research Agreement. While this approach met RAPID's requirements for the projects, it also surfaced the transformational challenge for open innovation. Across the series of relatively small and self-contained projects that made up RAPID, the proposed IP solutions worked reasonably well. For them to do so at scale would require significant structural and systemic changes to how business is done in the context of further developing open innovation.

Critical to early success of the RAPID initiative were support mechanisms that were established to help form relationships through problem identification. In the first year of operation — and six months before the launch — a series of industry breakfasts were held to outline the way the initiative would work. Academics and industry partners were invited to engage in dialogue about the kinds of wicked problems that would be of mutual interest. This process was gamified at the official launch, an event that explained the RAPID process, generated ideas for projects, and facilitated team formation. A second support workshop was held after the launch but before the application due date to assist with detailed project design and to help participants prepare for the pitch night. These support mechanisms were run again in the second year of RAPID but then significantly scaled back as academics and industry partners became familiar with the process.

These supporting mechanisms, funded by the school, were critical in ensuring RAPID was seen as a success from the outset and served to reinforce the "spirit" of RAPID as serious play, encouraging researchers to experiment in solving significant problems. Despite a relatively modest amount of project funding over six years, RAPID has demonstrated that transdisciplinary teams, working with engaged industry partners on shared problems in a genuinely collaborative way, can — with helpful support, loose rules, and insightful independent funding decisions — create significant value for the project stakeholders as well as the communities they strive to benefit.

REFERENCES

Baer, Hans A., and Merrill Singer. 2014. *The Anthropology of Climate Change*. Routledge.

Brem, Alexander, and Agnieszka Radziwon. 2017. "Efficient Triple Helix Collaboration Fostering Local Niche Innovation Projects: A Case from Denmark."

Technological Forecasting and Social Change 123: 130–141. https://doi. org/10.1016/j.techfore.2017.01.002.

Burton, Ian. 1987. "Report on Reports: Our Common Future." *Environment: Science and Policy for Sustainable Development* 29 (5): 25–29. https://doi.org/ 10.1080/00139157.1987.9928891.

Cai, Yuzhuo, Borja Ramis Ferrer, and Jose Luis Martinez Lastra. 2019. "Building University-Industry Co-Innovation Networks in Transnational Inno- vation Ecosystems: Towards a Transdisciplinary Approach of Integrating Social Sciences and Artificial Intelligence." *Sustainability* 11 (17): 4633. https://doi. org/10.3390/su11174633.

Chesbrough, Henry William. 2003. *Open Innovation: The New Imperative for Creating and Profiting from Technology*. Harvard Business School Press.

Crowther, Mathew S., Clive A. McAlpine, Daniel Lunney, Ian Shannon, and Jessica V. Bryant. 2009. "Using Broad-Scale, Community Survey Data to Compare Species Conservation Strategies Across Regions: A Case Study of the Koala in a Set of Adjacent 'Catchments.' " *Ecological Management & Restoration* 10: S88–S96. https://doi.org/10.1111/j.1442-8903.2009.00465.x.

Di Maria, Eleonora, Valentina De Marchi, and Katharina Spraul. 2019. "Who Benefits from University–Industry Collaboration for Environmental Sustain- ability?" *International Journal of Sustainability in Higher Education* 20 (6): 1022–1041. https://doi.org/10.1108/ijshe-10-2018-0172.

Dorst, Kees. 2018. "Mixing Practices to Create Transdisciplinary Innovation: A Design-Based Approach." *Technology Innovation Management Review* 8 (8): 60–65. https://doi.org/10.22215/timreview/1179.

Drummond, Jon, Mario Minichiello, Paul Egglestone, et al. 2022. " 'House We Build': Design Communication and Urban Planning." Presented at the Peer Review Proceedings of the 16th International Conference of Design Principles and Practices, Newcastle, January 19–21, 2022.

Egglestone, Paul. 2021. "Imagine Better." In *The Elephant's Leg: Adventures in the Creative Industries*, edited by Craig Hight and Mario Minichiello. Common Ground Research Networks.

Egglestone, Paul. 2022. "Applied Chaos: The Future Arts, Science and Technology Laboratory." *Design Principles and Practices: An International Journal—Annual Review* 16 (1): 19–30.

Hansson, Stina, and Merritt Polk. 2018. "Assessing the Impact of Transdisciplinary Research: The Usefulness of Relevance, Credibility, and Legitimacy for Understanding the Link Between Process and Impact." *Research Evaluation* 27 (2): 132–144. https://doi.org/10.1093/reseval/rvy004.

Harman, Grant. 2010. "Australian University Research Commercialisation: Perceptions of Technology Transfer Specialists and Science and Technology Academics." *Journal of Higher Education Policy and Management* 32 (1): 69–83. https://doi.org/10.1080/13600800903440568.

Killen, Chloe, Phillip McIntyre, Bernadette Drabsch, et al. 2022. "Communicating as Community: Examining Power and Authority in Community-Focused Environmental Communication Through Participatory Action Research in the Ourimbah Creek Valley." *Platform: Journal of Media and Communication* 9 (2): 6–21. https://doi.org/10.46580/p90707.

Leydesdorff, Loet. 1998. "The Triple Helix as a Model for Innovation Studies." *Science and Public Policy* 25 (3): 195–203. https://doi.org/10.1093/spp/25.3.195.

Leydesdorff, Loet. 2012. "The Knowledge-Based Economy and the Triple Helix Model." Arxiv.org, January. https://doi.org/10.48550/arXiv.1201.4553.

Lubbe, Berendien, Alisha Ali, and Jarmo Ritalahti. 2021. "Increasing Student Employability Through University/Industry Collaboration: A Study in South Africa, the UK and Finland." *Travel and Tourism Research Association: Advancing Tourism Research Globally*. https://scholarworks.umass.edu/ttra/2021/research_papers/42/.

Matthias, Philip, Mark Billinghurst, and Zi Siang See. 2019. "This Land AR: An Australian Music and Sound XR Installation." In *Proceedings of the 17th International Conference on Virtual-Reality Continuum and Its Applications in Industry*. Association for Computing Machinery.

Peters, B. Guy. 2017. "What Is So Wicked About Wicked Problems? A Conceptual Analysis and a Research Program." *Policy and Society* 36 (3): 385–396. https://doi.org/10.1080/14494035.2017.1361633.

Rajalo, Sigrid, and Maaja Vadi. 2017. "University-Industry Innovation Collaboration: Reconceptualization." *Technovation* 62–63: 42–54. https://doi.org/10.1016/j.technovation.2017.04.003.

Sachs, Jeffrey D., Guido Schmidt-Traub, Mariana Mazzucato, Dirk Messner, Nebojsa Nakicenovic, and Johan Rockström. 2019. "Six Transformations to Achieve the Sustainable Development Goals." *Nature Sustainability* 2 (9): 805–814.

Schmidt, Laura, Thomas Falk, Marianna Siegmund-Schultze, and Joachim H. Spangenberg. 2020. "The Objectives of Stakeholder Involvement in Trans-disciplinary Research: A Conceptual Framework for a Reflective and Reflex-ive Practise." *Ecological Economics* 176: 106751. https://doi.org/10.1016/j.ecolecon.2020.106751.

Siang See, Zi, Una Rey, Faye Neilson, et al. 2019. "Sodeisha Sculptural Ceram-ics: Digitalization and VR Interaction." In *Proceedings of the 17th International Conference on Virtual-Reality Continuum and Its Applications in Industry.* ACM.

Sjöö, Karolin, and Tomas Hellström. 2019. "University–Industry Collabora-tion: A Literature Review and Synthesis." *Industry and Higher Education* 33 (4): 275–285. https://doi.org/10.1177/0950422219829697.

Weaving, Simon. 2021. "Evoke, Don't Show: Narration in Cinematic Virtual Reality and the Making of Entangled." *Virtual Creativity* 11 (1): 147–162.

Witt, Ryan R., Chad T. Beranek, Lachlan G. Howell, et al. 2020. "Real-Time Drone Derived Thermal Imagery Outperforms Traditional Survey Methods for an Arboreal Forest Mammal." *PLoS ONE* 15 (11): e0242204. https://doi.org/10.1371/journal.pone.0242204.

Zafeirakopoulos, Mariana, and Mieke van der Bijl-Brouwer. 2018. "Exploring the Transdisciplinary Learning Experiences of Innovation Professionals." *Tech-nology Innovation Management Review* 8 (8): 50–59. https://doi.org/10.22215/timreview/1178.

CHAPTER 7

RAPID Case Studies

Paul Egglestone and Craig Hight

Introduction

This chapter presents brief case studies of five Research and Project Innovation and Development (RAPID) projects: Koala Quest, Backyard Detectives, Six Seasons, This Land AR, and Communicating as Community. These provide snapshots of the conceptualization, challenges, and outcomes of projects that successfully gained funding during a RAPID pitching round between 2017 and 2022. These collectively demonstrate the potential for industry–academy collaborations focused on rapid prototyping, offering insights into the process of participation in the RAPID program. They demonstrate highly innovative, valuable solutions particularly to local problems (with global implications), and are notable for fostering ongoing, productive collaborations between local industry partners and the University of Newcastle (UON).

Koala Quest: Innovation in Population Monitoring

RAPID Team 2017

Adam Roff, Senior Scientist, NSW Office of Environment and Heritage (OEH)
Michael Day, Senior Scientist, NSW OEH
Bob Denholm, Senior Team Leader, NSW OEH
Paul Egglestone, FASTlab
Grant Hamilton, Senior Lecturer in Ecology (Biosecurity), Queensland University of Technology (QUT)

In response to a declining koala population in NSW and predictions of their functional extinction in the near future, this 2017 RAPID project proposal was developed in collaboration with QUT and the NSW Office of Environment and Heritage. Its key objective was to develop technology that would help to accurately detect koalas in the field using drones. Koalas are cryptic animals, both widespread and unevenly distributed and consequently can be hard to detect (Crowther et al. 2009). Accurate estimates of their populations are essential to make effective and longer-term conservation decisions (Lunney et al. 2009; Phillips and Callaghan 2011; Predavec et al. 2015, 2017). This project proposed to trial a new method of koala detection using drones or unmanned aerial vehicles (UAVs). This opened new opportunities for data processing (drawing on crowdsourcing and AI-centered workflows) and new media for digital artists.

This project is notable for several reasons. Concern and anger surrounding the approval process for the development of large sections of koala habitat in NSW has been a recent feature of the local political and environmental landscape. Community groups have protested this approval process, but due to the difficulty in establishing a reliable method for documenting koala numbers, research commissioned to both oppose and support policy decisions has tended to generate conflicting results. Koala Quest exemplifies the goal of the RAPID program to identify local issues and challenges and enable collaboration between researchers from UON and industry partners, in this case the NSW Office of Environment and Heritage, as well as inviting members of the community to participate through crowdsourcing to identify better solutions to these local challenges. As Adam Roff and Bob Denholm from the NSW Department of Environment, speaking in 2019, noted, "It is difficult to take on projects that involve risk or innovation in an operational environment. RAPID funding would allow us to acquire new knowledge in preparation for further grant applications."

The findings of the Koala Quest project show that drones coupled with thermal imaging cameras are a promising, efficient and effective alternative method to systematic spotlighting and the Spot Assessment Technique (SAT) for detecting koala and estimating density at low density sites in the winter period. However preliminary, the project team highlighted the potential application of drones to garner new insights into koala behavior, movement, and tree utilization preferences. Further, they showed that drones combined with systematic spotlighting are likely to be more accurate methods to estimate population density at low density sites than the SAT and suggest that the SAT should only be used to calculate precursory density estimates where funding other methods is not possible. However, before drones will be able to supersede the SAT on a landscape scale, improvements are required to enhance battery life, flight time, and resolution quality of the visual and thermal imagery sensor (Witt et al. 2020).

One key insight from the project was that the RAPID program allowed research-ers to take risks within a program framework designed for experimentation and collaboration, rather than requiring researchers to produce immediately profitable or measurable outcomes. The focus on fostering collaboration and building lasting networks and relationships between university researchers and industry partners here fostered wider outcomes. A longer-term view of productive cooperation could provide the ideal conditions for generating ongoing research outcomes for devel-opment of sustainable solutions to industry challenges. In the case of the Koala Quest project, the findings of the project include identifying new knowledge that would suggest helpful areas for further research to develop better solutions, and some new information to build future solutions from. The project, as well as the relationships it established, continues to develop alongside evolving opportunities for further collaboration with the original RAPID funding providing the impetus for the NSW government to further invest in this new technology.

By 2022, the nascent Wildlife Drone Hub (WDF) at the Department of Envi-ronment had been funded AUD 2.3 million by the NSW Digital Restart Fund to demonstrate regional scale drone surveys and to train ecologists from universities, government, and industry to fly drones. The team published the methods (Witt et al. 2020) and teams from across the government and private sector ultimately began operating drones at scale. The program has also delivered a cloud platform with AI capabilities to support analyses of these new data. Drone pilots trained by the WDF have since completed over 1,440 scientific surveys across NSW. They have located over eleven thousand animals and the new technology has become an integral part of the AUD 20 million survey of koalas that were recently listed as endangered species in Eastern Australia. Such rapid development and scaling of new technology is unusual in the government sector, and it was inspired by the principles of the RAPID program at the UON.

Backyard Detectives: Crowdsourcing the Monitoring of Coal Dust Pollution

RAPID Team 2017

Nathaniel Bavinton, Smart City Coordinator, Strategic Planning, Newcastle City Council

Mario Minichiello, Professor of Design, FASTlab
Desirée Sheehan, Smart City Officer—Strategic Planning, Newcastle City Council
Michael Dickinson, Senior lecturer Design, FASTlab
Chris Hilderbrandt, Independent advisor—UON Innovation Program
Danielo Pati, Senior Technical Advisor—School of Creative Industries, UON

Backyard Detectives was initially a collaboration between FASTlab, City of Newcastle (CoN), Newcastle City Living Lab, and the Hunter Medical Research Institute (HMRI). It proposed an innovative and community based "science project" model to leverage the potential to crowdsource information that could respond to and help disrupt an environmental challenge. Whilst this challenge is specific to the Newcastle region, its application is globally relevant to any large city where there is pollution in the atmosphere, or the transportation of waste, and a community desire to trace and document the harmful effects it may have.

The CoN is a major center for coal transportation, significant as the largest coal port in the world.[1] A long-standing practice has been for coal trucks to be moved by rail through residential areas using uncovered containers. A consequence has been that coal dust can be found in most Newcastle homes, prompting community questions and concerns about the scale and distribution patterns of the dust and its potential impact on health. These concerns have been further heightened by the widely spread findings in the *Lancet* that a certain size of dust particle (PM2.5) had breached the blood–tissue barrier protecting the human brain (Seaton et al. 1995).

Ultimately, the aim of this project was to harness known local public health concerns through a crowdsource methodology to both prove the local reality of the coal dust phenomenon through indicative data sampling, as well as to build community momentum toward social change. The practical objective for the RAPID project was to develop a fine grain sensor-based DIY kit that can read how much coal dust is dispersed into the atmosphere from uncovered coal train loads. The project designed and deployed Internet of Things (IoT) sensor-based technologies to enable crowdsourced data as a citizen science project. The IoT core sensor kit is designed to be so simple that a 5-year-old can assemble it and be supplemented by everyday household items (toilet rolls, coat hangers, PVC pipe, etc.). RAPID funding helped resource a poster and email campaign inviting

---

[1] See https://en.m.wikipedia.org/wiki/Port_of_Newcastle and the regular reports provided by the Port of Newcastle: https://www.portofnewcastle.com.au/trade-and-business/trade-overview-reports/

school-age children and their families to come to an interactive workshop in the newly opened Maker Space at the City of Newcastle's library. During the initial workshop, which was heavily oversubscribed, children followed open-source instructions, to create a particulate matter sensor for measuring coal dust. In involving children and adopting the playful nature of a "community science project" to deal with a very serious local health issue, this project embodied the aims of the RAPID program in their research goals and methodology.

One of the challenges that this project highlighted was that all RAPID research projects are inevitably taking place within a sociopolitical context which inform and shape not only the urgency of community members but also diverse reactions from other stakeholders. The relationship between science and society is continually shifting including universities' relationships to private interests, technology, and conceptualizations of knowledge as a "public good." Understanding the material, political, and economic forces that enable, shape, or constrain knowledge is central to understanding contentious policy disputes (Hardie et al. 2016).

Figure 1: Assembled IoT Core Sensor Kit

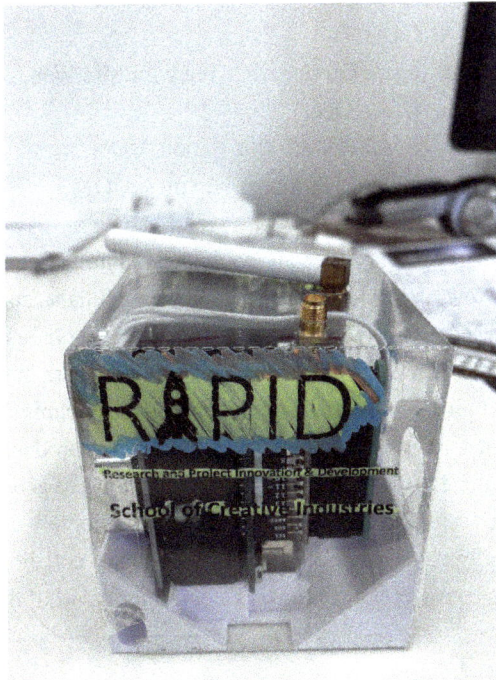

Source: Paul Egglestone

While university academics can and do produce research that is critical of government or industry policies or practices, within a broader setting they may find that industries or large corporations are hesitant to be involved in projects which appear too contentious or may have future negative implications for companies who align themselves with the project. For example, there is, historically, a close nexus between the coal industry and the federal and various state governments in Australia (Baer and Singer 2014). Despite the researchers on this project approaching many well-known Australian brands for potential collaboration or to help fund this project, all those approached declined, citing the "political" nature of the project.

Six Seasons: Investigating and Implementing Design and Digital Print Textile Solutions for a Sustainable Fashion Industry

RAPID Team 2019

Faye Neilson, Fine Arts, UON
Rowena, Juliana and Angela Foong, High Tea with Mrs Woo
Brett McMahon, Fine Arts, UON
Bernadette Drabsch, Natural History Illustration, UON
Giselle Penn, Technical Officer in Fibres–Textiles, UON

High Tea with Mrs Woo[2] has been an iconic Australian clothing label since its establishment in Newcastle in 2004 by sisters Rowena, Juliana, and Angela Foong. The Six Seasons RAPID project saw School of Creative Industries academics Faye Neilson, Bernadette Drabsch, and Brett McMahon work in partnership with the founders of High Tea with Mrs Woo to create a sustainable future in fashion by promoting waste reduction in three areas of garment production: the cutting of fabric to minimize offcuts, the selection and printing of eco-friendly fabric, and encouraging customized production. In Rowena Foong's words, speaking in 2021: "We really value the fact that we can actually collaborate not only as a way to achieve a project but actually as a community, all of this is part of the creative industries."

---

[2] https://highteawithmrswoo.com.au/

The overall aim of the project was to prototype a small collection of low-waste garments, using natural fabrics and unique digital printing methods designed to minimize the waste that generally occurs when cutting fabric for garment creation (Gam 2018; Rissanen and McQuillan 2016; Saeidi and Wimberley 2017; Teibel 2019). Custom printing the fabric for each piece means that the waste that is generated by pattern matching for aesthetic continuity is minimized. Acceptance into the RAPID program also enabled this project to compete in the 2020 We the Makers' Design for the Future: Sustainable and Ethical Textiles and Fashion competition, in which the Six Seasons project tied for first place. The judges "applauded the zero waste pattern techniques, natural fabrics, gender-neutral inclusivity and design philosophy to lengthen the life by being able to mix and match between the garments."[3]

Dr. Bernadette Drabsch, a senior School of Creative Industries lecturer and visual humanities researcher, worked on the Six Seasons project. She emphasizes the importance of open and clear communication between stakeholders and soft skills such as time management and respect for the ideas of others as crucial to the success of transdisciplinary research projects: "Good communication was vital to avoid any confusion. We determined from the beginning who would be doing what, who would be paying for what and the timeframe of delivery."

Figure 2: Rowena, Juliana, and Angela Foong

Source: https://highteawithmrswoo.com.au/pages/aboutS

[3] Australian Fashion Council (AFC), https://ausfashioncouncil.com/we-the-makers-designer-showcase-2020-winners-announced/, accessed 18 August, 2024.

Sigrid Rajalo and Maaja Vadi's (2017) research into university–industry (UI) innovation collaboration found that the particular case study that stood out as best practice of UI collaboration was built on a strong foundation of open and consistent communication. "These partners also described the importance of project management encompassing coordination, communication, risk, regular meetings, and so on…This was also the only case where partners discussed the demand-led aspects (client-driven approach) of their collaboration" (49). The responses from RAPID project participants support these kinds of insights from the literature about the importance of good communication as the foundation of transdisciplinary research. Making the expectations and aims of all contributors clear and explicit from the very outset of a project can provide clarity and focus and help avoid confusion and misadventure throughout the collaborative research process. The Six Seasons project was successful in their RAPID pitching round, in part, because the team had obviously developed a close and productive collaboration in a compressed time frame. In this case, a rapid prototyping approach perfectly suited a motivated collective of collaborators.

The Six Seasons project also provided professional opportunities for students to be involved through Studio Zed, a work-integrated design studio within the UON run by Dr. Simone O'Callaghan. The studio provided students the opportunity to work in a creative studio environment, getting first-hand experience with clients on a wide variety of professional design jobs. Dr. Drabsch commented that:

> The funding from RAPID allowed us to develop a prototype product that we otherwise wouldn't have been able to do. As we also brought in students from Studio Zed it became a wonderful medley of industry, staff and students—with everyone bouncing ideas off each other and pushing our creativity levels.

The project also fostered a range of potential future applications and collaborations that High Tea with Mrs Woo could engage in with other stakeholders in the fashion industry. The project's short-term prototyping achievements helped generate impetus to support further collaborative work with fabric design companies on a local or international level.

One of the main challenges the participants in the Six Season project encountered, however, was the continuing malfunction of a direct digital fabric printer that was sourced for the project. While this issue was eventually overcome by outsourcing the printing of the fabric, the space for experimentation and reiteration provided by RAPID arguably aids in industry innovation by absorbing some of the economic risk involved in developing new methods. The printer was eventually replaced by the manufacturer (with ambition at that stage to be used in ongoing experiments in the UON's textiles department to establish what possible sustainable solutions the technology could enable). Successfully printing low-waste garment layouts directly onto fabric has since proved to be an attractive measure for businesses such as Spoonflower or Digital Fabric, allowing for customized garment piece printouts to be overlaid on existing fabric designs, printed and produced for home production. Despite posing a difficult challenge for the researchers on the RAPID "sprints," the future potential of the ideas seeded in the Six Seasons project is significant for the sustainable fashion movement.

This Land AR: Indigenous Immersive Installation in a Regional Gallery

RAPID Team 2019

Philip Matthias, Music Lecturer, UON
Zi Siang See, Interaction Design Researcher, UON
Helena Bezzina, Creative Industries Professional
Akur Meta, Torres Strait Islander Corporation
Lauretta Morton, Director, Newcastle Art Gallery (NAG)
Toby Whaleboat, Land Services Officer, Hunter Local Land Services

This Land AR was successful as a RAPID funding project in 2019. It was a transmedia initiative, comprising an augmented reality (AR) Indigenous music, visual and sound installation. It also involved the use of an extended reality (XR) interactive approach to augment audible elements in the public exhibition "WAR-WAR: The Art of Torres Strait" an exhibition staged that year at the Newcastle Art Gallery. This Land AR was based on Australian Indigenous knowledge, histories, narratives, and performance, building from earlier creative collaborations particularly within the UON's music program. The project promoted the research expertise of Aboriginal and Torres Strait Islander collaborators, as a co-creation process and aimed to raise the profile of, and expand Australia's knowledge base and research capability in, the areas of heritage, inclusivity, transmedia storytelling, and creative technologies.

The research team for This Land AR partnered with Newcastle Art Gallery to investigate best practice use of innovative creative industries technologies and performance arts (including music, dance, narrative) and Australian Indigenous

Figure 3: A Visitor Using This Land AR at Newcastle Art Gallery as Part
of the WARWAR: The Art of Torres Strait Exhibition, May 2021

Source: Paul Egglestone

heritage and culture within a gallery installation/exhibition model. The longer-term
ambition was to create greater awareness of such cross-cultural exchanges and
instigate inspiration for further educational and social change in this area. This
project exemplifies some of the key benefits of participation in the RAPID project
and how "prototyping" facilitates not just impetus for technology innovations,
or traditional research outputs, but more immediate and meaningful benefits to
the local community.

   The collaboration structure of this project is distinct from the other case studies
discussed in this chapter. The researchers involved, Dr. Zi Siang See, Dr. Philip
Matthias, and Dr. Helena Bezzina from the UON, and Mark Billingshurst from
University of South Australia, took on a supporting role to project partners, the
Akur Meta Torres Strait Islander Corporation. Rather than active collaboration, the
researchers provided technical skills and specialized knowledge in a more technol-
ogy-centered translational role. The Akur Meta Torres Strait Islander Corporation
guided researchers on what was to be included, directing the decision-making

process around curation of the project's creative outcomes. Other partners in this project included the Wollotuka Institute and the Newcastle Regional Art Gallery. Through this structure, the project built a VR prototype to facilitate a virtual connection with specific sites (e.g., Murray Island in the Torres Strait, and Wollombi sacred sites), whereby a close-up connection to land and people is made. Of somewhat secondary concern, this project also produced several more traditional research outcomes including two peer-reviewed journal articles and the presentation of the project at SIGGRAPH VRCAI in Brisbane in 2019.[4]

Communicating as Community: Environmental Participatory Action Research in the Ourimbah Creek Valley

RAPID Team 2020

Phillip McIntyre, Communications, UON
Bernadette Drabsch, Natural History Illustration, UON
Chloe Killen, Communications, UON
Anita Chalmers, Plant Ecologist/Botanist, School of Environmental and Life Sciences, UON
Andrea Cassin, Communications, UON
Luke Foster and Lucinda Ransom, Senior Threatened Species Officers, Department of Planning, Industry and Environment
Kevina-Jo Smith, Artist

Within a broader context of a belated recognition of climate change, the contested term the Age of the Anthropocene, and its more localized manifestations as increasing urbanization, the biodiversity of NSW is becoming more precarious and needing more proactive and direct interventions. There is scientific consensus that close to one thousand species of animals and plants in NSW are at risk of lapsing into the endangered status. In the Hunter and Central Coast regions of the state, many such threatened species are found in areas where community and nature coexist, including backyard gardens.

---

[4] This conference was the 17th ACM Siggraph International Conference on Virtual-Reality Continuum and its Applications in Industry.

Despite, or because of, this proximity the principal industry partner of this project, the NSW Department of Planning, Industry and Environment (DPIE), has found it challenging to communicate to the public the need to actively contribute to the preservation of endangered species. Their RAPID project involved joining with researchers from the UON to engage community members in the Ourimbah Creek Valley in an action-based initiative. The project involved a multidisciplinary research team from communication, biodiversity, plant ecology, and public relations, began in 2021 and has become the most successful of the RAPID projects in terms of developing momentum and scale through external funding opportunities.

The project initially looked to leverage a range of techniques (including community art-making practices) to build community awareness about threatened species and build knowledge of local biodiversity. Along with the primary industry partner (DPIE), external participants included the Rainforest Sanctuary at the Forest of Tranquility, the Darkinjung Local Aboriginal Land Council, and internationally exhibited artist Kevina-Jo Smith, all of whom became "co-researchers" of the project through an open, collaborative research design.

The project involved engaging the community at the Ourimbah Creek site, exploring the flora in its natural state, making and eating bush tucker foods with a guided information session about their uses and value, and an art-making activity where participants made small sculptural components from upcycled household waste. Observation and informal interviews were collated in a research journal to help reflect upon and iterate the effectiveness of the project's storytelling approach.

The collaborative and highly transdisciplinary research approach proved a powerful way "for the research team to diffuse innovative ideas and encourage the community to begin thinking about themselves in a systemic relationship to their surrounding ecosystem" (Killen et al. 2022) and crucially helped the DPIE achieve several complex management objectives. The core of the team has subsequently gained NSW Environmental Trust Education Grant funding,[5] and an Australian Research Council (ARC) Linkage Grant in 2023.[6] This team demonstrates the broader ambition of the RAPID program: to foster innovative creative research but also to potentially scale approaches, workflows, and practices from local collaborations to engender broader impact beyond the narrow confines of the academy.

[5.] With a project titled 'Creating Community through Communication: Using a Systems-based Framework to Foster Community Engagement within the Biodiversity and Culturally rich Wonnarua Woodlands' ($250,000).

[6.] The project proposal title was 'Saving our Species: Creating Systemic Change in Regional Communities.' ($506,000). See https://rms.arc.gov.au/RMS/Report/Download/Report/a3f6be6e-33f7-4fb5-98a6-7526aaa184cf/247 for details.

REFERENCES

Baer, Hans A., and Merrill Singer. 2014. *The Anthropology of Climate Change*. Routledge.

Bédat, Maxine. 2016. "Our Love of Cheap Clothing Has a Hidden Cost—It's Time for a Fashion Revolution." World Economic Forum, April 22. https://www.weforum.org/agenda/2016/04/our-love-of-cheap-clothing-has-a-hidden-cost-it-s-time-the-fashion-industry-changed/.

Crowther, Mathew S., Clive A. McAlpine, Daniel Lunney, Ian Shannon, and Jessica V. Bryant. 2009. "Using Broad-Scale, Community Survey Data to Compare Species Conservation Strategies Across Regions: A Case Study of the Koala in a Set of Adjacent 'Catchments.' " *Ecological Management & Restoration* 10: S88–S96. https://doi.org/10.1111/j.1442-8903.2009.00465.x.

Gam, Hae Jin. 2018. "Zero Waste Fashion Design." *Family & Consumer Sciences Research Journal* 46 (3): 314–316.

Hardie, Liz, Naomi Smith Devetak, and Will Rifkin. 2016. "Universities in Contentious Energy Debates—Science, Democracy and Coal Seam Gas in Australia." *Energy Research & Social Science* 20: 105–116. https://doi.org/10.1016/j.erss.2016.06.008.

Killen, Chloe, Phillip McIntyre, Bernadette Drabsch, et al. 2022. "Communicating as Community: Examining Power and Authority in Community-Focused Environmental Communication Through Participatory Action Research in the Ourimbah Creek Valley." *Platform: Journal of Media and Communication* 9 (2): 6–21. https://doi.org/10.46580/p90707.

Lunney, Daniel, Mathew S. Crowther, Ian Shannon, and Jessica V. Bryant. 2009. "Combining a Map-Based Public Survey with an Estimation of Site Occupancy to Determine the Recent and Changing Distribution of the Koala in New South Wales." *Wildlife Research* 36 (3): 262–273.

McAlpine, Clive, Daniel Lunney, Alistair Melzer, et al. 2015. "Conserving Koalas: A Review of the Contrasting Regional Trends, Outlooks and Policy Challenges." *Biological Conservation* 192: 226–236.

Phillips, Stephen, and John Callaghan. 2011. "The Spot Assessment Technique: A Tool for Determining Localised Levels of Habitat Use by Koalas Phascolarctos Cinereus." *Australian Zoologist* 35 (3): 774–780.

Predavec, Martin, Daniel Lunney, Ian Shannon, John Lemon, Indrie Sonawane, and Mathew Crowther. 2017. "Using Repeat Citizen Science Surveys of Koalas to Assess Their Population Trend in the North-West of New South Wales: Scale Matters." *Australian Mammalogy* 40 (1): 47–57.

Predavec, Martin, Daniel Lunney, Ian Shannon, Dave Scotts, John Turbill, and Bill Faulkner. 2015. "Mapping the Likelihood of Koalas Across New South Wales for Use in Private Native Forestry: Developing a Simple, Species Distribution Model That Deals with Opportunistic Data." *Australian Mammalogy* 37 (2): 182–193.

Rajalo, Sigrid, and Maaja Vadi. 2017. "University-Industry Innovation Collaboration: Reconceptualization." *Technovation* 62–63: 42–54. https://doi.org/10.1016/j.technovation.2017.04.003.

Rissanen, T., and H. McQuillan. 2016. *Zero Waste Fashion Design*. Fairchild Books, an Imprint of Bloomsbury Publishing.

Saeidi, Elahe, and Virginia Schreffler Wimberley. 2017. "Precious Cut: Exploring Creative Pattern Cutting and Draping for Zero-Waste Design." *International Journal of Fashion Design, Technology and Education* 11 (2): 243–253. http://doi.org/10.1080/17543266.2017.1389997.

Seaton, Anthony, D. Godden, W. MacNee, and K. Donaldson. 1995. "Particulate Air Pollution and Acute Health Effects." *Lancet* 345 (8943): 176–178.

Teibel, Elisha, 2019. "Waste Size: The Skinny on the Environmental Costs of the Fashion Industry." *William & Mary Environmental Law & Policy Review* 43 (2): 595.

Witt, Ryan R., Chad T. Beranek, Lachlan G. Howell, et al. 2020. "Real-Time Drone Derived Thermal Imagery Outperforms Traditional Survey Methods for an Arboreal Forest Mammal." *PLoS ONE* 15 (11): e0242204. https://doi.org/10.1371/journal.pone.0242204.

CHAPTER 8

HEAD2ART: Establishing a Gallery-Based Wellbeing Program for Young People Through Industry Collaborations

Helena Bezzina

Abstract

Recent data from the Australian Bureau of Statistics highlight a concerning trend in youth mental health, with anxiety disorders being one of the most prevalent among young people. In response, the research project HEAD2ART aims to enhance museums' capacity to support the mental health and well-being of young people nationwide. Collaborating with "headspace Newcastle," a youth mental health service, and the Museum of Art and Culture, Lake Macquarie City Council, the program seeks to address the research question: How can museum-based programs best support young people's mental health and well-being? Industry professionals, including Jason Trethowan, CEO of headspace, emphasize the urgent need for alternative therapeutic support measures due to high levels of psychological distress and long waiting lists for mental health services. HEAD2ART proposes an innovative, evidence-based creative therapies program integrating museum-based learning theories with psychodynamic art therapy to provide accessible museum-based support for high school children experiencing mental health challenges. This chapter outlines the processes involved in establishing collaborations and the preparation undertaken for the HEAD2ART research project.

Introduction

Recent data indicate that around 1.1 million young people have experienced a mental disorder in the preceding twelve months; notably, anxiety disorders were the most prevalent among this demographic (Australian Bureau of Statistics [ABS] 2023). In response to this concerning trend, the research project HEAD2ART has been initiated to enhance museums' capacity to support the mental health and well-being of young people. The program aims to be scalable, evidence-based, and implemented nationwide through collaboration with museums (including galleries) and "headspace Newcastle," a youth mental health service. The guiding research question for this study is: How can museum-based programs be optimally designed to support the mental health and well-being of young people?

Specifically, this study aims to generate a prototype for a replicable, scalable creative therapy program, called HEAD2ART that is built on a collaborative approach between museums, the national youth counseling service "headspace," high schools, and young people, to support young people's mental health and well-being.

This chapter provides a concise history, outlining the research program's origin and the steps taken to establish industry collaborations leading to the HEAD2ART pilot. A description of the structure of the pilot is provided below. The HEAD2ART pilot involved ten students from Lake Macquarie High and took place at the Museum of Art and Culture (MAC), Lake Macquarie City Council in 2023.

Significance of Study

In 2022, one of the most common chronic conditions among young people aged 15–24 were anxiety disorders (26%) and depression (17%), both mental and behavioural conditions. (ABS 2023b)

As outlined by the Australian Institute of Health and Welfare (AIHW) (2022), almost one in seven (15%) Australians (18% of male and 12% females) were experiencing social isolation with the proportion of young people experiencing social isolation increasing. Social isolation and loneliness have emerged as significant health issues in Australia. Survey findings indicate that individuals in the 18 to 24 age group consistently reported the highest levels of loneliness, described as both "most of the time" and "occasionally" during the examined periods of April to August 2020, and April to August 2021. Notably, young people exhibited increased vulnerability resulting in heightened levels of loneliness during the COVID-19 (coronavirus disease 2019) pandemic compared to other age demographics (AIHW 2022).

This study involves collaboration with industry professionals to directly address real-world problems, such as youth mental health and loneliness. Jason Trethowan (2020), CEO of headspace, pointed out that "one-third of young Aussies are already reporting high or very high levels of psychological distress, treble what they were in 2007, but we're also seeing the impacts of a really challenging year affecting their sense of general well-being." Williams, headspace Newcastle's community officer, reports a long waiting list for young people to access their mental health services, highlighting the need for alternative therapeutic support measures (personal communication, 2022). This pilot aims to respond directly to this problem by prototyping an innovative, evidence-based creative therapies program. The program, HEAD2ART, integrates museum-based learning theories with psychodynamic art therapy to support the well-being of young people and school children who may require mental health services that are not readily accessible.

The HEAD2ART collaboration stems from my placement at MAC in 2018, as part of my master of art therapy. With a professional background in public programs and education, I have worked within teams in various museums, including the Asian Civilisations Museum, the National Portrait Gallery, and the National Museum of Australia. My firsthand experience highlighted the positive transformative influence of cultural institutions on a range of visitors. However, I have also seen this potential constrained by institutional caution and perceptions of the specialist skills required to support groups seeking well-being and mental health from their museum visit. This prompted me to pursue a master's in art therapy, building toward my research on exploring museums as potential sites for supporting mental health and well-being.

Like other museum practitioners (Ioannides 2016; Peacock 2012; Rochford 2017; Salom 2011), my roles in various institutions involved supporting research and innovation in educational and public programming, resulting in valuable insights into the role of learning within the museum context. A recognition of the interconnectedness of art therapy, education, curation, and public programming has fed into this research project aiming to synergize these fields within the HEAD2ART well-being program.

My understanding of museums as sites for transformation and well-being is not a new concept and aligns with Duncan (1995), who suggested that museums serve as transitional spaces, facilitating calming liminal experiences. Significantly, the very origins of museum can be traced to the Enlightenment with ideologies around improving citizenry, such as those of Buckingham, a nineteenth-century English social reformer, who chaired the Select Committee on Drunkenness and envisioned museums as a remedy for intoxication and a means of civilizing the morals and manners of the population (Bennett 1995). These perspectives in part underscore museums' founding role as institutions tasked with influencing human behaviors (Bennett 1995; Duncan 1995; Hooper-Greenhill 1992).

More recent perspectives, exemplified by Silverman (2010), advocate for museums as sites for promoting justice and social change. Silverman recognized that museums inherently encourage therapeutic practices, fostering self-reflexivity, reducing isolation, and promoting social cohesion. Importantly, Silverman's study (2010) quantitatively establishes a link between museum visits and reduced levels of stress hormones, demonstrating the calming effect of museum's liminal spaces (Duncan 1995). In the past decade, the intersection of art and health has witnessed significant growth, extending to public museums, which have shifted from providing access programs to visitors with physical disabilities to actively exploring the potential development of a range of mental health and well-being programs (Roland 2010).

Setting Up the Collaboration with the Museum of Art and Culture (MAC) – Lake Macquarie City Council and headspace Newcastle

I pitched the art therapy placement and the development of well-being programs at MAC to the then gallery director Deb Abraham in 2019. Recognizing the potential benefits, Abraham directed me to Joanne Davies, MAC's Visual Arts and Public Program leader. Collaborating closely during my placement, Davies brought over a decade of institutional knowledge to the project, essential for gaining approval, staff, and funding for the development of HEAD2ART. As a practicing artist and public program leader, she also understood the potential of art therapy in museums and was interested in developing programs that would make MAC accessible to its diverse communities while supporting MAC's KPIs (key performance indicators) and strategic priorities.

The onset of the COVID-19 pandemic during my placement prompted us to explore innovative ways of designing a well-being program using the museum's collection and temporary exhibitions. This exploration led to the emergence of the *MAC Collection Connections*—a well-being program based on art education and group interactive art therapy, initially delivered via Zoom to individuals isolated in their homes during the pandemic. This program allowed participants to view art works, carefully selected from the collection based on their themes, via zoom and respond with both discussion and artmaking. Post the COVID-19 pandemic, positive feedback encouraged the expansion of the program within gallery spaces drawing on current exhibitions, receiving further acclaim from seniors (the main participants given the program was run during business hours).

headspace Newcastle community development officer Byron Williams initially attempted to recruit young people ranging from 18 to 25 into the gallery-based program. The success of *MAC Collection Connections*, meshed with Lake Macquarie City Councils strategic plan (2020) to better support the well-being needs of young people, especially considering the rise in post-COVID-19 mental health issues within this age group. Williams, with a background as a professional musician and mental health worker, understood the potential of creativity to support mental health and became instrumental in establishing the youth well-being program at MAC, leveraging resources and expertise within headspace Newcastle. Given the extended waiting list for young individuals seeking assistance from clinicians at headspace, Williams could see the advantages of being able to offer them an art-based well-being program. Davies also recognized the gap in programs for young people at MAC.

To support the development of a well-being program for young people, a AUD 10,000 Research and Project Innovation and Development (RAPID) grant was obtained through collaboration with Davies, Williams, and myself. We were awarded the grant to pilot the gallery-based young people's well-being program, HEAD2ART, in collaboration with the School of Humanities and Social Science, College of Human and Social Futures, University of Newcastle, MAC, and headspace Newcastle. The program HEAD2ART was structured to run for eight weekly, two-hour sessions, with participants aged 18 to 24 both via Zoom and within the gallery. After considerable time and effort with headspace Facebook and Instagram posts plus the circulation of physical flyers, it became apparent that recruiting twenty headspace clients into the research project was a significant challenge.

Responding to these challenges, Jo Davies pointed instead to the local interest of Lake Macquarie High School in collaborating more extensively with MAC, to foster more students utilizing the gallery as a community resource. After careful consideration, it became evident that the HEAD2ART program could be equally as beneficial for high school students as for headspace clients, particularly those grappling with challenges post-COVID-19. Significantly, this aligned with the NSW Education's Wellbeing Framework (2015) which actively encourages schools to collaborate with community organizations to build support structures, facilitating students to "Connect, Succeed, and Thrive" (1).

An additional AUD 14,000 in funding was secured from the "Children and Young People Wellbeing Recovery Initiative Grant" (2022), focusing on the need for evidence-based programs that support the mental health and well-being of children and young people. The collaboration with Newcastle University provided capacity for a sustained evaluation within the grant application, aligning HEAD2ART with broader research into the potential of publicly funded museums to support the well-being and mental health of young people. The revised research objective was to pilot the HEAD2ART program but now with high school students, aiming to establish an evidence-based, repeatable, and scalable well-being program.

Establishing the Collaboration with Lake Macquarie High School

To initiate collaboration with Lake Macquarie High School, crucial staff members, including principal Brenden Maher, wellbeing head teacher Bronwyn Svihla, and other key personnel, were invited to an informative afterschool session. During this meeting, I, with the assistance of Davies and Williams, outlined the aims, objectives, and therapeutic outcomes of the HEAD2ART research program. The school staff expressed keen interest in supporting the initiative. To satisfy University ethics requirements, participating high school students were not to have a preexisting diagnosed mental illness but should still be deemed to potentially benefit from a well-being program. Maher could see the clear benefits of a nonclinical preventive program like HEAD2ART that empowered students rather than claiming to "treat" students' mental health illnesses.

Svihla undertook the responsibility of recruiting students, inviting those she described as "missing in plain sight"—i.e., students not fully engaged with school, with poor attendance, and those seemingly struggling with social anxiety and isolation. Svihla noted that such student issues had become more pronounced in the post-COVID-19 era. She put together an initial group of ten students from years nine and ten whom she thought would benefit from the program. Participation in the pilot was voluntary with Svihla responsible for distributing participant information sheets and collecting the consent forms signed by both the parents and students prior to the start of the program. As this study was conducted within the NSW school system, ethics clearance was also required from the NSW State Education Research Applications Process (SERAP), a process delayed by eight months over post-COVID-19 stress on schools' resources.

Theoretical Underpinnings of HEAD2ART

The prototype for the pilot HEAD2ART drew on a *group interactive art therapy* model (Waller 2015). Hogan (2016) describes this approach as an integrative model, bringing together a number of methods and ideas, such as psychodynamic and analytic art therapy, interpersonal group psychotherapy and system theories. This approach is based on a philosophy that humans construct an individual inner world, constantly in flux, rebuilt through interactions with others. The group interactive art therapy model enables the use of a space for people to interact, promoting interpersonal learning through the responses of others in a safe therapeutic space (Waller 2015). Waller (2015) argues that therapy takes place as feedback from others in the group illuminates' aspect of the self in the here-and-now.

I feel the group interactive art therapy model naturally lends itself to integrating Vygotsky's (2020) concepts of socially mediated inquiry-based learning and Csikszentmihalyi's (1990) flow theory as they systematically build upon participant interactions. The amalgamation of art therapy principles and museum-based learning theories aims to offer a comprehensive strategy for supporting the mental health and well-being of young people, capitalizing on the unique environment and exhibits offered by the museum setting.

What follows is a brief literature review summarizing the shifting role of museums in the arts, health, and well-being movement, as it more formally aligns with changes in healthcare policy. The primary objective here is to critically assess gaps in existing literature, particularly the exclusion of art therapy from some of the broader discussions surrounding the art, health, and well-being movement. The following abbreviated review covers a range of studies, ranging from long-term, well-funded programs (The Museum of Modern Art 2009) to one-off art therapy interventions tailored to support young people and school groups.

While museums have traditionally been seen as elitist institutions (Bourdieu et al. 1991), they have evolved to remain relevant and connect with new audiences (Vicars-Harris 2018). Initiatives like "Meet Me at MoMA" (The Museum of Modern Art 2009) highlight the shift from a "sickness culture" to a "wellbeing culture" (All-Party Parliamentary Group on Arts 2017; Ander et al. 2011; Chatterjee and Noble 2013; Dodds and Jones 2014). The champion Museums in Health identify museums as providing a safe space for reflection reducing stress hormones and offering educational programs supporting mental health, Alzheimer, cancer, and social isolation, although they omit art therapy from their studies.

Art therapy utilizes active artmaking, the creative process, and applied psychological theory within a psychotherapeutic relationship to enhance the lives of individuals, families, and communities (American Art Therapy Association 2023). Until the last ten to fifteen years, art therapy commonly operated out of art studios or within clinical environments. As mentioned earlier, art therapy has been swept along by the art and health movement shifting into community environments such as museums. This has resulted in organizations like The British Association of Art Therapists established the Specialist Interest Group: "Art Therapy in Museums and Galleries" (n.d.). Literature since 2010 now emphasizes the collaborative relationship between art educators and art therapists. While most programs are one-off and reliant on grants, exceptions like the Montreal Museum of Fine Art demonstrate the potential of established integrated art therapy and well-being programs within a cultural institution.

Existing literature on art therapy approaches for young people typically focus on pilot initiatives, emphasizing the need for further research to establish evidence-based programs. Notable contributions outline the overarching advantages of group art therapy for young people, emphasizing group dynamics, image-making, and fostering a sense of belonging. Most recently, Hartman (2022) provides a comprehensive review of all published journal articles directly addressing Art Therapy within Museums, demonstrating a significant growth since COVID-19. Specifically, Hartman (2022) found that the programs that directly addressed adolescence "aimed to provide an outlet and space for a particular underrepresented population," which included programs for individuals with conditions such as high-functioning autism, (Hartman 2019), emotional behaviour disorders (Treadon et al. 2006), aggressive behaviour issues (Marxen 2009), pregnant teens facing self-esteem issues (Stiles and Mermer-Welly 1998), and middle school students and family members (Linesch 2004). Hartman (2022) describes such programs as creative interventions, "adopting different therapeutic objectives, structures and theoretical approaches based on the mission and needs of the museum programming and the therapeutical benefits being addressed" (16).

Initiatives addressing young people and school groups tend to be ad hoc and one-off. There is an obvious need for evidence-based, scalable, and replicable well-being programs specifically tailored to support the well-being of young people. The brief review above highlights the urgent need for further research in this area, emphasizing the importance of a robust theoretical framework.

Effective learning in museums involves active engagement, incorporating socio-cultural constructivist frameworks. There is a need to more formally identify the intersection or synergies between group interactive art therapy and sociocultural constructivist inquiry-based learning to support the legitimacy of well-being high school programs within museums. The literature also makes clear that museums are adapting programs to align with national arts, health, and well-being agendas and that collaborations between curators, educators, artists, and therapists is imperative.

HEAD2ART: Program Design

HEAD2ART was piloted with ten students aged 14 to 16, over eight weekly two-hour sessions, culminating in an exhibition within MAC community galleries. The weekly sessions followed a clear structure while allowing students to an open-ended response to allow for maximum agency in creative expression:

> *Setting the Stage: Williams, Davies, Svihla, and Dr. Bezzina were all in attendance, along with the eight students. I led the program as the key facilitator, reiterating the aims of the sessions: to pilot a well-being program where students are asked to look at and respond to art within exhibitions through making and discussion. Davies had organized an array of good-quality materials for students to easily access.*

> *Introduction: The program started with a relaxation activity, inviting participants to be present and focus on the two-hour session as self-care.*

> *Making Art: I then ask participants to consider their "here-and-now," introducing and explaining the concept briefly—i.e., how they are feeling in that moment. She then invited them to undertake a ten-minute art response, picturing their "here-and-now" as a way of checking in (Figure 1), breaking the ice, and getting to know each other (Figures 2 and 3).*

Figure 1: Collaborators, Byron Williams and Bronwyn Svihla, Participating with Students on Check-In Drawings

Source: Dr. Helena Bezzina 2023

Figure 2: HEAD2ART Participants, Working on Check-In Drawings

Source: Dr. Helena Bezzina 2023

Figure 3: Check-In Drawings from Year 9

Source: Dr. Helena Bezzina 2023

Evoking Expression: I invited the students to show and discuss their drawings, encouraging comments on each other's artworks and sharing thoughts. She and her co-facilitators modeled this process, then invited participants to volunteer sharing and nominate the next person in the group to share, providing participants with agency while maintaining a structure.

Experiencing Art: In the second part of the program, I invited students to view the exhibition and requested they identify a work they are drawn to and explore the work beyond their first impressions drawing on tools from student-centered, inquiry-based museum learning (Figure 4).

Figure 4: Students Explore the Gallery as They Select a Work That They Find Interesting

Source: Dr. Helena Bezzina 2023

Responding to Art: This was followed by a twenty/thirty-minute art response, where students made art in response to what they see in the gallery, choosing from a range of materials, after which they were invited to show and discuss their artwork (Figure 5).

Figure 5: Students Are Given an Array of Materials to Choose from to Respond to Their Gallery Experience

Source: Dr. Helena Bezzina 2023

Self-Care: After each session, participants were invited to briefly describe forms of self-care they had planned for the following week

Community Art Exhibition: After eight weeks, the program concluded with an exhibition of participants' artworks within MAC's community art gallery, celebrating the students' efforts and supporting awareness addressing youth mental health and resilience. MAC put on a morning tea as an opening celebration for participating students and their family and friends. This was a successful event with the school principal acknowledging the students' achievements while some parents were clearly proud and moved to see their children's art on display. The students themselves looked very pleased to have their work seen and validated in the gallery.

HEAD2ART Program Goals

The ultimate aim of the study is to establish an online HEAD2ART training package containing resources such as museum protocols, collaboration protocols, risk assessments, evaluation measures, permission slips, exhibition, post-program follow-up suggestions, and exhibition guidelines. Following the pilot, the team aims to work with different museums and headspace offices to ensure the program is replicable, scalable and can be supported via other museums and headspace collaborations.

Initial qualitative feedback from the teachers, student evaluation forms and empathy maps, observations, independent exit interview with students, and pre- and post-pilot focus groups provide rich triangulation data indicating that the program benefited students' overall well-being. Teachers also reported that some students showing an improved attitude and higher levels of engagement to school. However, with such a small sample, before and after quantitative assessments are largely meaningless; hence, we hope to establish HEAD2ART as an ongoing researcher project, resulting in much larger sample sizes in order to also provide valid quantitative findings.

Conclusion

This ongoing research project HEAD2ART emerges as a proactive response to the concerning trend of youth mental health issues, particularly prevalent anxiety disorders among young individuals. With over 1.1 million young people experiencing mental disorders in the 2023 alone, there is a pressing need for innovative interventions (ABS 2023). HEAD2ART, in collaboration with headspace Newcastle and the Museum of Art and Culture, Lake Macquarie City Council, aims to actively promote and facilitate museums' role in supporting the mental health and well-being of young people nationwide.

As noted, the program's theoretical underpinnings draw from group interactive art therapy models, integrating museum-based learning theories and psychodynamic art therapy. By synergizing these approaches, HEAD2ART offers a proactive approach to address the mental health challenges faced by young individuals, leveraging the unique environment and exhibits provided by museum settings.

The establishment of collaborations with key stakeholders, including headspace, museums, and educational institutions, underscores the program's commitment to scalability, evidence-based practice, and to community engagement. Through strategic partnerships and funding initiatives, such as the RAPID grant and the Children and Young People Wellbeing Recovery Initiative grant, HEAD2ART continued to evolve a replicable, scalable, and evidence-based creative therapy program.

In summary, HEAD2ART represents a collaborative effort to address the real-world problem of the mental health needs of young people, recognizing the transformative potential of museums as spaces for healing, self-discovery, and community support. As the program develops, it holds the promise of not only supporting individual well-being and resilience but also fostering broader societal awareness around youth mental health issues.

REFERENCES

ABS (Australian Bureau of Statistics). 2023a. "Two in Five Australians Have Experienced a Mental Disorder." Media Release, October 5. https://www.abs.gov.au/media-centre/media-releases/two-five-australians-have-experienced-mental-disorder.

ABS (Australian Bureau of Statistics). 2023b. "National Health Survey 2022–Table 3: Long-Term Health Conditions, by Age and Sex-External Site Opens in New Window [Data Set]." abs.gov.au.

AIHW (Australian Institute of Health and Welfare). 2022. *Social Isolation and Loneliness: A Snapshot—In AIHW's 15th Biennial Welfare Report*. AIHW. https://www.aihw.gov.au/reports/australias-welfare/social-isolation-and-loneliness-covid-pandemic.

All-Party Parliamentary Group on Arts. 2017. *Health and Wellbeing Inquiry Report Creative Health: The Arts for Health and Wellbeing*. All-Party Parliamentary Group on Arts. http://www.artshealthandwellbeing.org.uk/appg-inquiry/Publications/Creative_Health_Inquiry_Report_2017.pdf.

American Art Therapy Association. 2023. "What Is Art Therapy?" https://arttherapy.org/.

Ander, E., L. Thomson, G. Noble, A. Lanceley, U. Menon, and H. Chatterjee. 2011. "Generic Well-Being Outcomes: Towards a Conceptual Framework for Well-Being Outcomes in Museums." *Museum Management and Curatorship* 26 (3): 237–259. https://doi.org/10.1080/09647775.2011.585798.

Bennett, T. 1995. *The Birth of the Museum: History, Theory, Politics*. Routledge.

Bourdieu, P., A. Darbel, and D. Schnapper. 1991. *The Love of Art: European Art Museums and Their Public*. Polity Press.

British Association of Art Therapists Museums and Galleries Specialist Interest Group. n.d. "Art Therapy in Museums and Galleries." http://www.atmag.org.

Chatterjee, H., and P. M. Camic. 2015. "The Health and Well-Being Potential of Museums and Art Galleries." *Arts & Health: An International Journal for Research, Policy and Practice* 7 (3): 183–186. https://doi.org/10.1080/175330 15.2015.1065594.

Chatterjee, H., and G. Noble. 2013. *Museums, Health and Well-Being*. Taylor & Francis.

Csikszentmihalyi, M. 1990. *Flow: The Psychology of Optimal Experience*. Harper & Row Publishers.

Dodds, J., and C. Jones. 2014. "Mind, Body, Spirit: How Museums Impact Health and Wellbeing." Research Centre for Museums and Galleries. https://www2. le.ac.uk/departments/museumstudies/rcmg/publications/mind-body-spirit-report.

Duncan, C. 1995. *Civilizing Rituals: Inside Public Art Museums*. Routledge.

Hartman, A. 2019. "The Museum as a Space for Therapeutic Art Experiences for Adolescents with High Functioning Autism (HFA)." Unpublished diss., Abstracts International Section A: Humanities and Social Sciences. ProQuest Information & Learning.

Hartman, A. 2022. "Exploring Museum-Based Art Therapy: A Summary of Existing Programs." In *Collaborative Effort with Access, Education and Public Programs*, edited by M. R. Ghadim and L. Dougherty. Routledge.

Hogan, S. 2016. *Art Therapy Theories: A Critical Introduction*. Routledge.

Holttum, S. 2020. "Art Therapy in Museum and Galleries: Evidence and Research." In *Art Museums and Galleries: Reframing Practice*, edited by A. Coles and H. Jury. Jessica Kingsley Publications.

Hooper-Greenhill, E. 1992. *Museums and the Shaping of Knowledge (Heritage)*. Routledge.

Ioannides, E. 2016. "Museums as Therapeutic Environments and the Contribution of Art Therapy." *Museum International* 68(3/4): 98–109.

Kapitan, L. 2007. *Introduction to Art Therapy Research*. 2nd ed. Taylor & Francis Publishing.

Lake Macquarie City Council. 2020. "#LAKEMACNEXTGEN: Youth Strategy 2020–2023." https://www.lakemac.com.au/files/assets/public/v/4/council/lake-macquarie-city-youth-strategy-2020-2023.pdf.

Linesch, D. 2004. "Art Therapy at the Museum of Tolerance: Responses to the Life and Work of Friedl Dicker-Brandeis." *Arts in Psychotherapy* 31: 57–66. https//doi.org/10.1016/j.aip.2004.02.004.

Marxen, E. 2009. "Therapeutic Thinking in Contemporary Art: Or Psychotherapy in the Arts." *Arts in Psychotherapy* 36 (3): 131–139. http://doi.org/10.1016/j.aip.2008.10.004.

NSW Department of Regional NSW. 2022. "Children and Young People Wellbeing Recovery Initiative: Large Grants Program for Regional NSW." https://www.nsw.gov.au/grants-and-funding/children-and-young-people-wellbeing-recovery-initiative/large-grants-program-for-regional-nsw.

NSW Ministry of Health. 2015. "NSW Health Framework: Improving the Health of the Community Through Integrating the Arts into the Design and Delivery of Health Services and Public Health Messaging." https://www.health.nsw.gov.au/arts/documents/nsw-health-and-the-arts-framework-report.pdf.

Peacock, K. 2012. "Museum Education and Art Therapy: Exploring an Innovative Partnership." *Art Therapy: Journal of the American Art Therapy Association* 29 (3): 133–137. https://doi.org/10.1080/07421656.2012.7016042012.

Rochford, J. S. 2017. "Art Therapy and Art Museum Education: A Visitor-Focused Collaboration." *Art Therapy* 34 (4): 1–6. https://doi.org/10.1080/07421656.2017.1383787.

Roland, D. 2010. "Creating a Wellness Culture." *Museums & Social Issues* 5 (2): 166–174. https://doi.org/10.1179/msi.2010.5.2.166.

Salom, A. 2011. "Reinventing the Setting: Art Therapy in Museums." *Arts in Psychotherapy* 38 (2): 81–85. https://doi.org/proxy.ulib.uits.iu.edu/10.1016/j.aip.2010.12.004.

Silverman, L. H. 2010. *The Social Work of Museums*. Routledge.

Stiles, G. J., and M. J. Mermer-Welly. 1998. "Children Having Children: Art Therapy in a Community-Based Early Adolescent Pregnancy Program." *Art*

Therapy: Journal of the American Art Therapy Association 15 (3): 165–176. https://doi.org/10.1080/07421656.1989.10759319.

The Museum of Modern Art. 2009. *The MoMA Alzheimer's Project: Making Art Accessible to People with Dementia—A Guide for Museums.* The Museum of Modern Art. https://www.moma.org/momaorg/shared/pdfs/docs/learn/Guide-forMuse ums.pdf.

Treadon, C. B., R. Marcia, D. Viki, and T. Thompson Wylder. 2006. "Opening the Doors of Art Museums for Therapeutic Processes." *Arts in Psychotherapy* 33: 288–301.

Trethowan, J. 2020. "Young People Risk More Mental Health Issues as Wellbeing Declines." headspace Media Release, October 21. https://headspace.org.au/our-organisation/media-releases/young-people-risk-more-mental-health-issues-as-wellbeing-declines.

Vicars-Harris, O. 2018. "Making Connections: Future Museum Project." http://museum-id.com/the-futuremuseum-project-what-will-museums-be-like-in-the-future-essay-collection/.

Vygotsky, L. S. 2020. *S. Vygotsky's Pedological Works, Foundations of Pedology*, 3 vols. First Translated by David Kellogg and Nikolai Veresov. Perspectives in Cultural-Historical Research. Springer.

Waller, D. 2015. *Group Interactive Art Therapy: Its Use in Training and Treatment.* Routledge.

SECTION III:

Using Creative Practice to Explore and Shift Cultural Patterns

Introduction

The projects collected in this section all deploy creative research within cultural spheres and are focused on small-scale and/or longer-term social and cultural impact. More specifically, these play out within training examples within secondary and tertiary education, rethinking design practices and new musical research.

In the first chapter (Chapter 9), Ari Chand and Tamara Blakemore outline success in intersecting a social work and design practice as a transdisciplinary social justice initiative for youth offenders. At the center of this project, Chand worked as a design practitioner with youth in custodial settings, using drawing practice as a support and alternative to discussion, allowing participants to express themselves through image-based storytelling. This generated knowledge which could later inform training programs for social workers.

Then, Paul Egglestone, Duncan Burck, and Jon Drummond (Chapter 10), detail an innovation program for high school students, providing them with experience in real-world problems, skills in representing these through data workflows, and then the capacity to translate these workflows through creative design. The discussion details the broader learning and innovation frameworks embedded in the project, and a specific instance of the program which resulted in a piece of data-driven design later embedded within a public interactive installation.

Rachael Unicomb, Joanne Walters, and Angus Stevens, in the third chapter (Chapter 11), discuss a collaboration with an industry partner to develop an innovative training resource for speech pathology students. This utilizes a VR (virtual reality) platform to provide an immersive environment for these emerging health professionals to encounter realistic scenarios for engaging with patients, allowing them to better prepare them for moving into the industry. The project serves as a case study in on-campus innovative collaboration which anticipates long-term real-world impact within speech pathology practice.

The fourth chapter (Chapter 12) covers Ralph Kenke and Ari Chand's insight into one element of design practice integral to relationships with clients, and core to students acquiring competency within design training. They detail the notion of "visual territories" to help formalize an element of practice which operates as tacit knowledge within design but is not clearly articulated in the literature. They use an example of engagement with a health industry collaborator as a case study.

In the following chapter (Chapter 13), Adam Manning and Ray Kelly outline their creative negotiation with the Sydney Symphony Orchestra, introducing a distinctive and innovative rhythmic "Acknowledgement of Country" into a national cultural performance space. Manning's practice centers on clapsticks of his own design, and the chapter suggests the difficulty of capturing and articulating the key insights of this kind of cross-cultural collaboration.

In the sixth chapter (Chapter 14), Martin K. Koszolko and Paul Egglestone report on an experimental musical collaboration initiative, centered on the staging of an online contest which attracted global participants. The focus for these researchers was partly on testing the effectiveness of software tools in facilitating the kinds of short-hand intuitive cultural exchange and collaboration required to foster musical collaborations, and partly on the direct and indirect benefits for participants.

The final chapter (Chapter 15) from Vincent Sebastian Labra is an account of his doctoral research project into Afro-Cuban elements within Australian electronic music. This is an example of practice-based creative research, with Labra scaffolding on his existing musical expertise and engaging in other practices to explore the implications of cross-cultural exchange within an Australian context. This project serves as a reminder of the diversity of new creative research surfacing within the doctoral space, as creative practitioners are both training in the management of substantial research projects and engaging in cutting-edge topics which serve as a key frontier for new knowledge. As with Manning and Kelly, Labra also outlines the challenges of capturing research insights generated through creative practice.

CHAPTER 9

Not Just Art Therapy: A Case Study Embedding a Design Practitioner in Youth Violence Intervention Program "Name.Narrate.Navigate" (NNN)

Ari Chand and Tamara Blakemore

Introduction

Design and illustration continue to be unique practices for the transmission of ideas, experiences, and lived realities. This chapter details a unique collaboration between a design researcher-practitioner and social work researcher-practitioners in an Australian social justice initiative for young people. The project was generated out of the restrictive environments of youth justice programs in custodial settings and the complexity of explaining the how, what and why of these programs to outsiders. The project sought to develop a strong narrative of how scaffolded drawing can be used, not just as an art therapy or diversional activity but as a reflexive and research generative intervention enhancing outcomes for both participants and practitioners.

The social justice initiative discussed in this chapter; Name.Narrate.Navigate (NNN) (Blakemore et al. 2021, 2022), is a trauma-informed and culturally safe intervention that works with young people aged 12 to 18 years who have used and experienced violence. Alongside experiential learning and mindfulness activities, the eight-week group work program intentionally uses creative methods as a safe and inclusive way to prompt narrative storytelling. The sharing of stories provides an opportunity for young people to feel seen and heard and the spectrum of their experiences recognized. Information shared in the program (with appropriate ethics approval) is then used to inform specialist practitioner training for workers who support young people impacted by violence.

Partnership between the first author (a design researcher-practitioner) and the NNN project team provided an opportunity to explore the potential of an embedded creative in delivering the program in custodial settings. Impetus for this partnership was twofold. First, expansion of NNN to a custodial setting meant it was subject to restrictions on the use of technology, including cameras. To date, delivery of the NNN program has incorporated Photovoice (Wang and Burris 1997), as a key method of creative engagement and stimuli for discussion, exploration, and reflective data capture. Hence, an emerging need for alternative approaches was identified. Second, evaluation of the NNN program (Rayment-McHugh 2021) identified that key to its effectiveness were the often-intangible aspects of practice that supported young people to feel safe enough in the program to engage, participate, and, ultimately, consider change. The NNN project team embraced the opportunity to work with the design researcher-practitioner to explore whether an embedded creative in the delivery of the program could assist in capturing and communicating the till now unseen dynamics of the work.

Three key tasks were identified to achieve the aims of the partnership. First, the existing NNN program required adaptation to remove Photovoice content and activities. This involved the design researcher-practitioner developing a visual cultural probe kit, previously untested in social justice settings, and working with the NNN project team to adjust activities to meet specific limits of a restricted environment. Second, to ensure efficacy in delivery of the adjusted model, the design researcher-practitioner was embedded in the delivery of NNN in the custodial setting. The design researcher-practitioner assisted with facilitating the developed creative adaptations, namely, scaffolded drawing work, allowing accompanying facilitator practitioners to observe how these activities enhanced the group work and elicitation of narrative storytelling among the young men involved.

Finally, the design researcher-practitioner acted as an observer of the program, using reportage illustration to compile additional visual notation of the happenings of all program participants; researchers, psychologists, case workers, and young men alike. Reportage illustration explains and constructs a visual experience of societal reflections, in which pictures, language, and meaning are entwined in the evaluation of a complex preventative intervention for youth violence. Embury notes Reportage combines sketching the appearance of a scene as well as striving to understand and communicate a story through visual language (Embury 2018).

This aspect of the project involved the illustrator drawing stories with a unique lens into the complex array of elements at play: a sense of immediacy, observation, gesture, and embedded opinion on storying the custodial setting as scene/situation (Reim 2019). Collectively, reportage illustration, drawing, and studio practice were then used to communicate the experience of the NNN program more broadly.

This chapter sketches the background and context to this unique project, sharing examples of creative work produced by participants and the design researcher-practitioner. Also presented are quotes sourced from practitioner reflections done directly after sessions. Consistent with Literat (2013), these data are presented to triangulate observations on the engagement of young people with the drawing activities, cross-validate findings, and prevent the overinterpretation of images as data. The chapter concludes by discussing learnings arising from the project that identify the value of live drawing as an elicitor of personal and collective narrative as well as a tool for exploring narratives of others.

Background and Context

The use of creative practices in custodial settings has a lengthy history (Teasdale 1999; Ursprung 1997). Often, these practices can be easily categorized as *art therapy* programs or *diversional* practices. These practices have been shown to have positive benefits for prisoners, and for prison management with improved outcomes identified across therapeutic, educational, quality of life, and pro-social engagement (Johnson 2008). There is a suggestion that art therapies are useful because they respond to basic human needs for creative self-development, autonomy, and expression (Johnson 2008).

While a distinction has been made between forensic art therapy and art therapy that occurs in forensic settings, with the former distinguished by its utility in fact-finding in forensic settings (Gussak and Cohen-Liebman 2001), less attention has been paid to the conceptual distinction between art as a tool for eliciting narratives in trauma-informed and culturally safe ways as a part of psychoeducational interventions. This project attends to this gap and significantly differs from existing work.

The NNN program was developed in response to a gap in available interventions for youth violence that adequately address the fact that upward of 90% of justice-involved young people have experienced some form of trauma (Malvaso et al. 2022). The potential adverse impact of trauma on young people's mental health and well-being has been well documented (Finkelhor

Figure 1: Postcards to Practice Example

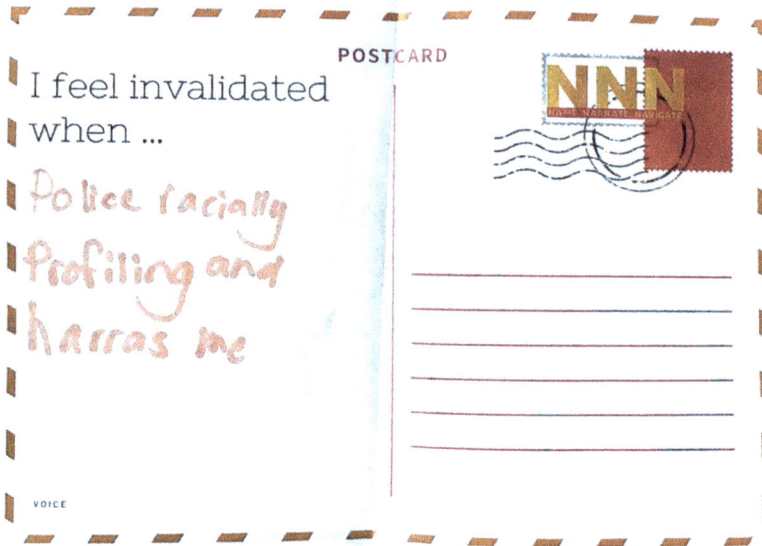

et al. 2009; Gellman and Delucia-Waak 2006; Malvaso et al. 2022; Ng-Mak et al. 2002). Justice-involved young people, perhaps because of trauma, often report negative educational experiences, problems with literacy, and often demonstrate a lack of confidence and ability to articulate experiences and feelings (Dallos 2016). The NNN program (Blakemore et al. 2021, 2022) merges the neuroscience of trauma with Aboriginal ways of knowing and doing to enhance self-awareness, self-regulation, and skills for connection in justice-involved cohorts. Creative methodologies are central to the NNN program. These methods position young people at the center of the intervention process and give voice and visibility to their experience in the context of their culture and communities.

In the existing NNN program, each session includes the use of Photovoice activities to explore concepts identified as drivers of violence. Photovoice involves a combination of photography and focus group discussions to gain rich, multidimensional understandings of social phenomena (Fitzgibbon and Healy 2019). The theory and method of Photovoice emerged from the health promotion work of Caroline Wang; thereafter Wang and Burris (1997) established it as a valid method to enable people to record and reflect their concerns and passions in their community, promote critical dialogue and knowledge about issues in inter-action with photographs, and inform research and policymakers. Fitzgibbon and Stengel (2018) point out that distinct from other forms of intervention/research, Photovoice positions participants as central to the method, empowering them to storify their own lives and in doing so speak directly to policies and practice that impact on their experiences and outcomes (Liebenberg 2018).

Photovoice activities in the program begin with an exploration of the use of the camera and a discussion about the ethics of taking photographs of people and places. Young people in the program are encouraged to take practitioners on a walking excursion to explore the theme of each session. Prompts for these excursions are presented in language that focuses on visualization. For example, "show me what shame looks like around here." Consistent with the observa-tions of Fitzgibbon and Healy (2017), facilitators of the NNN program have observed that Photovoice seems to "speed up" the process of engagement with young people. The photos act as elicitors for reflection, and as sessions progress, young people become more confident in selecting and storying their photo work, quickly moving into roles as "experts" on experiences and their social, cultural, and contextual meanings and enjoying "educating" the practitioners in the room. Consistent with the findings of Chonody et al. (2013), Fitzgibbon and Healy (2017), and Budig et al. (2018), facilitators of the NNN program note that Photovoice involves skill building, knowledge development, and self-awareness that often translates into self-efficacy and, ultimately, positive behaviors. Moreover, the collaborative experience of Photovoice in the NNN program can inspire the kind of bridge building necessary to relegitimize meaningful connections to services and support for the young people.

The NNN program has been delivered to 150 young people across the Hunter and Central Coast (New South Wales, Australia). On completion of the NNN program young people tend to reduce their offending (especially violent crime), often associated with shifts in their relationships, their engagement with edu-cation, training, or employment and migration of their identity toward better, healthier living. The strength of the outcomes of the program seem to relate to the program's connection-based approach to working with young people to get to the core of their experience. The custodial setting of a recent imple-mentation of the program provided an impetus and opportunity to examine how drawing assists and allows for narrative elicitation and rich discussion to aid in trauma-informed and culturally safe work. Designerly approaches to narrative elicitation are becoming recognizably useful across a variety of discipline areas. Although design has not been purely situated in the realm of visualization, and image making for quite some time. Design has long been emerging as a third area of knowledge, distinct from sciences and humanities (Chand 2021). Designers are fundamentally socially active agents. They must be transformational members of social life in order to engage with the design process. This project is an exemplary of how design-specific knowledge and approaches were embedded in the adjustment and rethinking of an intervention program for alternative contexts.

The embedded creative's role in this iteration of the NNN is not just as an artist but as a key investigator who uses visual communication systems and approaches to stimulate dialogue, elicit opinion, and reveal insights (Gwilt 2011). Their practice reveals research reflections on social and inclusive practices. Visual communication approaches to research and various forms of illustrative methods have become complex tools for the transmission of meaning, ideas, and insights surrounding multifaceted issues concerning social life. Designers and illustrators as social agents often bring a range of alternative skills to research situations, bringing an alternative methodological approach to established disciplines like social work (Grant and Clark 2021). In this case study, visual approaches assist in the way drawing and responding to drawings can make immaterial concepts/experiences material to discuss complex sociocultural relationships and help young men articulate their experiences and social work researchers elicit authentic insight. Uniquely, analysis of data is collaborative and undertaken with participants as they select, story, and codify their work as part of the NNN program or as part of ongoing practitioner reflection on their work.

Second, the project was explicitly interested in understanding how and why the embedded creative can enhance implementation of the psychoeducation program NNN as well as how their work can communicate the NNN program and the new knowledge it elicits to others. Reportage illustration was used for this purpose. Reportage illustration explains and constructs a visual experience of societal reflections, in which pictures, language, and meaning are entwined in the evaluation of a complex preventative intervention for youth violence. Third, the project seeks to translate its findings into a practical tool to aid trauma-informed and culturally safe practice with youth violence, by scaffolding creative methods to elicit narratives and enhance engagement.

The following sections of the chapter outline the adaptations made to the NNN program and present examples of the creative works produced by participants and practitioners.

A Drawing Adaptation

With restrictions on the use of cameras and technology in the custodial setting an alternative to the Photovoice components of the NNN program were needed. Lending itself well to a scaffolded drawing adaptation, NNN has a strong focus on the visualization of experience, and what things "look like." Visual relationality draws on embodied knowing and how reality is constructed. How "vision and visibility, seeing, and being now dominate how we inter-subjectively recognise ourselves and perform our world" (Grushka et al. 2022). Bryant emphasizes the nature of creative research within social work settings having the ability to negotiate the reflexivity in working with participants. They highlight the role creative approaches have in diversifying the modes of inquiry.

> Interagency between and among people and things suggests a power and force in the way individuals and objects may come together to deliver the unknown, and it is in the interaction where the power to create or bring something new is located. (Bryant 2015, 2 [original emphasis])

Drawing is an immediate practice interrelated with the ongoing tension between seeing in the world and acting. It operates as a reflexive and phenomenological practice. The act of drawing brings together the notion of the mind and body intertwining as a reflexive act (Merleau-Ponty and Smith 1993). Often, we explain the world with words, but the tension between words and the explanation are often difficult in bridging experience. Drawing as an immediate medium is the closest connection to thought, not a transcript of thought like writing or speaking, but the formulation of the thought through the act of material thinking (Fisher 2003). The process of drawing itself can be defined as the performative unification between immaterial and material thinking (Chand 2018). The drawing-as-artefact acts as a boundary object in which participants can explain their experience, perspective(s), and responsive thinking to activity prompts to social work practitioners as a performative demonstration of their thinking and perceptions.

Drawings as an embedded immersive and reflexive activity alongside other activities in the session operated as reflective and thoughtful moments in which key insights were elicited. The heart rates slow down, and the process of drawing allows for drawing-as-reflection to be engaged with. Although historically drawing is a strong element of creative practice in many forms, it is also a useful tool for thought at all ages. Drawing is an essential and critical reflection tool (Calvo 2017). There are several established commentaries on the cognitive foundations and benefits of drawing within design at expert and novice levels (Fava 2014; Fish and Scrivener 1990; Goldschmidt 1991, 2003; Kavakli et al. 1999; Minichiello 2005; Purcell and Gero 1998; Rodgers et al. 2000; Suwa et al. 1998; Suwa and Tversky 2003).

Drawing operates in four ways within this project:

1. Drawn images as stickers (cultural probe kit) are used as stimulus material for participant drawing activities used for narrative elicitation — particularly in weeks 1 and 2 of program delivery.
2. Drawing is used as a narrative elicitation device with young people in documented journals, drawings as an undocumented act and final object acts as performative sites.
3. Drawing as a documentative practice is unobtrusive and relies directly on the perceptive nature of the design practitioner's unique perception and reflection-in-action. This contributed significantly to observational practices linked to traditional social worker research strategies and insights assist ethnographic practitioner notes as reflection-on-action.
4. Refined illustrative studio practices assist in communicating the research program itself.

Table 1 shows the themes explored in sessions in the program, followed by the prompts used to frame exploration of the themes and the drawing activity developed.

Table 1: Drawing Adaptation of the NNN Program for Custodial Settings

Theme	Narrative Prompt (Where Used)	Drawing Activity
Emotional Recognition	"Show me what strong emotions look like on you?"	A drawing activity based on prede-signed sticker requiring scaffolded assemblage for participants to compose their most common strong emotions.
Invalidation	"Show me what it looks like when you feel heard/not heard?"	Participants use designed stickers and drawing to make a new self-portrait with sticker speech bubbles for what "I" hear/that makes me feel invalidated/unheard/unseen.

Theme	Narrative Prompt (Where Used)	Drawing Activity
Empathy	"If I walked a day in your shoes, I would know…"	Participants draw on and decorate plain canvas shoes with symbols, words and patterns whilst discussing with young people what would symbolize them—their identity, who they are, what they represent and stand for.
Power and Control	"Show me what power looks like"	Participants use pre-made silhouettes to collage with a landscape drawing to display self and who in their life has power and who does not.
Shame	"Show me what shame looks like"	Participants undertake an experiential learning activity using a coat covered in Post-it notes of descriptive words associated with shame. They then draw themselves in the coat and put patches of color on the coat to represent various statements they associate with shame.
Choice		Participants draw themselves meeting their future self-shaking hands. Annotating the drawing to explain what words, signs, and symbols might represent them now and in the future.
Evaluation and Exit		An individual post-activity interview with the participant. Illustrated portrait.

The following images showcase the illustrator developing a sticker set that explores different possibilities of combinations of facial features that can be used to express a variety of emotions. These stickers were to "template" the key features of the face, in the workshop on drawing the face. It helped facilitate a discussion a round how emotions are recognized, like anger, alongside photography cards of different people's faces. This meant the design practitioner was involved in the adjustment phases of the program for the new settings.

Figure 2: Vinyl Cut Cultural Probe/Sticker Set (Weeks 1 and 2 Focus)

Emotional recognition

The activity situated contextual discussions about emotional states, including what it felt like when they were first inside or first arrested."

-Practitioner Reflective Notes: 14th September 2022

Creative Work Developed by Participants

Figure 3 shows work developed by a program participant in weeks exploring emotional recognition and the experience of invalidation. The drawing activities in these weeks focused on how we identify the emotional states of others through close inspection of facial features. Participants created sticker combinations of emotive traits representing how they felt most of the time, and what it looks like when they feel, or do not feel heard.

The activity attends to evidence that justice-involved young people are at increased risk of experiencing difficulties recognizing and naming emotional states (Wilcox et al. 2022), and further that these difficulties might be associated with less direct attention to facial features (Halty 2019). Wegrzyn et al. (2017) found that violent offenders present with a reliable, hostile, attribution bias such that they rate ambiguous facial expressions as angrier compared to control populations. Similarly, Kret and de Gelder (2013) found violent offenders misjudge fearful body movements as expressing anger significantly more often than control groups.

Figure 3: Participant Journal (Weeks 1 and 2 Focus)

As noted by Linehan (2015), Cioffi (1993) identified that an important first step in learning to regulate emotions is being able to accurately identify and label emotions experienced by yourself and others. Emotion recognition training has been shown to significantly improve justice-involved young people's ability to accurately recognize fear, sadness, and anger and to significantly reduce the severity of recidivist crime (Hubble et al. 2015). Underpinning the effectiveness of this type of training is the link between observing and describing what we see in others. While observing is a means of noticing something, describing is a way of processing what we see. This drawing activity provided a tactile experience of both observing and describing emotions, with the drawings themselves becoming a tangible outcome of discussions around emotional recognition and states of emotional regulation.

> They were quite engaged in the activity and try to recreate the sticker drawing. They were interested in the mechanics of drawing a face. There was some good discussion during the drawing. For example, there was talk about which eyes or mouth looked sadder or angrier. The activity situated contextual discussions about emotional states, including what it felt like when they were first inside or first arrested. (Practitioner Reflective Notes: September 14, 2022)

Figure 4: Participant Drawing: "Drawing Activities Silhouette
and Landscape" (Week 4)

Power and Control

The process and product of participant drawing allowed for deep, mindful, and rich narrative elicitation.

"They really got into it. Did the paced breathing in the drawing when Ari got them to draw dots while holding their breath and then when out of breath draw a line back while letting out a line your breath."

– Researcher/Practitioner Notes: 12th October 2022.

Allows for relational conversations and youth narrative

Participant Drawing: 'Drawing Activities Silhouette and Landscape' (Week 4)

As noted in the above practitioner reflection, young people engaged well with this activity. The inclusion of tactile prompts from which to choose between, alongside psychoeducation about emotional states, supported autonomous and individualistic reaction to the prompts. Development of this activity was mindful of not placing performative expectations upon participants but instead providing safe opportunities to explore concepts in a playful and low risk way. In a custodial context, the small choices that participants made between different stickers could be indicative of positive engagement with the intervention. Their observed persistence with the task was observed to contribute to developmental learning in and across sessions.

This drawing was developed in week 4 interrogating power. The participant used the drawing alongside silhouettes to articulate an emotional landscape of social connections with place and familial relationships. Particularly identifying that their mother had a lot of power and influence in their world. In the drawing the key connections around metaphor are represented as a way of relationally connecting the sense of power, distance, and processes of understanding their positionality in a Justice setting.

The process and product of participant drawing allowed for deep, mindful, and rich narrative elicitation.

> *They really got into it. Did the paced breathing in the drawing when Ari got them to draw dots while holding their breath and then when out of breath draw a line back while letting out a line your breath. (Researcher/Practitioner Notes: October 12, 2022)*

Figure 5: Reportage Drawing of Activity and the Outcome/Large Collaborative Map of Participant Responses

Practitioners facilitate discussion, making conscious links between possible sources of power, individual experience, and social and structural understandings of power and control. The map created is treated as an externalised narrative object to prompt reflection on the utility and experience of power and control.

The narratives shared, consistent with findings associated with the delivery of NNN to date, by young people described both explicit and implicit experiences of power and control. Young people described explicit experiences of power and control in recounting interactions with systems and implicit experiences in relation to accepted (or acculturated) behavioral norms among peers, families, culture, and community. Common and consistent with Batchelor (2005) was the lived and reported experience of their communities (and indeed their current contexts) as dangerous and hostile places where violence can erupt at any moment. In these contexts, young people had learned that violence was an acceptable and necessary means to establish respect and reputation and ensure self-preservation.

Creative Work Developed by the Design Researcher-Practitioner

Visual approaches blur the line between subjectivity, semiosis, visual observation, and the performative reflection-in-action required of both social work researchers and the designer practitioner-researcher. The participatory nature of the drawing requires all—researchers, the illustrator, the psychologist/caseworker, and the young person—to engage on an open and discursive narrative playing field within the activity.

The drawing open ups the potential for storytelling and reflective sharing within the activities. Representing knowledge of program activities is central to this project—not only the participation for a design practitioner but the participant's engagement with the drawing as a way to capture the narrative engagement.

Figure 6: Select Reportage Style Drawings (Week 2) and Portrait (Evaluation: Week 8)

One participant remarked:

> *Really good story telling. I get you, you want us to think what it is like being in somebody else's shoes. (Practitioner Reflective Notes: September 28, 2022)*

This is a further developed studio illustration of one scene of the program. In this section, the illustrator is observing the engagement of participants in the notion of understanding empathy. Participants engaged in an experiential learning activity exploring the idea of "putting yourself in someone else's shoes." They are presented with a collated shoebox containing visual and tactile prompts and asked to think about what it might be like to walk in this person's shoes, what their story might be, what might be happening in their life, and how they might be feeling. The activity prompts imagining alternate realities and allows for the contemplation of another's experience in a safe space free from judgement or immediate connection to their own experience. Young people readily engaged in this activity exploring ingroup and outgroup identification and the links between this and displays of empathy versus violence. Themes of ingroup and outgroup identification continued to be discussed in the follow-up drawing activity in this session where participants decorated canvas shoes with symbolic representations of their own identity.

Figure 7: Narrative Elicitation: Shoebox Illustration
(Week 3: Empathy) – Work in Progress Illustration

"If I walked a day in your shoes, I would know..."

Studio Practice (Work in Progress)

Empathy

Discussion

Increasingly, there is an understanding that regardless of the value of interventions, the use of effective strategies to implement such interventions into practice is necessary to ensure participants achieve the intended intervention outcomes (Eldh et al. 2017). This project explored a unique opportunity to embed a design researcher-practitioner in the delivery of NNN, a trauma-informed and culturally safe intervention for youth violence to meet the challenges of work in restrictive social justice settings.

The embedded creative adapted existing program content, facilitated scaffolded drawing activities, and recorded in situ drawings of program practice. These drawings set up possibilities of dynamic interpretation for practitioners in the moment and in narrative conversation, as well as post-event objects for evaluation. This project relied on these images as central to the instigation of narrative, conversation, and clear communication between program facilitators and all participants, including case workers and psychologists also engaging in the program in the justice setting. Interrogation of practitioner reflections recorded after each program session identified three key learnings, which are discussed briefly in the following.

A Creative Calm

Inclusion of the embedded creative as well as the adaptation of the program was assessed as a constructive way to address realities of delivering NNN in a custodial setting. The activities developed were engaging for participants and achieved their aims of stimulating narrative discussion of program content. More so, the activities induced a calming effect on the group space. When fully engaged in the activities participants were more open to share stories and engage in reflexive conversation about experiences of violence. Opportunities have been identified to strengthen these activities through consistent formatting and display, as well as delivery which embraces NNN practice principles of mindful engagement.

An Unpredictable Fit

The idea of the embedded design practitioner arose from managing unpredictability in the activities by utilizing expertise. Creative methods and approaches were needed to engage with the unpredictability of the custodial settings and the young men's participation. Indeed, the context of this work is immersed in unpredictability that mirrors the lives of young people involved. Structure to the affordances of freedom of expression offered by the creative activities in the program both contrasted and complemented the unpredictability of human behavior in the experiences of the program. This affirmed the utility of creative methods in working with youth violence. Effective intervention for youth violence is important considering more than one in ten 13- to 15-year-olds reporting they have acted violently in the previous twelve months (Hemphill et al. 2013) and almost 10% of 15- to 19-year-olds reporting they had been victims of violence the year prior (Australia Bureau of Statistics [ABS] 2006).

Insider/Outsider Experience

An unexpected finding was the juxtaposition of the embedded creative as an outsider actively observing participants being welcomed and included as an insider to experiences within the work. Participants were noted to be interested and engaged in the creative's work, often taking time out to observe his practice, and seeming (surprisingly) unbothered by his observational drawings of them in the program. This resulted in reportage illustrations that will be further developed to communicate the importance of the NNN program more broadly, attending to the recognition that, increasingly, alternative methods are needed to enhance research, impact engagement, and dissemination.

Conclusion

This chapter outlined a pilot case study of an embedded design practitioner in the NNN program for youth violence specific to limits of a restricted environment. This project is novel in its design, data analysis, and intended outputs. Data are drawn from NNN and include visual work created by participants and embedded creatives and qualitative narrative reflections from practitioners. Learnings from the project affirm that the inclusion of a design practitioner in restricted justice settings intervention program resulted in new narrative conversations and novelty arising from new conversations and collaboration between program practitioners and an embedded creative. Although the NNN program uses creative methods, the alignment with a practitioner assisting in the facilitation tends to assist in validating methods included in the program design and raise authentic practitioner insights that connect with participant capacity for pro-social experiences. Previously untested in juvenile custodial settings, the program helps interrupt the intergenerational cycle of violence, abuse, and trauma played by systems of service and support in that cycle. We believe that the adjustment to the NNN program to include a design/creative practitioner as a collaborative investigator in the study is an approach to be further explored in a variety of social work intervention and research settings. This project's outcomes will contribute to social justice policy and practice by developing visual tools for intervention/research to scaffold creative methods in youth justice interventions in a trauma-informed and culturally safe way. Further, outcomes help highlight the value of embedded creatives in industry sectors seeking to elicit and communicate new or emerging knowledge.

Acknowledgments

We acknowledge the contributions of NNN participants, and funders Westpac and the Australian Government Department of Industry, Science, Energy and Resources and the wider NNN project team: Shaun McCarthy, Louise Rak, Graeme Stuart and Chris Krogh, and Aunty Elsie Randall. Ethics approval was provided by AIATSIS, the University of Newcastle and the NSW Department of Justice. The work took place on Awabakal, Worimi, and Darkinjung lands. We acknowledge the traditional owners of these lands and pay our respects to Aboriginal elders, past, present, and emerging. The project acknowledges cultural trauma—past and present, the proud histories of our lands and waters, and that the overrepresentation of young Aboriginal and Torres Strait Island persons in the criminal justice system is a national crisis.

REFERENCES

ABS (Australia Bureau of Statistics). 2006. *Personal Safety Survey Australia.* ABS cat. No. 4906.0. ABS.

Batchelor, S. 2005. "'Prove Me the Bam!': Victimization and Agency in the Lives of Young Women Who Commit Violent Offences." *Probation Journal* 52 (4): 358–375.

Blakemore, T., S. McCarthy, L. Rak, J. McGregor, G. Stuart, and C. Krogh. 2021. *Postcards from Practice: Initial Learnings from the Name.Narrate.Navigate Program.* University of Newcastle. https://nova.newcastle.edu.au/vital/access/manager/Repository/uon:37573.

Blakemore, T., E. Randall, L. Rak, and F. Cocuzzoli. 2022. "Deep Listening and Relationality: Cross-Cultural Reflections on Practice with Young Women Who Use Violence." *Australian Social Work* 75 (3): 304–316.

Bryant, L., ed. 2015. *Critical and Creative Research Methodologies in Social Work*. Ashgate Publishing.

Budig, K., J. Diez, P. Conde, M. Sastre, M. Hernán, and M. Franco. 2018. "Photovoice and Empowerment: Evaluating the Transformative Potential of a Participatory Action Research Project." *BMC Public Health* 18 (1): 1–9.

Calvo, M. 2017. "Reflective Drawing as a Tool for Reflection in Design Research." *International Journal of Art & Design Education* 36 (3): 261–272.

Chand, A. 2018. "Habitus, Tacit Knowledge and Design Practice: The Context of the Designer as Illustrator." PhD thesis, The University of Newcastle.

Chand, A. 2021. "Developing a Designerly Way of Being, or at Least Trying." In *Elephant's Leg: Adventures in the Creative Industries*. Common Ground.

Chonody, J., B. Ferman, J. Amitrani-Welsh, and T. Martin. 2013. "Violence Through the Eyes of Youth: A Photovoice Exploration." *Journal of Community Psychology* 41 (1): 84–101.

Cioffi, D. 1993. "Sensate Body, Directive Mind: Physical Sensations and Mental Control." In *Handbook of Mental Control*, edited by D. Wegner and J. W. Pennebaker. Prentice-Hall.

Dallos, R. 2016. "Narratives of Young Offenders." In *Narrative Therapies with Children and Their Families*, edited by Arlene Vetere and Emilia Dowling. Routledge.

Eldh, A. C., J. Almost, K. DeCorby-Watson, et al. 2017. "Clinical Interventions, Implementation Interventions, and the Potential Greyness in Between—A Discussion Paper. *BMC Health Services Research* 17 (1): 1–10.

Fava, M. 2014. "Understanding Drawing: A Cognitive Account of Observational Process." Doctoral diss., Loughborough University.

Finkelhor, D., H. Turner, R. Ormrod, and S. L. Hamby. 2009. "Violence, Abuse, and Crime Exposure in a National Sample of Children and Youth." *Pediatrics* 124 (5): 1411–1423.

Fish, J., and S. Scrivener. 1990. "Amplifying the Mind's Eye: Sketching and Visual Cognition." *Leonardo* 23 (1): 117–126.

Fisher, J. 2003. "On Drawing." In *The Stage of Drawing: Gesture and Act*, edited by C. De Zegher. Tate Publishing and The Drawing Centre.

Fitzgibbon, W., and D. Healy. 2019. "Lives and Spaces: Photovoice and Offender Supervision in Ireland and England." *Criminology & Criminal Justice* 19 (1): 3–25.

Fitzgibbon, W., and C. M. Stengel. 2018. "Women's Voices Made Visible: Photovoice in Visual Criminology." *Punishment & Society* 20 (4): 411–431.

Goldschmidt, G. 1991. "The Dialectics of Sketching." *Creativity Research Journal* 4 (2): 123–143.

Goldschmidt, G. 2003. "The Backtalk of Self-Generated Sketches." *Design Issues* 19 (1): 72–88.

Grant, P., and G. Clark. 2021. *Graphic Storytellers at Work: Cross-Industry Opportunities for Cartoonists, Illustrators and Comics-Makers*. Australia Council for the Arts.

Grushka, K., M. Lawry, A. Chand, and A. Devine. 2022. "Visual Borderlands: Visuality, Performance, Fluidity and Art-Science Learning." *Educational Philosophy and Theory* 54 (4): 404–421.

Gussak, D., and M. Cohen-Liebman. 2001. "Investigation vs. Intervention: Forensic Art Therapy and Art Therapy in Forensic Settings." *American Journal of Art Therapy* 40 (2): 123.

Halty, L. 2019. "Impairment in the Processing of Fear Gaze in Adolescents with Callous-Unemotional Traits." *Psychology, Crime & Law* 25 (8): 792–802.

Hemphill, S. A., A. Kotevski, T. I. Herrenkohl, R. Smith, J. W. Toumbourou, and R. F. Catalano. 2013. "Does School Suspension Affect Subsequent Youth Non-Violent Antisocial Behaviour? A Longitudinal Study of Students in Victoria, Australia and Washington State, United States." *Australian Journal of Psychology* 65 (4): 236–249.

Hubble, K., K. L. Bowen, S. C. Moore, and S. H. M. van Goozen. 2015. "Improving Negative Emotion Recognition in Young Offenders Reduces Subsequent Crime." *PLoS ONE* 10 (6): e0132035.

Johnson, L. M. 2008. "A Place for Art in Prison: Art as a Tool for Rehabilitation and Management." *Southwest Journal of Criminal Justice* 5 (2): 122–135.

Kavakli, M., M. Suwa, J. Gero, and T. Purcell. 1999. "Sketching Interpretation in Novice and Expert Designers." In *Visual and Spatial Reasoning in Design*, vol. 99. University of Sydney.

Kret, M. E., and B. de Gelder. 2013. "When a Smile Becomes a Fist: The Perception of Facial and Bodily Expressions of Emotion in Violent Offenders." *Experimental Brain Research* 228: 399–410.

Liebenberg, L. 2018. "Thinking Critically About Photovoice: Achieving Empowerment and Social Change." *International Journal of Qualitative Methods* 17 (1): 1609406918757631.

Linehan, M. M. 2015. *DBT Skills Training Manual*. 2nd ed. The Guilford Press.

Literat, I. 2013. " 'A Pencil for Your Thoughts': Participatory Drawing as a Visual Research Method with Children and Youth." *International Journal of Qualitative Methods* 12 (1): 84–98.

Malvaso, C., A. Day, L. Hackett, J. Cale, P. Delfabbro, and S. Ross. 2022. "Adverse Childhood Experiences and Trauma Among Young People in the Youth Justice System." *Trends and Issues in Crime and Criminal Justice [Electronic Resource]* 651: 1–19.

Merleau-Ponty, M., and M. B. Smith. 1993. *The Merleau-Ponty Aesthetics Reader: Philosophy and Painting*. Northwestern University Press.

Minichiello, M. 2005. "Head, Heart and Hand." *International Journal of Diversity in Organisations, Communities & Nations* 5 (3): 23–52.

Ng-Mak, D. S., A. Stueve, S. Salzinger, and R. Feldman. 2002. "Normalization of Violence Among Inner-City Youth: A Formulation for Research." *American Journal of Orthopsychiatry* 72 (1): 92–101.

Purcell, A. T., and J. S. Gero. 1998. "Drawings and the Design Process: A Review of Protocol Studies in Design and Other Disciplines and Related Research in Cognitive Psychology." *Design Studies* 19 (4): 389–430.

Rayment-McHugh, S. 2021. *Name.Narrate.Navigate: A Preventive Initiative for Youth Violence: Evaluation Report*. Sexual Violence Research and Prevention Unit. University of the Sunshine Coast.

Reim, M. 2019. "Reportage: 'Drawing the Stories.' " *A Companion to Illustration*, edited by Alan Male. John Wiley & Sons.

Rodgers, P. A., G. Green, and A. Mcgown. 2000. "Using Concept Sketches to Track Design Progress." *Design Studies* 21 (5): 451–464.

Suwa, M., J. S. Gero, and T. A. Purcell. 1998. "The Roles of Sketches in Early Conceptual Design Processes." In *Proceedings of the Twentieth Annual Conference of the Cognitive Science Society*. Routledge.

Suwa, M., and B. Tversky. 2003. "Constructive Perception: A Metacognitive Skill for Coordinating Perception and Conception." *Proceedings of the Annual Meeting of the Cognitive Science Society* 25 (25): 1140–1145.

Tan, X. 2021. "Speed, Subjectivity and Visual Conventions in Ethnographic Reportage Drawings." *Drawing: Research, Theory, Practice* 6 (1): 153–170.

Teasdale, C. 1999. "Report: Developing Principles and Policies for Arts Therapists Working in United Kingdom Prisons." *Arts in Psychotherapy* 26 (4): 265–270.

Ursprung, W. A. 1997. "Insider Art: The Creative Ingenuity of the Incarcerated Artist." In *Drawing Time: Art Therapy in Prisons and Other Correctional Settings*, edited by D. Gussak and E. Virshup. Magnolia Street Publishers.

Wang, C., and M. A. Burris. 1997. "Photovoice: Concept, Methodology, and Use for Participatory Needs Assessment." *Health Education & Behavior* 24 (3): 369–387.

Wegrzyn, M., S. Westphal, and J. Kissler. 2017. "In Your Face: The Biased Judgement of Fear-Anger Expressions in Violent Offenders." *BMC Psychology* 5 (16): 1–12.

Wilcox, M., N. Frude, and L. Andrew. 2022. "Emotion Recognition and Perceived Social Support in Young People Who Offend." *Youth Justice* 22 (2): 125–144.

CHAPTER 10

The Sustainnovation Challenge: Empowering Youth Civic Engagement Through Creative Collaboration and Scalable Data-Driven Innovation

Paul Egglestone, Duncan Burck, and Jon Drummond

Abstract

The Sustainnovation Challenge combines experiential learning, data-driven problem-solving, and civic engagement, offering high school students the opportunity to co-create solutions to real-world challenges alongside industry, academia, and government partners. One of the challenge's significant outcomes was the development of City Pulse, an interactive art installation created by FASTlab that transformed data into an interactive civic dialogue platform. This installation exemplifies how the initiative goes beyond theoretical learning, allowing students to directly influence community engagement and local governance strategies. Rooted in rights-based empowerment and developmental approaches, the Sustainnovation Challenge nurtures leadership, critical thinking, and civic literacy. Projects like "Unity Within Our Community" have demonstrated the tangible impact of youth-driven innovation by shaping local governance discussions and addressing public concerns, such as urban sustainability and social inclusion. By integrating technology, public art, and cross-sector collaboration, the challenge offers a scalable model adaptable to diverse social and geographic contexts, promoting sustained youth engagement in both local and global issues like climate change and political polarization.

Introduction

Traditional governance processes, such as voting, often limit youth partic- ipation, which in turn fosters disengagement among younger generations (Harris and Wyn 2009; Vromen et al. 2016). Newer approaches, however, are empowering young people to become active agents of change through advocacy, participatory governance, and digital activism. One such initiative is the Sustainnovation Challenge, a program that merges creativity, data, and collaboration with government, academia, and industry to address local and global challenges.

This chapter examines the Sustainnovation Challenge, focusing on how it engages high school students in solving civic issues through cross-sector collaboration. A key example is the Wollondilly Sustainnovation Challenge, where collaboration with FASTlab demonstrated how student ideas could be brought to life through data art. FASTlab developed a flip-dot display prototype, dubbed "City Pulse," to showcase the potential of transforming data into a dynamic, interactive art installation. Engaging students in the formation and delivery of projects like City Pulse gives them a sense of ownership and agency, ultimately enhancing their civic literacy and partic- ipation (Shier 2001).

The program's success lies in its adaptability, as demonstrated through its implementation in various contexts, such as the Wollondilly Sustainnovation Challenge.

This chapter explores how the Sustainnovation Challenge leverages creativity and collaboration to enhance youth civic participation, examines its tangible outcomes, and evaluates the model's scalability across different settings. By addressing these points, this chapter will demonstrate the broader potential of the Sustainnovation Challenge to shape future civic engagement models and foster sustained youth participation in governance.

The Sustainnovation Challenge engages students, local governments, and communities to tackle real-world civic issues through creative and data-driven approaches. The program adapts to local needs, with a key example being the Wollondilly Sustainnovation Challenge, where a collaboration with FASTlab led to the creation of the City Pulse prototype, a flip-dot display that transformed civic data into a dynamic, interactive visual installation.

Not all Sustainnovation Challenges focus on data and public art, but the program is adaptable to various themes, from environmental sustainability to social inclusion, depending on the community's needs. This flexibility makes the program scalable and relevant across different contexts.

Grounded in theories like the *rights-based empowerment approach* (Lansdown 2001) and the *developmental approach* (Youniss et al. 1997), the program fosters leadership, critical thinking, and civic engagement among young people. By turning student ideas into public-facing projects, the program not only empowers youth but also promotes inclusive civic discourse and community involvement.

Beyond the local impact of programs like the Sustainnovation Challenge, digital technologies are increasingly central to how young people engage with civic processes globally. Digital platforms democratize political participation, enabling youth to mobilize around causes that resonate with them, often bypassing traditional gatekeepers (Loader et al. 2014). High-profile movements like the climate strikes led by Greta Thunberg exemplify how digital tools empower youth to coordinate across borders, amplify their voices, and influence policy discussions internationally.

In restrictive political environments, digital activism also provides young people with alternative ways to challenge governance structures. Structural barriers and socioeconomic inequalities often limit youth engagement in formal political processes, as highlighted by scholars like Bessant (2014) and Norris (2002). Digital technologies help mitigate these barriers by providing marginalized youth with platforms to express their views, organize movements, and challenge exclusionary norms, thereby fostering social change.

Framing the Chapter

The Sustainnovation Challenge, in partnership with FASTlab, demonstrates the power of integrating experiential learning with public engagement to foster youth civic participation. By combining civic education, creative problem-solving, and cross-sector collaboration, the challenge empowers students to co-create solutions to local challenges. The Wollondilly Sustainnovation Challenge serves as a key case study, showing how students work alongside government and community stakeholders to design practical, community-driven projects that address real-world issues.

The chapter also highlights how technologies, such as FASTlab's flip-dot display prototype (City Pulse), can enhance the visibility and impact of these initiatives. Through this case study, the chapter explores both the local outcomes and the broader scalability of the model, demonstrating its potential to sustain youth participation in civic life on a global scale.

The Sustainnovation Challenge program offers new avenues for meaningful youth participation in civic life by blending creativity, data-driven solutions, and public engagement. These initiatives introduce students to innovative problem-solving while actively involving them in shaping their communities. By working alongside local governments and community stakeholders, the program provides a platform for students to address real-world issues, fostering a sense of agency and civic responsibility.

What sets these initiatives apart is their ability to transform abstract civic challenges into tangible, interactive experiences. For example, FASTlab's involvement in the Wollondilly Challenge, through the development of a prototype artwork, translates students' ideas into engaging formats that make complex civic issues accessible to the wider community.

Theoretical Foundations of Youth Participation

The Sustainnovation Challenge applies key theoretical frameworks — such as the Rights-Based and Empowerment approaches — to practically foster youth civic engagement, exemplified by initiatives like the City Pulse project. In the digital age, these frameworks intersect with the growing role of AI and data-driven tools in civic participation. Emerging technologies, including AI, machine learning, and IoT (Internet of Things) sensors, are transforming how communities interact with civic spaces, offering new pathways for participation. Public art projects like City Pulse illustrate how AI technologies, combined with civic data, can amplify youth voices and democratize access to public discourse, fostering more inclusive participation in governance processes.

- *Rights-Based Approach:* This approach emphasizes that young people have the right to participate actively in decision-making processes, a principle enshrined in the United Nations Convention on the Rights of the Child (Lansdown 2001). The Sustainnovation Challenge applies this by treating young people as legitimate stakeholders in governance, ensuring their voices are heard and their contributions valued.
- *Empowerment Approach:* This framework focuses on equipping young people with the skills, confidence, and opportunities they need to shape

their political environments. In the Sustainnovation Challenge, participants engage in creative problem-solving, leadership development, and community-building, gaining hands-on experience in addressing civic issues (Shier 2001).

- *Developmental Approach:* The developmental approach highlights the importance of youth participation for personal and social growth. By involving students in experiential learning, the Sustainnovation Challenge helps them develop critical thinking, collaboration, and communication skills — key components of active citizenship (Youniss et al. 1997).
- *Sociological Approach:* The sociological approach looks at how community and social structures affect youth participation. In the Sustainnovation Challenge, this means understanding how initiatives like City Pulse provide spaces for young people to connect, share their perspectives, and help shape their own environment.

The Sustainnovation Challenge offers a highly adaptable framework for fostering youth civic engagement across diverse contexts. Two key features make this scalability possible: the integration of data-driven public art and the use of the triple helix model (Etzkowitz and Leydesdorff 1995), of cross-sector collaboration.

Data-driven public art transforms complex civic issues into accessible, visually compelling formats, allowing young people to creatively communicate real-time data to their communities. Projects like City Pulse demonstrate how public spaces can be used to visualize civic data, making it easier for communities to engage with local issues. This approach is not only adaptable to various themes — such as environmental sustainability and social inclusion — but also scalable across different geographic and sociopolitical contexts, providing a flexible platform for engagement.

The Triple Helix model which fosters collaboration between industry, academia, and government, further enhances the program's adaptability. By leveraging each sector's unique resources, the model ensures that projects remain grounded in practical, real-world challenges while benefiting from academic insights and government support. This cross-sectoral framework can be replicated in different regions, ensuring that the Sustainnovation Challenge is adaptable to local needs and capacities while maintaining its core focus on youth empowerment and civic participation.

These features position the Sustainnovation Challenge as a scalable model for promoting sustained youth engagement, adaptable to both local governance challenges and global issues such as climate change and social inequality.

Interplay of Theoretical Frameworks

The *rights-based*, *empowerment*, and *developmental* approaches, along with a *sociological perspective*, offer unique insights into youth civic engagement. The *rights-based approach* emphasizes youth participation as a legal and ethical right, while the *empowerment approach* focuses on equipping young people with the skills to influence governance (Shier 2001). The *developmental approach* highlights how civic participation fosters personal and social skills essential for active citizenship (Youniss et al. 1997). Lastly, the *sociological perspective* addresses the structural inequalities that often limit participation, particularly for marginalized groups (Harris and Wyn 2009).

Together, these frameworks provide a comprehensive understanding of youth civic engagement. They illustrate that fostering participation requires not only a focus on rights and empowerment but also creating developmental opportunities and addressing systemic barriers. The initiatives in the Sustainnovation Challenge embody these principles in practice, showing how theory can be applied to cultivate sustained youth engagement and civic involvement.

While these theoretical frameworks provide valuable insights, each has limitations in contemporary political environments.

The *rights-based approach* emphasizes youth participation as a legal right, but enforcement mechanisms are often weak. Many political institutions, though legally bound, are ill-equipped or unwilling to genuinely engage young people in decision-making (Norris 2002). This gap between theory and practice hinders the realization of youth rights in governance.

Similarly, the *empowerment approach* assumes that providing skills and opportunities is enough to overcome systemic barriers. However, without addressing broader socioeconomic inequalities, such initiatives may disproportionately benefit privileged youth, leaving marginalized groups with fewer opportunities (Bessant 2014). As a result, empowerment initiatives can unintentionally reinforce existing disparities.

The *developmental approach* also presumes equal access to civic opportunities, which is rarely the case. Disparities in education, socioeconomic status, and access to civic platforms often prevent disadvantaged youth from fully participating (Harris and Wyn 2009). Consequently, these programs may fail to reach those most in need.

The *sociological perspective* adds valuable insight by addressing the structural inequalities that limit youth participation, particularly for marginalized groups (Bessant et al. 2016). Youth from lower socioeconomic backgrounds or minority communities often face significant barriers, leading to political exclusion and alienation, especially when traditional governance structures fail to accommodate their voices (Harris and Wyn 2009).

While this perspective highlights structural barriers, it often lacks practical solutions for dismantling entrenched inequalities. This underscores the need for an integrated approach, combining empowerment, developmental, and rights-based frameworks to create adaptable civic engagement initiatives.

Efforts like the Sustainnovation Challenge (Figure 1) address these barriers by providing inclusive platforms that engage diverse groups of young people. Through collaboration with local governments, educators, and community leaders, these initiatives foster a more equitable civic environment.

Figure 1: Students from Birrong Girls High School in NSW Answer Questions from the Expert Panel of Local Government, Business, and Community Representatives at the City of Canterbury Bankstown Sustainnovation Challenge.

Schools and civic institutions also play a vital role in this process, creating opportunities for meaningful youth engagement. By addressing structural barriers, initiatives such as this one help reduce inequalities in civic participation. These principles are exemplified in projects like the Wollondilly challenge, where students co-created community-driven solutions based on these frameworks.

Case Study: Wollondilly Sustainnovation Challenge

The *Sustainnovation Challenge* embodies the principles of the *developmental approach*, which views civic participation as essential for developing critical thinking, collaboration, and problem-solving skills (Youniss et al. 1997). Through hands-on engagement with real-world issues, participants gain these competencies in an experiential learning environment that combines civic education, creativity, and data-driven problem-solving.

The *Wollondilly Challenge* (Figure 2) shows how the initiative operates in practice. Workshops, facilitated by representatives from the New South Wales Government, Wollondilly Council, and local businesses, introduced students to key environmental challenges. These sessions emphasized the role of data and creativity in addressing civic issues. Students investigated how technology, public art, and data could be combined to address urgent local challenges.

Figure 2: High School Students Receiving Mentoring and Expert Feedback on Their Ideas During the Wollondilly Sustainnovation Challenge

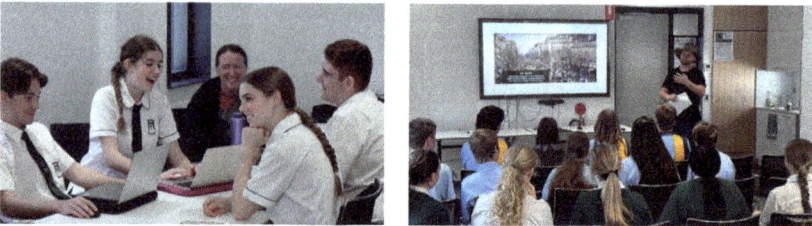

Day 1 of the Sustainnovation Challenge sets the stage for students by grounding them in the broader context of the issues, challenges which they are to address and their local relevance. Through guided exploration, participants learn to apply critical thinking skills to probe beneath surface-level symptoms and understand root causes. This involves engaging with individuals who have lived experiences related to these challenges, providing invaluable insights into the complexity of the problems or opportunities. By asking questions and listening to those closest to the issues, students are equipped to build a more authentic understanding of the challenges they aim to solve.

Central to the Sustainnovation Challenge is the idea that emotional connection to a problem enhances resilience and commitment in the innovation process.

Students are encouraged to look within themselves when exploring the challenge topic and reflect on which topic resonates with them personally. By identifying a challenge they care about, students are more likely to persist through setbacks and obstacles, as their passion for the issue fuels their resilience and creativity throughout the process.

On the second day, students worked in teams to develop solutions combining civic learning with innovative approaches. One standout project, *Unity Within Our Community—A Voice for All*, created by Picton High School, transformed community survey data into a concept for an interactive public art installation. The development of the *City Pulse* prototype, a flip-dot display, illustrated the potential of using data-driven tools to engage the public by visualizing community voices.

The FASTlab Data Art Project played a key role in this Challenge by supporting the transformation of the winning idea into a public art concept that bridged creative problem-solving with public engagement. The City Pulse flip-dot display (Figure 3) was developed as a prototype to explore how public art could foster civic dialogue by visualizing community data in an interactive manner. While the prototype was not used in the final implementation, it demonstrated the potential for transforming student ideas into dynamic public engagement tools. Instead of limiting student outcomes to presentations, FASTlab ensured that the project embodied a practical vision of civic dialogue, highlighting the importance of turning theoretical knowledge into actionable insights.

Figure 3: The City Pulse Flip-Dot Display—An Interactive Public Art Installation That Visualizes Real-Time Community Data. The Project Was Part of the Wollondilly Sustainnovation Challenge Designed to Illustrate How Data-Driven Public Art Fosters Civic Engagement

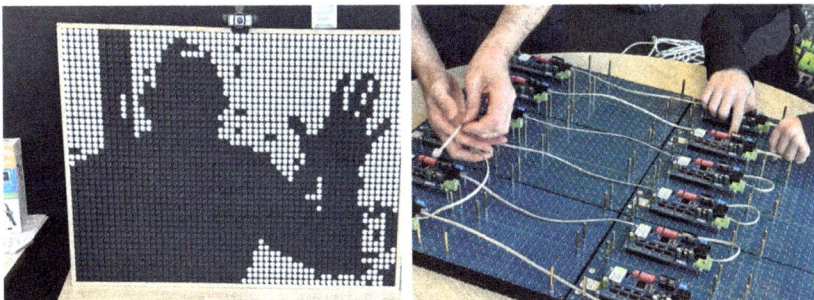

Through a combination of workshops, mentorship from professionals in fields like technology, the arts, and governance, and project-based learning, students gained practical skills and the confidence to take active roles in shaping their communities. This approach offers a scalable template for fostering civic engagement and creative problem-solving across diverse regions and contexts, adaptable to various challenges and community needs.

Data Art as a Tool for Civic Engagement

Data visualization and public art have become effective tools for fostering community engagement in civic discourse. By transforming complex datasets into visually compelling formats, data art bridges the gap between abstract civic issues and accessible public engagement. Grounded in the principles of data visualization (Card et al. 1999), this approach not only enhances comprehension but also supports informed decision-making by presenting civic data in relatable ways.

Data-driven public art empowers youth by enhancing their ability to visualize and communicate civic data creatively, fostering ownership and participation in public discourse. By guiding participants through the process of turning abstract data into accessible visual narratives, these projects build the capacity for young people to lead civic discussions and drive community change.

Participatory art practices, which involve public collaboration in creating art, are increasingly valued for their ability to democratize public spaces and foster civic discourse (Bishop 2012). By engaging communities in the creative process, these practices provide platforms for marginalized voices and encourage collective reflection on social issues. As public art intersects with data visualization and AI-driven technologies, these practices are further enhanced. For example, AI algorithms can transform complex datasets into real-time interactive public art installations, making abstract civic issues accessible to wider audiences. Initiatives like the Sustainnovation Challenge, through projects like City Pulse, demonstrate how AI and data visualization foster deeper public engagement by turning civic data into tangible, visual experiences.

Data art, in this context, becomes both a tool for communication and a form of participatory governance, opening new pathways for public involvement (Manovich 2011). The Sustainnovation Challenge leverages this intersection of data art and civic participation, enabling youth to create visual representations of data that reflect their communities' experiences. This creative approach aligns with global trends, such as the *Data Canvas* initiative, which uses sensor-driven data to produce public art that visualizes environmental information in urban spaces (Ciuccarelli et al. 2014).

Public art has long shaped civic identity and fostered community dialogue. Art displayed in public spaces reflects community values, offering platforms for interaction and reflection. In the context of the digital age, public art is now leveraging AI and emerging technologies to foster even richer dialogues. Art installations, such as City Pulse enable real-time data interaction, making public spaces more dynamic and responsive to civic concerns. These technologies not only visualize community issues but also adapt based on ongoing input, creating a continuous feedback loop between the public and the artwork, deepening civic engagement.

The use of data-driven public art is a particularly scalable element of the Sustainnovation Challenge. The combination of data visualization and participatory art has broad applicability, making this model easily replicable across different regions and settings.

The Wollondilly Sustainnovation Challenge is part of a growing global movement that leverages data-driven public art to enhance civic engagement. International projects such as the Data Canvas initiative and Smart Citizen Kit offer compelling examples of how real-time environmental data can be transformed into public art, sparking community discussions and inspiring action on pressing social and environmental issues (Ciuccarelli et al. 2014; Gabrys 2014). The Data Canvas project, a collaboration between cities like San Francisco and Geneva, used air-quality sensors to gather environmental data, which was then visualized through public art installations. This approach facilitated community dialogue around urban environmental health. Similarly, Barcelona's Smart Citizen Kit enabled residents to monitor air-quality and noise levels, with the data publicly displayed to encourage civic participation and activism.

These examples demonstrate the scalability of data-driven public art as a tool for civic participation, making complex issues more accessible through visual storytelling and encouraging collective action. The Sustainnovation Challenge aligns with these principles, empowering young people to engage their communities and transform public spaces through creative, participatory public art.

The Triple Helix Model in the Sustainnovation Challenge: Industry Leadership and Collaboration

The triple helix model (Etzkowitz and Leydesdorff 2000) of collaboration between industry, academia, and government underpins the Sustainnovation Challenge.

Key partners, including MCB Business Partners, FASTlab, and government bodies like the NSW State Department of Education, demonstrate how cross-sector cooperation engages youth in solving real-world challenges.

Industry Leadership: MCB Business Partners. As the principal industry partner and creator of the Sustainnovation Challenge, MCB Business Partners shapes the program by grounding it in real-world issues. MCB ensures that students acquire skills relevant to future career demands, emphasizing the intersection of sustainability and economic innovation. This industry involvement shows how business leadership can align educational initiatives with practical needs, making the triple helix model adaptable to real-world applications (Galvao et al. 2019).

Academic Collaboration: FASTlab at the University of Newcastle. FASTlab enhances the program's creative dimension by transforming student data into interactive public art, underscoring academia's role in fostering innovation and addressing societal challenges. By integrating academic knowledge with industry and government efforts, FASTlab exemplifies how academia drives civic problem-solving (Trencher et al. 2013).

Government Support: NSW State Department of Education and Wollondilly Council. The NSW State Department of Education and Wollondilly Council support student projects with resources and community engagement, ensuring alignment with local issues and fostering meaningful civic participation.

Outcomes and Impact

The Sustainnovation Challenge has delivered both qualitative and quantitative outcomes, demonstrating its success in engaging students, fostering civic literacy, and driving local governance collaborations. While earlier discussions emphasized the theoretical and qualitative aspects of the challenge, the following section highlights specific metrics to provide a clearer picture of the initiative's tangible impact.

Since its inception, the Sustainnovation Challenge has engaged a total of 173 students from fourteen schools across the Southwest Sydney region. This exceeded the minimum participation target of 150 students, with an average of forty-three students per event, surpassing the expected participation range of twenty-five to fifty students per challenge. The initiative included students from diverse educational institutions, such as Picton High School, Wollondilly Anglican College, and All Saints Catholic College. Moreover, these students worked on community-centric projects and delivered twenty-four cumulative student pitches. Out of these pitches, five student projects were selected by councils and partners for further exploration, with the potential for real-world implementation. This demonstrates the direct influence of the program in shaping local governance strategies and providing youth with a platform to contribute meaningfully to their communities.

The program significantly improved civic literacy among participants, equipping students with hands-on experience in local governance and problem-solving. Although the evaluation report does not include precise survey data, anecdotal feedback indicates that the students developed a stronger understanding of how local government functions. For instance, through workshops with local council members and industry leaders, students were able to tackle challenges such as sustainability, inclusiveness, and public safety. Additionally, students expressed an increased sense of empowerment and a deeper connection to their communities. The willingness of several students to remain engaged in the follow-up activities of their proposed solutions further underscores the challenge's success in fostering long-term civic engagement.

Real-World Implementation and Scaling Success

A key indicator of the Sustainnovation Challenge's success is its scalability and the adoption of student-led ideas by local councils. For example, in Wollondilly, the Unity Within Our Community project, developed by students from Picton High School in collaboration with the local council and FASTlab at the University of Newcastle, is being implemented to create public art that fosters civic engagement. This project demonstrates how student ideas move from conceptual pitches to actionable community projects.

In Liverpool, the Green Gateway initiative, proposed by students to encourage sustainable business practices through practical, in-curriculum learning experiences, is under consideration for implementation in partnership with local councils and innovation stakeholders. These examples illustrate how the Sustainnovation Challenge is more than just an educational experience — it is a catalyst for real-world change, driving local governance and community development.

Another recent example of real-world impact comes from the South West Sydney Sustainnovation Challenge in May 2023, held in collaboration with the City of Canterbury Bankstown (Figure 4). More than fifty students from five local schools worked alongside council officers, community leaders, and industry experts to generate solutions for "creating places where women and girls feel safer." The standout proposal, the Breaking Bread Program, aimed to foster cross-cultural understanding and boost community confidence through

multicultural pop-ups. Other proposals, such as a women's wellness space, a safe travel app, and a male etiquette program, further highlighted the students' creativity and practical problem-solving.

As noted by City of Canterbury Bankstown Mayor Khal Asfour, these innovative ideas have the potential to be realized through future programs and urban improvements. The Sustainnovation Challenge continues to provide a platform for students to influence local governance, with councils actively exploring how to bring these ideas to life, underscoring the program's ongoing contribution to community development and social change.

Beyond the immediate outcomes, the challenge has laid the groundwork for continued collaboration between students and local governments. Five student ideas from the Southwest Sydney series are currently being pursued for further development by councils and industry partners. This commitment to exploring student innovations highlights the long-term potential of the Sustainnovation Challenge as a scalable model for fostering youth civic engagement and leadership.

Expanding the Impact of the Sustainnovation Challenge and the Triple Helix Model

The Sustainnovation Challenge program brings together industry, academia, and government to engage young people in civic life while preparing them for future professional challenges. The initiative empowers students to craft innovative solutions to local challenges by combining creative thinking, technology, and collaboration. Projects like "Unity Within Our Community—A Voice for All" and the subsequent "Pennies and Nellies" installations demonstrate how diverse approaches—ranging from art and data to technology and social innovation—can address critical societal challenges such as environmental sustainability, social inclusion, and public safety. This flexible, adaptable model can be applied across different regions and contexts, ensuring it remains relevant to a wide range of community needs.

The Pennies Installation in Penrith (Figure 5), co-designed with local women and girls, integrates sensor technology to collect real-time data on space usage and perceptions of safety. This data-driven approach not only informs urban design but also invites community members to actively participate in improving public spaces. The Pennies and Nellies projects highlight the role of inclusive data collection in fostering safe environments for women and girls. As D'Ignazio and Klein (2020) emphasize, data tools in participatory governance can challenge existing power structures, empowering marginalized communities, including women, to actively shape public spaces. The collaboration among industry partners, academic institutions like FASTlab, and government entities exemplifies how collaboration can create scalable, impactful initiatives that foster engagement and community empowerment.

Figure 5: The Pennies Installation in Penrith—This Public Art Installation Was Co-designed with Local Women and Girls, Integrating Sensor Technology to Collect Real-Time Data on Space Usage and Perceptions of Safety

By working across these three sectors, the Sustainnovation Challenge can leverage each partner's unique strengths — industry insights, academic expertise, and government support — to create a holistic model for youth engagement. This approach provides a replicable framework that can be adapted for similar initiatives globally, promoting youth empowerment and active citizenship.

The impact of the Sustainnovation Challenge extends beyond the local context, providing a scalable framework for addressing global challenges. Initiatives like Pennies and Nellies, which transformed public spaces through interactive public art that fosters reflection on environmental and social issues, can be adapted to tackle broader issues such as climate change and social equity. By engaging young people in data-driven public art and civic problem-solving, the Challenge offers a model that can be replicated to foster community dialogue and action on global sustainability issues.

In addition, the Challenge's creative approach to public engagement has the potential to address rising political polarization. By creating shared spaces for dialogue through art and data visualization, the Sustainnovation Challenge promotes inclusive civic discourse, offering diverse communities the opportunity to engage with and understand different perspectives. The integration of civic education, public art, and technology provides a powerful tool for bridging divides and fostering a more inclusive democratic process.

As the Challenge expands, its focus on art and technology creates opportunities for young people to connect with their communities in meaningful ways, addressing issues that matter to them. The emphasis on community co-design and data-driven storytelling makes this model adaptable to different contexts, allowing it to respond to the specific needs and challenges of each community it serves.

The scalability of the Sustainnovation Challenge lies in its ability to harness the triple helix model and create a platform where youth can contribute to addressing critical societal challenges. By providing young people with the skills and opportunities to participate actively in governance, this initiative demonstrates the power of integrated learning models to foster youth leadership, promote equity, and address complex social challenges.

Future Research and Evolution of the Initiatives

The Sustainnovation Challenge, through collaboration between industry, academia, and government, offers a scalable blueprint for future civic engagement initiatives. By combining creativity, practical problem-solving, and civic education, the program empowers youth to address a wide range of local and global challenges, including climate change and political polarization.

Future research should explore the long-term impact of these programs on sustained civic participation. Specifically, understanding how involvement in initiatives like the Sustainnovation Challenge influences participants' civic behavior and leadership development over time can offer valuable insights into how such models can be refined and scaled. Additionally, investigating the integration of emerging technologies, such as AI and virtual reality, can reveal new opportunities to enhance engagement, deepen interaction, and expand the program's reach to diverse audiences.

Further research can also explore how these initiatives can adapt to different cultural and socioeconomic contexts. By understanding the nuances of community needs and building culturally responsive frameworks, the Sustainnovation Challenge can evolve to support young people worldwide, providing them with the skills and tools necessary to shape their environments actively.

No program is without its challenges, so it is important to recognize and discuss potential limitations faced during the Sustainnovation Challenge to provide a balanced perspective. While the Sustainnovation Challenge has shown success in specific contexts, scaling the model to different communities presents certain challenges. For instance, the program relies heavily on cross-sector partnerships, which may not always be feasible in regions with fewer resources or less access to academic and governmental collaborators (Bessant 2014).

Moreover, there are structural barriers that could limit the participation of marginalized youth. Programs that engage students from privileged backgrounds might unintentionally reinforce existing inequalities, leaving less advantaged groups with fewer opportunities for meaningful civic engagement (Norris 2002). Addressing these barriers requires a more deliberate focus on inclusivity and outreach to ensure that all young people, regardless of their socioeconomic background, can participate fully in the program.

One solution could be the introduction of alternative pathways for participation, such as digital or remote options, which allow students from different regions to engage with the program even if in-person resources are limited. These alternative pathways would democratize access and offer broader inclusion for students from disadvantaged communities (Gabrys 2014).

The Sustainnovation Challenge could also benefit from further research into the long-term impact on participants, including whether students continue to engage in civic activities after completing the program. This would help identify areas for improvement and measure the sustained impact of the initiative on civic literacy and engagement.

Conclusion

The Sustainnovation Challenge and the FASTlab Data Art Project exemplify the transformative potential of integrating rights-based, developmental, and empowerment approaches to foster youth civic engagement. By harnessing creativity, collaboration, and data-driven problem-solving, these initiatives empower young people, building long-term civic literacy and active participation. Drawing on theoretical foundations like the rights-based approach (Lansdown 2001), empowerment approach (Shier 2001), and developmental approach (Youniss et al. 1997), they demonstrate how abstract concepts of youth participation can evolve into practical and impactful frameworks.

The case study explored in this chapter showcases how experiential learning and public art can bridge the gap between youth and governance. Through scalable and adaptable models like the Sustainnovation Challenge, young people are equipped to contribute meaningfully to their communities. The triple helix model, which brings together the expertise of industry, academia, and government, plays a crucial role in fostering environments where youth can learn, innovate, and contribute to civic life. FASTlab's support in transforming student projects into prototypes, including the City Pulse art installation, showcases how creative and data-driven approaches can enhance civic engagement across various regions and contexts.

The Sustainnovation Challenge offers a scalable and flexible blueprint for enhancing youth engagement in civic life (Figure 6). By integrating digital tools, creative practices, and cross-sector collaboration, it empowers young people to actively participate in governance and community-building. This adaptable model addresses a wide range of societal challenges, from local governance to global issues like climate change and social inequality, ensuring that youth remain at the forefront of societal transformation. As the initiative continues to evolve, it provides a pathway for sustained global impact, equipping the next generation of civic leaders to navigate and lead in an increasingly interconnected world.

Figure 6: Students from High Schools across South West Sydney, NSW, Work in Teams to Develop Solutions to Real-World Problems, Combining Civic Learning with Innovative Approaches

Acknowledgments

We would like to extend our heartfelt thanks to all the high schools, local government bodies, businesses, and educational institutions whose collaboration made the Sustainnovation Challenges possible. Their collective contributions, insights, and support have been instrumental in empowering young people and fostering civic engagement across communities.

We would also like to acknowledge the valuable contributions of the director of MCB Business Partners, Duncan Burck, who not only played a key role in the development of the Sustainnovation Challenge series but also served as a coauthor of this paper, providing vital insights and expertise that enriched this work.

References

Bessant, J. 2014. *Democracy Bytes: New Media, New Politics and Generational Change*. Palgrave Macmillan.

Bessant, J., R. Farthing, and R. Watts. 2016. "Co-Designing a Civics Curriculum: Young People, Democratic Deficit and Political Renewal in the EU." *Journal of Youth Studies* 19 (7): 921–937. https://doi.org/10.1080/13676261.2015.1098776.

Bishop, C. 2012. *Artificial Hells: Participatory Art and the Politics of Spectatorship*. Verso Books.

Cai, Y., and H. Etzkowitz. 2020. "Theorizing the Triple Helix Model: Past, Present, and Future." *Triple Helix* 7 (2): 189–226.

Card, S. K., J. D. Mackinlay, and B. Shneiderman. 1999. *Readings in Information Visualization: Using Vision to Think*. Morgan Kaufmann.

City of Canterbury Bankstown. 2023. "Making Women and Girls Feel Safer: What Students Think." May 7. https://www.cbcity.nsw.gov.au/your-council/media-centre/making-women-and-girls-feel-safer-what-students-think.

Ciuccarelli, P., G. Lupi, and L. Simeone. 2014. *Visualizing the Data City: Social Media as a Source of Knowledge for Urban Planning and Management*. Springer.

D'Ignazio, C., and L. F. Klein. 2020. *Data Feminism*. MIT Press.

Etzkowitz, H., and L. Leydesdorff. 1995. "The Triple Helix — University-Industry-Government Relations: A Laboratory for Knowledge-Based Economic Development." *EASST Review* 14 (1): 14–19.

Etzkowitz, H., and L. Leydesdorff. 2000. "The Dynamics of Innovation: From National Systems and 'Mode 2' to a Triple Helix of University–Industry–Government Relations." *Research Policy* 29 (2): 109–123.

Gabrys, J. 2014. "Programming Environments: Environmentality and Citizen Sensing in the Smart City." *Environment and Planning D: Society and Space* 32 (1): 30–48.

Galvao, A., C. Mascarenhas, C. S. Marques, and J. J. M. Ferreira. 2019. "Triple Helix and Its Evolution: A Systematic Literature Review." *Journal of Science and Technology Policy Management* 10 (3): 812–833.

Harris, A., and J. Wyn. 2009. "Young People's Politics and the Micro-Territories of the Local." *Australian Journal of Political Science* 44 (2): 327–344.

Hullman, J., and N. Diakopoulos. 2011. "Visualization Rhetoric: Framing Effects in Narrative Visualization." *IEEE Transactions on Visualization and Computer Graphics* 17 (12): 2231–2240.

Lansdown, G. 2001. *Promoting Children's Participation in Democratic Decision-Making*. UNICEF Innocenti Research Centre.

Lawrence, R. J. 2015. "Advances in Transdisciplinarity: Epistemologies, Methodologies, and Processes." *Futures* 65: 1–9.

Loader, B. D., A. Vromen, and M. A. Xenos. 2014. "The Networked Young Citizen: Social Media, Political Participation and Civic Engagement." *Information, Communication & Society* 17 (2): 143–150. https://doi.org/10.1080/1369 118X.2013.871571.

Lupi, G., and S. Posavec. 2016. *Dear Data*. Princeton Architectural Press.

Manovich, L. 2011. *The Language of New Media*. MIT Press.

Norris, P. 2002. *Democratic Phoenix: Reinventing Political Activism*. Cambridge University Press.

Ribeiro, A. B., and I. Menezes. 2022. "Youth Participation and Citizenship Education: An Analysis of Relations in Four European Countries." *JSSE—Journal of Social Science Education* 21 (1): 4–32. https://doi.org/10.11576/jsse-1454.

Shier, H. 2001. "Pathways to Participation: Openings, Opportunities and Obligations." *Children & Society* 15 (2): 107–117.

Trencher, G., M. Yarime, and A. Kharrazi. 2013. "Co-Creating Sustainability: Cross-Sector University Collaborations for Driving Sustainable Urban Transformations." *Journal of Cleaner Production* 50: 40–55.

Vromen, A., M. Xenos, and B. D. Loader. 2016. "Beyond the Youth Citizenship Dichotomy: The Role of Social Media and Human Agency in Young People's Political Engagement." *Social Media + Society* 2 (1): 2056305115622483.

Youniss, J., J. A. McLellan, and M. Yates. 1997a. "What We Know About Engendering Civic Identity." *American Behavioral Scientist* 40 (5): 620–631.

Youniss, J., J. A. McLellan, and M. Yates. 1997b. *Community Service and Social Responsibility in Youth*. University of Chicago Press.

CHAPTER 11

Virtual Reality (VR) Oral Musculature Assessment (VOMA): Using VR to Solve a Real-World Problem in Health Practice

Rachael Unicomb, Joanne Walters and Angus Stevens

Abstract

In 2019, educators/researchers in speech pathology at the University of New-castle (UON) were awarded internal funding (Digital Simulation Technology Evaluation Pilot—STEP1) to support the development of an innovative teaching technology using virtual reality, Virtual Reality Oral Musculature Assessment (VOMA). VOMA is used as a teaching and learning resource to teach a fundamental clinical skill to undergraduate speech pathology students. The technology was developed in collaboration with key university stakeholders and an external industry partner, Start Beyond. Since development, VOMA has been delivered to over two hundred undergraduate students and has won three UON awards, been the subject of presentations at national stakeholder and Australian Defence Force-based conferences, facilitated cross-college collaborations, formed the basis of journal article publications, as well as further equipment and college funding grant support. Recently, the research and development team has grown and now includes university and industry (technology and health) stakeholders. The team is expanding the project to roll out a new addition to VOMA to strengthen its robustness and to consider worldwide commercialization and future research application of the technology. This chapter will discuss the project from the perspectives of early/mid-career researchers, and their industry partners, who have navigated both university and industry systems to develop an innovation that started as a small project and continues to have wider impact and value.

In the Beginning

An oral musculature assessment (OMA) is a fundamental assessment performed by speech pathologists and is conducted out on individuals suspected of (certain types of) communication and swallowing/feeding issues, to identify potential underlying structural and functional causes (McLeod and Baker 2016). An OMA can be carried out on both children and adults; however, a pediatric OMA is very different to an adult OMA as there are significant differences in pediatric oral cavity anatomy compared to adult oral cavity anatomy. Conducting an OMA is crucial for any child referred for speech, swallowing, feeding, and voice issues to identify possible underlying causes for these issues. An OMA can also aid clinical decision making, as it provides valuable information for differential diagnosis and classification of a pediatric speech sound disorder. Therefore, OMA assessment and interpretation is an important and essential clinical skill that needs to be taught to speech pathology students.

This content area and clinical skill is currently taught to students at University of Newcastle (UON) in the course SPTH2080 — Professional Practice. This course takes place in the students' second year (of four) of their undergraduate studies. The course involves the students' first practice education (placement) experience and is pediatric in nature. Students attend placement (off-site) for one day per week for around fifteen weeks, and attend a weekly tutorial on campus, where they have an opportunity to reflect on, and consolidate their clinical learning. It is within these tutorials that students are initially taught how to conduct an OMA on a child, and this is done early in the tutorial series, often before students conduct a live OMA on a child. This timing is important, as conducting an OMA is a hands-on, invasive procedure that can lead to behavior and compliance issues in children, which students often lack confidence in managing (American Speech-Language-Hearing Association [ASHA] 2022).

Up until 2019, the content was taught in the tutorial series via direct teaching methods (provision of information and an OMA checklist), use of visual materials to demonstrate OMA administration, and basic simulation activities (e.g., role-playing OMA on adult peers). Students are required to demonstrate the administration of an OMA by role-playing the assessment of the three main areas of an OMA: function, structure, and coordination of the oral cavity and articulators. Students are also required to consider what information they can get by investigating the structure and/or function of the oral mechanism and oral motor skills and whether minor and/or major structural variations have an impact on speech production.

The lead educators/researchers in speech pathology at UON (the current authors) reflected on this method of teaching and recognized some insufficiencies in the current method of addressing the students' learning goals in this area.

Pediatric OMA taught using adult peers as models is problematic because of the following reasons:

- Significant differences in pediatric versus adult oral cavity anatomy and function.
- Adult model not being able to replicate issues in relation to child behavior and compliance during this assessment.
- Impossible to replicate or demonstrate difficulties within the oral cavity such as minor and/or major structural variations that are commonly observed in clinical practice related to issues with the oral anatomy including lips, tongue, teeth, and palate. Adult peers are more likely to have a typical presentation of function and structure of the oral cavity and oral skills.

In 2019, these educators recognized an opportunity to enhance student learning in relation to how students are taught to conduct a pediatric OMA, using more current pedagogical and technological approaches — that is, use of simulation, specifically with virtual reality (VR), to teach this clinical skill.

Why Virtual Reality

Simulation is a learning technique applied across many disciplines that provides immersive experiences and aims to supplement realistic situations (Gaba 2004). Simulation can be used to target specific clinical skills and provide students with opportunities to engage with cases that may be rare and complex in nature (MacBean et al. 2013). Simulation-based learning can facilitate knowledge and skill development in a controlled, safe learning environment. Simulated experiences can be repeated, so students can safely make errors and learn from these experiences before re-attempting tasks with new knowledge (Hewat et al. 2020). Simulation in health education can therefore provide students with life-like scenarios without real-world consequences, without posing risk to patient safety (Gaba 2004).

Simulation techniques range from low- to high-fidelity with examples ranging from written case-based scenarios to use of simulated patients in the form of actors or mannequins, to use of VR at the higher-end of the fidelity scale.

VR offers a uniquely immersive experience, where the 3D visual display utilizes real-world visual stimuli within a simulated world. VR technologies involve computer-generated simulation of a 3D image and/or environment that a person can interact within using electronic devices such as goggles, controllers, sensors, and gloves. They simulate the human experience through use of multisensory feedback options such as auditory, visual, and/or tactile feedback. VR also allows individuals to step into someone else's shoes, through a perceptual illusion called embodiment, so users can feel empathy via a way of feeling someone else's experience.

There are known pros and cons to the use of VR, particularly when being used in an educational setting. The pros are that this type of technology is new, it is exciting, and it is innovative and fun. It is also highly visual and highly immersive, and it allows for teaching of skills that can be repeated in a safe environment for students. The cons around VR use relate to cost and accessibility, and there is potential for motion or cyber sickness. Technology hardware and software need to be reliable as well as maintained and updated.

Use of VR within the field of speech pathology is a fairly recent phenomenon and is a novel area, particularly in relation to student education. A review conducted by Bryant and colleagues (2020) aimed to explore current research using VR in speech pathology. VR has been used in several health care fields including physiotherapy and psychology and mostly for rehabilitation interventions. Education, psychiatry, and speech pathology have also utilized VR as an intervention tool for social skills training in people with autism. In terms of application of VR in speech pathology, most of the research has reported its use for language intervention in people with aphasia.

There is a real paucity of research on using VR as a teaching tool to teach a specific clinical skill in speech pathology, however, use of VR in tertiary education is a growing area that can overcome pedagogical limitations including those related to ethics, funding, and logistics. It has been used as a teaching tool for this purpose in other health areas, including with medical students to teach them how to take a case history, in nursing to teach interprofessional communication skills, and there is emerging research in dentistry taking place at the UON where VR is being used to teach students how and where to accurately administer anesthesia in people's mouths.

In speech pathology, use of simulated placement experiences is an emerging area and has largely involved use of role plays and simulated patients to date. Exploration of fully immersive VR experiences in SP education is limited; most of the research focuses on virtual learning environments to develop general communication and rapport building skills rather than specific clinically based skills.

As learning to conduct an OMA on a child patient is a fundamental clinical skill there was potential that given the complex and multifaceted nature of this assessment, a high-fidelity approach like VR could be an effective way to present this student learning.

The Opportunity

In 2019, the authors were awarded Digital Simulation Technology Evaluation Pilot STEP1 (internal UON) funding to support the development of an innovative teaching technology utilizing VR, to address the shortcomings of traditional teaching in relation to an OMA. The purpose behind the funding was to acknowledge the UON's dedication to implementing technology into curriculum as it is the way of the future in higher education. The STEP1 steering committee acknowledged utilization of these technologies requires significant, sustained investment, and this funding aimed to develop and implement digital simulation teaching tools using VR for identified appropriate projects with well-defined teaching and learning objectives. The OMA project was one of only a small handful of projects funded by the UON at the time, and it was the only project to utilize the funding to support development of the teaching technology by an external stakeholder. The VR application was therefore designed and developed in collaboration with external industry partner Start Beyond, as a teaching and learning resource to teach a specific clinical assessment skill to students.

By using VR digital simulation technology in this area, educators hoped to improve the teaching content and clinical skill of administration and interpretation of pediatric OMAs by:

- Allowing students to more realistically engage with a complex clinical procedural task compared with traditional teaching methods. An OMA is a procedure involving a number of tasks that need to be carried out to make up the total assessment. Students would be able to train for this assessment prior to administration on a real child.

- Providing an opportunity for students to practice administration of an OMA on a simulated pediatric client in a consistent and standardized manner that can be repeated for skill acquisition.
- Providing experience with pediatric oral cavity anatomy and potential variations related to structure and function.
- Enabling students to make comparisons more realistically between adult and pediatric oral cavity anatomy.
- Facilitating clinical placement readiness for students prior to undertaking their first pediatric clinical placement.
- Ensuring all graduates have the same experience in relation to pediatric OMA administration and interpretation, thereby standardizing the learning process.

The End Product: Virtual Reality Oral Musculature Assessment

The end product of VOMA was an immersive learning experience delivered on Meta's Quest VR headsets. It combined 360° and 180° video with interactive design, allowing the user to select two different experiences. Students could choose to either conduct an OMA on a 4-year-old boy, "Hendrix," or a 6-year-old girl, "Ciara." Student users were able to select different stages of the OMA and see from a first-person point of view, that is, the perspective of the speech pathologist conducting the assessment, the child's response to the specific OMA requests, as well as see inside the child's mouth.

VOMA was initially implemented in the SPTH2080 professional practice course in one of the students' weekly tutorials with around twenty students in the tutorial. Students were provided with a Quick Access Guide orientating them to the VR headset and controller with instructions on hardware setup, starting the application and navigating within the application. Health and safety issues were highlighted including use of a hygiene mask under the headset and what to do if the student felt nauseous or dizzy at any time throughout the experience. Following this orientation, students put on the headsets and immersed in the VOMA experience. Students were instructed to undertake the OMA with Ciara first. Following all students completing the first OMA there was a break from the VR experience and a quick debrief provided by the tutor(s) as to what they had just experienced. Typically, students were "buzzing" and amazed at the clarity and the complete immersion of the experience. Then the students went back into VOMA to undertake the OMA with Hendrix with direction around recognizing the similarities and differences in conducting OMAs on children of different ages.

Figure 1: View of the Virtual Clinic Room and Menu Options Available Once Inside VOMA

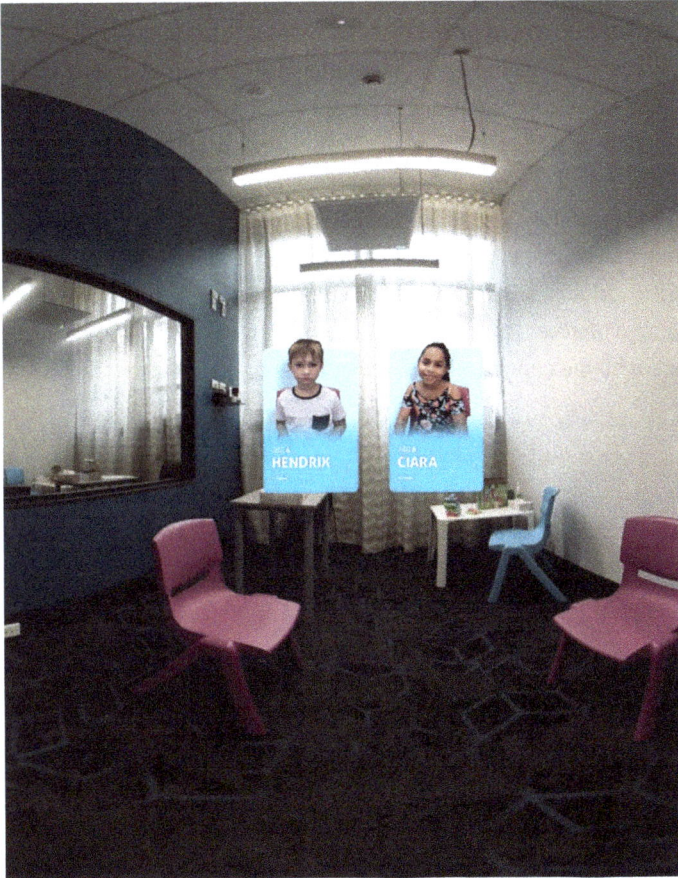

Early Outcomes and Impact

Ongoing Collaboration and Development of VOMA: Module 2

The successful implementation of VOMA and positive feedback on its use from students and practice educators led to ongoing discussion with Start Beyond to continue working together to develop VOMA. The initial VOMA application was designed to teach students the procedural aspects of conduct of an OMA, but not the anatomical variations a child could present during an OMA. Therefore, a second phase of VOMA was considered essential to develop which would allow students the opportunity to experience what anatomical variations a child could present with during an OMA. The extension to VOMA built on the initial content and extended the delivery platforms. When considering which anatomical variations children would be the most likely to present with in clinical practice, we surveyed speech pathologists internationally (Walters et al. 2024). The three prominent anatomical variations reported by clinicians were tongue tie, high narrow palate, and enlarged tonsils. These were used to build the content of VOMA (module 2). With each of these sections the user can engage with an interactive 3D model illustrating the specific features of the examples as well as supporting video, imagery, and audio. This immersive learning experience within VOMA is available across mobile, desktop as well as VR, thereby providing a greater range of access points for learners of all types (students, clinicians, etc.) to engage with the content.

Figure 2: Students at the UON Using VOMA in a Learning Environment (Tutorial)

Commercialization Opportunities and Collaborative Research Opportunities

Recently, our industry partner, Start Beyond, has realized the potential commercial value of this teaching tool and have made negotiations with education facilities internationally. Some of these education organizations have also expressed interest in collaboration in relation opportunities with the research team around research projects using VOMA. Potential collaborative research could involve projects investigating things like student satisfaction, student competence, and student confidence, as well as outcomes of traditional versus nontraditional pedagogies.

Nontraditional Research Outputs

Traditionally, research reporting has recognized outputs in the form of journal publications and the impact of these publications on individuals, communities, organizations, and governments including policies and procedures. However, increasingly, research has expanded beyond publications to include a range of other outputs such as software applications, licenses and patents, performances, architecture, and exhibitions. These outputs are known as "nontraditional research outputs" (NTROs). VOMA as a software application, and therefore an NTRO, has far-reaching impacts on the way teaching is delivered and students learn.

The Overall Experience

UON Researcher Perspectives

Our journey into the world of teaching and learning pedagogy, VR, industry partners, software application development and implementation, NTROs, impact, an end product with commercialization potential, has been incredibly complex, challenging and rewarding.

It has been incredibly rewarding to have worked so closely with our industry partner Start Beyond who were able to take our initial ideas around OMAs and possibly use VR as a teaching tool and develop an application that met our students' learning needs. Angus Stevens (CEO) came into the collaboration with the ability to take an initial, undeveloped idea, understand it, and introduce us to the technology of VR. His knowledge, experience, and ability to explain and simplify technology allowed us as a team to work collaboratively, achieving all we had envisaged and more. Josef Heks (head of capture and postproduction) from Start Beyond became our trusted film-making partner as he easily worked with us as academics, our speech pathology students, and the children from our clinic.

Challenges predominately were around sourcing and securing funding to support the project, and our time to commit to the project. Initially, we were fortunate to gain UON grant funding, however, to continue the development of VOMA (module 2), we had to be creative and innovative in our search for suitable funding opportunities through ad-hoc support from our college and targeted equipment grants through the school. Gaining the support of Knowledge Exchange and Enterprise (KEE) was instrumental in sourcing appropriate funding (through the Australian Government) for our industry partner, allowing them to continue on with the development of VOMA. Negotiating the space of intellectual property, patents, and commercialization was initially confronting however with support from KEE we developed our own understanding and knowledge of these areas. Finally, as early/mid-career researchers, sourcing support and navigating various university systems was at times, challenging, and time-consuming and at times we would have appreciated more guidance in this area. However, universities working with industry partners are a dynamic space, and it can be difficult for universities to keep up with the intricacies and complexities of working with nonuniversity organizations.

Industry (Start Beyond) Partner Perspectives

Q. What made you consider working with the University of Newcastle on this project?

A. Through my experience with different educators, it has been brought to my attention that the University of Newcastle has a reputation for being an organization that is proactive in seeking out new ways of learning, that also has a dynamic educational ethos. Start Beyond is Australia's leading VR and AR immersive learning studio. So, it felt like a great collaborative opportunity for two like-minded organizations to build a brilliant innovative VR experience that transports students out of the classroom and into a complex real-world situation.

Q. What have you enjoyed most about working on this project?

A. From a content development and execution perspective, working with Rachael Unicomb and Joanne Walters (Speech Pathology, UON) has been enjoyable and rewarding. Their knowledge and passion for the subject matter, as well as the rich understanding of both their curriculum, and how the students respond to the teaching material, has made the process a really positive and successful collaboration. Outside of the content development and alongside the Speech Pathology team, the support of Murielle Kluge (strategy and research coordinator, STEP1; Centre of Advanced Training Systems, UON) in the initial stages of the VR deployment, as well as more recently Danielle Neale (director, Knowledge Exchange and Enterprise [KEE], UON) in other facets of the project has also been really enjoyable, but they could never eclipse the heart and soul of VOMA which the intellect and insights of Joanne and Rachael.

Q. What have been some of the challenges you have encountered working on this project/with the University?
A. The primary challenges have come from understanding some of the processes of the university itself especially in relation to the commercialization of VOMA and the ability to extend this offering as an immersive learning experience beyond the university, worldwide. Thankfully, through persistence and support with different folks at the University of Newcastle, we have been able to work through these challenges and are now in a really strong position to take this project and offer it as a world-leading immersive learning experience to organizations around the globe. This will not only raise the profile of the University of Newcastle, and the brilliant work of Rachael Unicomb and Joanne Walters, but will also provide the university with additional revenue.

Acknowledgments

The authors would like to acknowledge the Knowledge Exchange and Enterprise (KEE) and Simulation Technology Evaluation Pilot Program (STEP1) teams at the UON for their valuable input and support at various points throughout the VOMA project. We would also like to acknowledge the funding support provided to our wider research team from the University of Newcastle (university, school, and college levels), and the Australian Government (Innovations Connections grant).

REFERENCES

ASHA (American Speech-Language-Hearing Association). 2022. *Orofacial Myofunctional Disorders*. ASHA. https://www.asha.org/practice-portal/clinical-topics/orofacial-myofunctional-disorders/#collapse_5.

Bryant, L., M. Brunner, and B. Hemsley. 2020. "A Review of Virtual Reality Technologies in the Field of Communication Disability: Implications for Practice and Research." *Disability and Rehabilitation: Assistive Technology* 15 (4): 365–372. https://doi.org/10.1080/17483107.2018.1549276.

Gaba, D. M. 2004. "The Future Vision of Simulation in Health Care." *BMJ Quality & Safety* 13 (suppl. 1): i2–i10. https://doi.org/10.1136/qshc.2004.009878.

Hewat, S., A. Penman, B. Davidson, et al. 2020. "A Framework to Support the Development of Quality Simulation-Based Learning Programmes in Speech-Language Pathology." *International Journal of Language & Communication Disorders* 55 (2): 287–300. https://doi.org/10.1111/1460-6984.12515.

MacBean, N., D. Theodoros, B. Davidson, and A. E. Hill. 2013. "Simulated Learning Environments in Speech-Language Pathology: An Australian Response." *International Journal of Speech-Language Pathology* 15 (3): 345–357. https://doi.org/10.3109/17549507.2013.779024.

McLeod, S., and E. Baker. 2016. *Children's Speech: An Evidence-Based Approach to Assessment and Intervention.* Pearson Education.

Walters, J., R. Unicomb, and T. Wenger. 2024. "Anatomical and Structural Variations Observed by Speech-Language Pathologists in an Oral Musculature Assessment Conducted on Children Suspected of Having a Speech Sound Disorder (SSD)." [Manuscript in Preparation].

CHAPTER 12

Visual Territories: Perspectives on Domain Knowledge Acquisition in Design for Health

Ralph Kenke and Ari Chand

Introduction

Designers often find it difficult to articulate domain-specific knowledge acquired over years of practice — the embodied design lexicography linked to tacit knowledge and visual knowledge acquired in practice. In an increasingly mediated world, visual communication design is a substantial form of global and local communication into the twenty-first century. This chapter outlines the role of "visual territories" as an identifiable frame of reference for the investigation of associated or linked aesthetics within visual identities for health. It explores notions of resonance, perceptual and cognitive mechanisms, and recognition and misrecognition. Domain knowledge and expertise in the negotiation or presentation of a "visual territory" influence the way in which visual communication design emerges within society. Visual territories are implemented in the early stages of concept development in design studios and branding agencies for more than two decades since Wally Olins, the father of territory branding, invented the cognitive concept to enhance collaboration between creative practitioners. Despite its importance in the design industry to articulate and facilitate the iterative process which supports the visual dialogue between studios and clients, visual territories have mostly been ignored in visual communication design education.

Representing the complex facilitation of designers with clients around interests, expectations, domain knowledge, emotions and aesthetics, subjective perception, and visual design principles and practices. Within the design discipline, there is an identifiable intellectual chasm between design practice and theoretical and research-led practice (Bennet 2006; Chand 2021). A project entitled "Visual Aids for Helicopter Rescue" funded by the University of Newcastle School of Humanities, Creative Industries, and Social Sciences *Rapid* Funding Scheme. This chapter presents design theory framed in a practical case study "Visually Designing for Health" by designer-researchers to showcase the implemented role of creativity in action. It sets out to inform design educators, designers, and students as a case study.

Background

Researchers investigating the notion of visual territories were intrigued by the way groupings of visual communication practices resonated with those who work in health care. That the field of visual iconography and symbolism is historically developed as a strong visual territory. Those working in health care identify with specific visual semiotic language as symbols, indexes, and icons. The project worked with the Hunter Retrieval Service. The Hunter Retrieval Service (HRS), critical care doctors and nurses have been delivering inter-hospital retrieval services to the Hunter region for more than twenty-five years. The Hunter Retrieval Service (HRS) is one of three partners involved in the Westpac Helicopter Rescue Service, providing qualified doctors for rescue operations. The other two partners are Westpac Helicopters—which provides the aircraft and pilots—and NSW Ambulance Service—which provides paramedics. A rescue crew comprises four people: a pilot and co-pilot, a paramedic, and a doctor.

Medical organizations are often underfunded to engage designers or studios in configuring more effective visual aids or a consistent visual identity to interface with the public and public interest. Doctors are often required to try and develop their own nonvisual approaches in quick fix Band-Aid solutions that ignore visual approaches to developing strong visual identities. Our industry partner has identified a key problem that their service was little known within the public domain because it lacked a clear and consistent visual identity.

In working directly with the doctors, key insights from their profession and an ongoing dialogue about design language and design language acquisition, and practices assisted the process of collaboration in developing outcomes. This case study looks at the way visual designers can begin to take up the role of facilitator and researcher (Napier and Wada 2015). In making ideas a tangible thing through visualizing and image-making, Designers are Information mediators: they can organize information and help make it meaningful (Beonhart 2018). Design researchers have called for a more explicit approach to democratizing the learning of design (Augustin and Coleman 2012; Conole and Wills 2013; Cross 2001; Friedman 2000, 2012; Norman 2000; Oxman 2001). While embracing an explicit approach, there remains the need to accommodate the inherently tacit nature of much design knowledge.

Looking at wider integrated design approaches to health, perception, and emergency prehospital response care, this research design uses a practice-based design research approach to "design for health" and develops an insider perspective through design ethnography to identify the key pressure points for the user.

> *The visual communicator can be regarded as a key investigator who uses visual communication systems and approaches in the context of research to stimulate dialogue, elicit opinion and reveal insights. (Gwilt and Williams 2011, 2)*

Researchers used studio-based methods of inquiry to visually test appropriate visual territories and identity design. This project engages design thinking, visual communication, co-design, and iterative prototyping methods alongside documentative studio practices (Nusem et al. 2020). Centralizing visual communication thinking strategies will be core to emphasizing the visual identity responses needed to respond to the key stakeholders requirements.

Visual Territories in Health Domains

Images are the soft power of the twenty-first century and the way we attract, co-opt, and communicate to an audience as visual designers. Designers are constantly operating within domain-specific knowledge and practices inherent to the field and domain of design. Designers operate in reconstituting practices and approaches to working in which they draw from the body(ies) of knowledge within the field. The primary function of this role is that communication designers have to engage in articulating the value proposition and often "*invisible*" processes and practices to a client or project partner.

> *A domain is the symbol system that the person and others working in the area utilises. It is the culture, the sets of conventions, the knowledges the person becomes immersed in. (McIntyre 2007, 5)*

An initial key goal in a client-oriented design project is to establish a visual dialogue within the domain-specific field, as in this case, health and medical emergency. A convenient first step to visualize are charts, or diagrams or even maps. However, such abstractions are, unfortunately, at an early stage, too vague in terms of aesthetic directions and too specific as they can lead to expectations that are incoherent with the domain-specific knowledge that excites already in the field and design.

> *[Maps] have become embedded in society as an unquestioned truth, a reality—they have become the territory. However, the territory, its inhabitants and their behaviours are inevitably more complex than conventional maps illustrate. (Noble and Bestley 2005, 76)*

By accumulating and organizing domain- and design-specific visuals, researchers are able to prevent stagnation during the critical phase of domain-specific knowledge exchange. Such visual territories are made up of both existing and digital or hand-drawn sketches; they are single boards or sheets that aim to capture the core characteristics of a visual language. In essence, visual territory accommodates the written definition of a design brief.

In this project, symbolism and typographical features are part of the essential visual assets that make up a future design proposition. It is partly the researcher's challenge to imagine a visual solution as much as it is to research and find exciting features as an adequate reference to articulate potential alternative concepts for "design for health."

> *While it is theoretically true [that most design problems are unique], it is also misleading since most design problems have features they share in common with others. [Designers] are more able to recognise [these features it seems] through the possible similarity of potential solutions than through some abstract description of the problem. (Lawson 2004, 118)*

The visual territories facilitate a collaborative process that requires basic technical skills but intricate knowledge that enables the deconstruction, analysis, and comparison of graphic features. In a commercial studio, this process offers an economic benefit, while in the educational environment, it is a timesaver where time constraints with large student groups and clients are often limited to an hourly class schedule. This approach enables researchers to guide the HRS doctors in identifying relevant aspects within existing "design for health" implementations and other design elements, such as typography, which are critical to defining the project scope. This iterative process is a negotiation between domain-specific knowledge in health and domain-specific knowledge in design, which contributes to a truly unique visual identity, a framework for HRS communication to appear recognizable within its field.

Negotiating Territories

The visual territories function as a temporary lens toward "design for health" with consideration of the essential requirements to display HRS as a unique entity that is a key partner of the Westpac Helicopter Rescue Service. To accomplish a successful visual identity design, it is critical to respect the significance of the name Hunter Retrieval Service, and its typographical legibility and visual recognition in the health domain. A visual audit (Figure 1) of the current state of the HRS visual identity (HRS jacket, shirt, and vehicle) concluded that the use of graphics and text, and application of color appear cluttered and there are inconsistencies, making HRS difficult to recognize as a group of doctors and nurses that provide medical attention in critical circumstances as a unique service.

Figure 1: Inconsistent Visual System

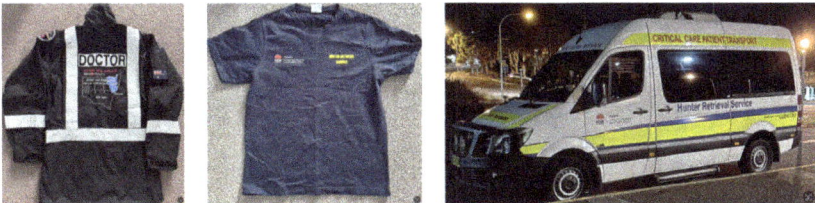

Not only is the team trained to provide critical care, doctors and nurses are proficient in aeromedical operations. HRS expressed that cluttering and inconsistencies do not align well with the team's mission to act and appear calm and professional in high-stress scenarios such as a helicopter rescue mission, for example in remote terrains or the open ocean; therefore, the proposed visual identity required to capture such qualities within its domain. Simultaneously, it was required that its visuals represent a local community service that operates in the Hunter Region in NSW both on the road and in collaboration with the Rescue Helicopter team.

Addressing the essential requirements, such as a logotype with the wording Hunter Retrieval Service on which the visual identity can expand, initiated the development of fifteen visual territories. The HRS team required a recognizable logotype that considered an appropriate tone of voice and attracted its target audience. The overall visual direction needed to represent a visual identity that is Caring, Trustworthy — but Serious and Calm. Visual representations here assist in bridging between the concrete and abstract (Ewenstein 2009).

All visual territories (Figure 2) with their foundational typographic references indicate multiple drafts, and images that drive the ideation process toward a visual identity that carries a logotype as its core graphic communicating qualities such as Caring, Trustworthy but Serious and Calm in relation to health rescue operations.

Figure 2: Results from HRS Survey

How would you describe the current state of the Hunter Retrieval Service branding/visual identity?
12 responses

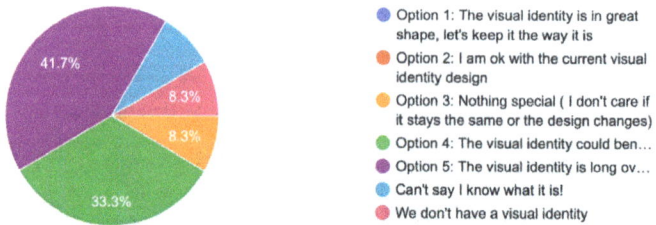

- Option 1: The visual identity is in great shape, let's keep it the way it is
- Option 2: I am ok with the current visual identity design
- Option 3: Nothing special (I don't care if it stays the same or the design changes)
- Option 4: The visual identity could ben...
- Option 5: The visual identity is long ov...
- Can't say I know what it is!
- We don't have a visual identity

In addition, HRS conducted an internal questionnaire to seek advice from their colleagues and as understanded their attachment to their current visual identity. Two key outcomes were found in this qualitative outcome. First, there was very little visual recognition with the current visual elements as stated by HRS staff. "Jackets and branding is inconsistent, too many varying elements" and "Lack of unifying logo."

And second, HRS staff indicated that HRS should have a more unified visual identity that appears of high quality. The issue with the name and its connotation as well as its lack of symbolism was raised multiple times by HRS team members. Staff expressed, "the name is correct but confusing. Hunter has multiple implications. Retrieval is a very strange word but we don't have a better one. No symbol or interesting font." One response captured the complexity of the design challenges ahead in detail, providing an example of the real-life impact a visual identity can make on the care of a patient: "The concept of 'retrieval' isn't understood by our community. I guess a visual identity should elicit an appropriate recognition response of service provision, i.e. if you see our vehicle, the community should have awareness there is a very sick person on board to ensure road consideration and urgency or transit."

The HRS team indicated in their last survey question a clear interest in progressing with a contemporary design for their visual identity (not a single team member wanted to keep the current designs according to the responses, see chart in Figure 2).

Interesting suggestions that later influenced the decision-making narrowing down the visual territories were made, too; for example, to the question, What should a symbol look like? one response was, "I feel like its closest to RED CROSS — saving lives, care," and to the question, Is there anything that bothers you about the Hunter Retrieval Service visual identity? a perspective shifting statement was made: "HRS is related directly to the helicopter but it's so much more than that it includes the HRS van, women and men, nurses, doctors and paramedics and transport drivers."

With the HRS responses and the base information that determined the requirements of the brief, the design researcher and students were accumulating visual references and making sketches that align with the proposed qualities and their aesthetics.

All visual territories (Figure 2) with their foundational typographic references indicate multiple drafts, and images that drive the ideation process toward a visual identity that carries a logotype as its core graphic communicating qualities such as Caring, Trustworthy but Serious and Calm in relation to health rescue operations.

Alongside the designers' ability to research visual material and forms of cultural capital as defining visual territories for the design process, the question around the notion of design fixation as problematic occurs. Design fixation can be defined as follows:

> The term 'design fixation' is ofteEn used to refer to this broad set of phenomena, or is used more narrowly to refer to the way in which designers inadvertently carry over specific and unhelpful features from a previous example when they are designing something new. (Crilly 2015)

Figure 3: Developed Visual Territories

Crilly offers a comprehensive overview of design fixation and its pervasive nature (2015, 2017), with key observations in design research, noting its limiting cognitive role in the ability to produce a range of creative ideas (Agogué et al. 2014).

Some of the methods of visual research and making employed included found material, mind mapping, thumbnailing, sketching, photography, sketch-noting, visual analysis, mood boarding, and prototyping. Designers engage design practices as an instrument for the transformation of the artificial world (Clark and Brody 2009; Crouch and Pearce 2012; Roxburgh 2013; Simon 1969). The use of the visual territories enables researchers to explore a wide range of different graphics, designs fonts, as well as combinations of symbols integrated in words or letters. Its details within existing letter forms that can inspire unusual new combinations of a given name such as HRS that can lead to a visual identity that represents the desired quality when "visually designing for health."

Importantly, a critical documentative approach to visual material as data was taken (Sadokierski 2020), in which visual work as data doesn't need to be represented visually, rather as a documentative part of practice-based research. Crouch notes, "it is a fallacy to think that because data was collected visually (either through drawing or by cameras) it has to be presented visually" (Crouch and Pearce 2012, 333). At this early stage of the design process, the visual territories enable the expansion of ideas, while simulations help to maintain a dialogue with the client. It is important to note that at this stage, no definite designs are established, which is critical to define common expectations for both the design researcher and the client to agree on artistic directions. Visual territories play a diplomatic role in the negotiations of aesthetics as the visual identity influences the conversation around domain knowledge and shapes the future of the HRS brand and its visual communication assets.

> *Art directors search for ownable visual elements that are recognisable and unique within the competitive space. Art directors require examples of previous brand advertising and visual mandatories to start ideation, both to bolster personal creativity and to understand a client's visual preferences. (Phillips 2014)*

Figure 4: Client Meeting with Fledgling Designers

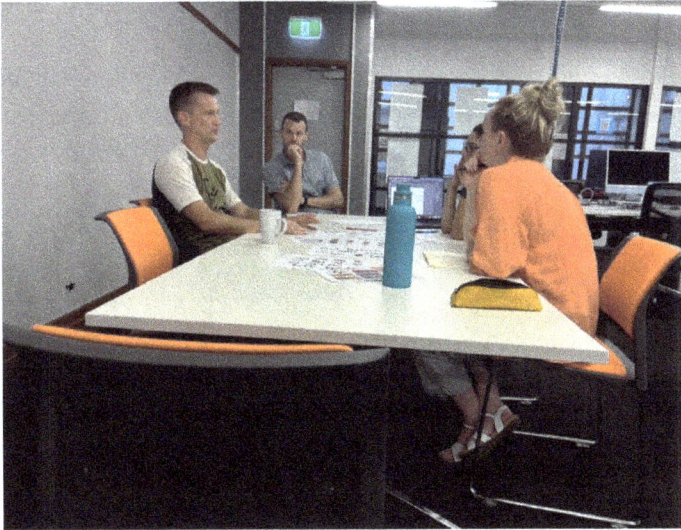

While such practice is common in commercial studio and client-oriented processes, the implementation of visual territories in design education is less common, partly because education institutions tend to apply text instructions, which often lean toward a linear approach due to the linearity of writing, but also due to the complexity such a multiplication factor of visual ideas can cause in the context of a school or university class environment.

Traditionally, design processes are illustrated as linear processes or at least processes that make progress towards an optimum through trial and error, as the notion of iteration suggested. (Lotz 2008)

While iteration takes place with the implementation of visual territories during the design process of visual identities, it is more like a vehicle that enables the exploration of multiple visual solutions simultaneously, expanding the ideation process with some graphics indicating greater promises than others. The visual territories can also cross-correlate features as they progress into visual identities. It exhausts the potential variation that could lead to a successful design outcome. In a way, designers do not necessarily follow a traditional problem-solving approach. Instead, they generate multiple visual challenges that question the linear solution process. By exploring the inherent clues within the visual components of a client's name (Hunter Retrieval Service), designers aim to uncover an overarching concept that serves as a core representation of the identity. The territories drive a visual investigation of associated aesthetics within the various visual identity propositions while aligning their graphic elements to the regional health sector and its global competitors.

In the case of the HRS designs, multiple design student teams explored and refined the visual territories through critical choice-making. Arranged client meetings enabled students to receive feedback and make informative decisions to create coherent results that could meet the expectations of designers and HRS doctors. Apart from enabling designers and clients to discuss and analyze their commonalities and differences concerning the proposed visual identities, the individual visual territories enable students to form groups based on a visually recognizable concept instead of a purely written design brief. The advantage of such an approach is that it allows students to identify their commonality and address challenges at the beginning of a design project to develop a collaborative learning environment.

"Brief" Options Narrowed to…

Design students developed critical design skills, negotiating a distinctive visual direction with the support of visual territories. The physicality of presenting rough design concepts, and implementing client feedback during their iterative process, revealed to most students a surprisingly different visual aesthetic than most expected at the beginning stage of the project.

Figure 5: Mock-ups for HRS

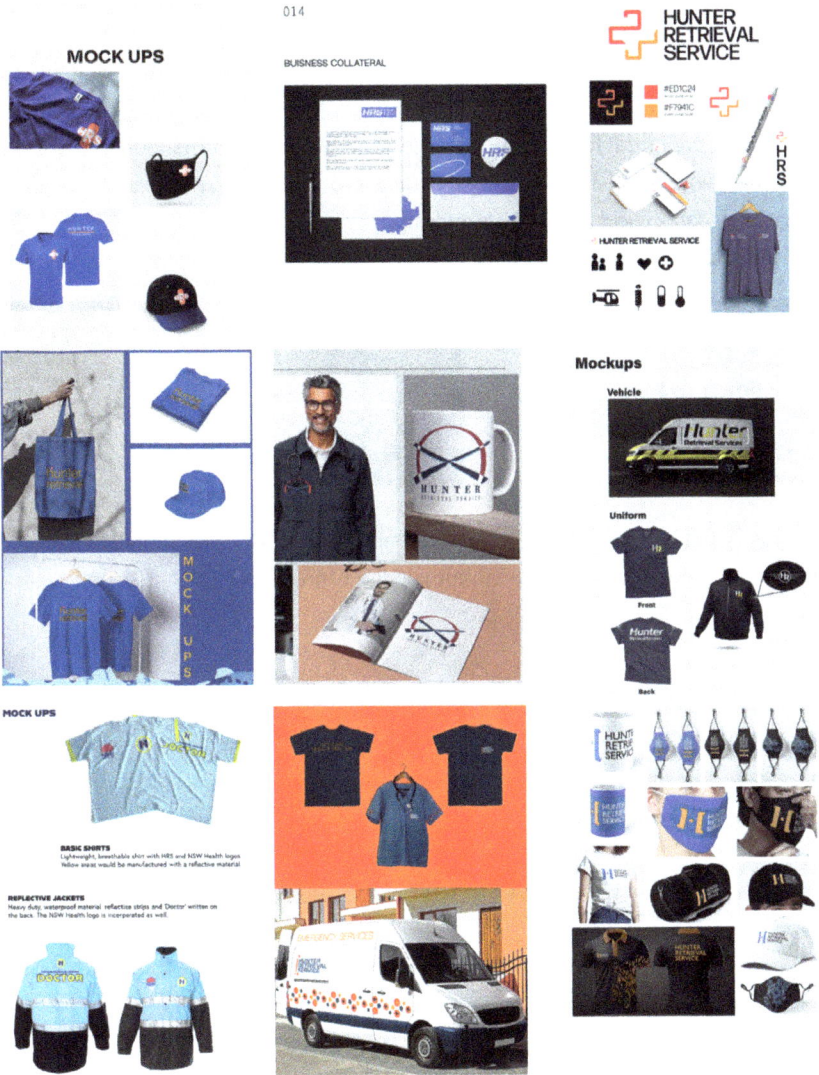

Equally surprising to students was the broad feedback they received during their client meetings; while their visuals, overall, had resonated positively with the HRS team, the more detailed feedback did not provide instructions to alternate graphic elements or make typographical amendments but rather resulted in raising new questions, such as, What signifies that HRS is a medical emergency entity?

What makes a logotype appear Calm and Trustworthy while linking its quality to a team of doctors that respond fast and professionally in case of an emergency?

This dialogue provided critical information that enabled design students to make crucial changes and even eliminate some of the visual territories altogether, narrowing the initial fifteen visual territories down to nine visual identities — all presented with mock-ups that provide context to enable the HRS team to imagine what they can expect from a future design.

The HRS team narrowed down...

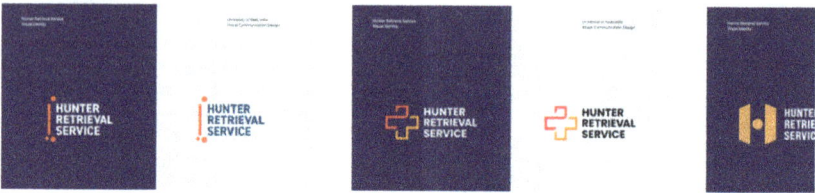

This is linked to the practice-oriented nature of design, operating in a realm where tacit and nonpropositional knowledge is preferred.

Conclusion

Understanding the inner design lexicon is challenging for those unfamiliar with the implicit and iterative design processes. This chapter presented a case study exploring visual territories in health design as a framework for acquiring and applying domain-specific knowledge, bridging gaps between designers, clients, and collaborators.

This approach enhances designer–client consultations by structuring expectations and serves as a critical educational tool. It enables students to navigate complexities in real-world challenges, balancing technical skills, aesthetics, and domain demands through iterative development and refinement.

Visual territories facilitated collaboration for the Hunter Retrieval Service, addressing challenges to create a unified visual identity that embodied trust, care, and professionalism. This process emphasized iteration, adaptability, and the reciprocal relationship between design and its context, fostering creative problem-solving.

Visual territories serve as an integrative tool, supporting both practical and conceptual dimensions of design. They empower designers to articulate their creative processes effectively, bridging theory and practice. This study highlights their potential for broader application, particularly in health-focused design, contributing to design discourse and advancing its role in addressing specific domain needs.

Acknowledgment

We would like to acknowledge the HRS team who generously contributed their time and insights into the process.

REFERENCES

Agogué, Marine, Nicolas Poirel, Arlette Pineau, Olivier Houdé, and Mathieu Cassotti. 2014. "The Impact of Age and Training on Creativity: A Design-Theory Approach to Study Fixation Effects." *Thinking Skills and Creativity* 11: 33–41. https://www.sciencedirect.com/science/article/pii/S1871187113000710.

Augustin, Sally, and Cindy Coleman. 2012. *The Designer's Guide to Doing Research: Applying Knowledge to Inform Design.* John Wiley & Sons.

Bennett, A. 2006. "The Rise of Research in Graphic Design." In *Design Studies Theory and Research in Graphic Design*, edited by Audrey Bennett. Princeton.

Brenner, Andrea. 2005. "Collaborative Insight: Fostering Communication Between Designers and Their Clients." *Critical and Creative Thinking Capstones Collection* 31, Master of Arts project, University of Massachusetts.

Buswell, G. T. 1935. *How People Look at Pictures: A Study of the Psychology and Perception in Art*. University of Chicago Press.

Chand, A. 2021. "Developing a Designerly Way of Being, or at Least Trying." In *The Elephant's Leg: Adventures in the Creative Industries*. Common Ground.

Clark, H., and D. Brody. 2009. *Design Studies: A Reader*. Berg.

Conole, G., and S. Wills. 2013. "Representing Learning Designs: Making Design Explicit and Shareable." ro.uow.edu.au/cgi/viewcontent.cgi?article=1407&context=asdpapers.

Crilly, N. 2015. "Fixation and Creativity in Concept Development: The Attitudes and Practices of Expert Designers." *Design Studies* 38: 54–91.

Cross, Nigel. 2001. "Designerly Ways of Knowing: Design Discipline Versus Design Science." *Design Issues* 17 (3): 49–55.

Crouch, C., and J. Pearce. 2012. *Doing Research in Design*. Berg.

Friedman, K. 2000. "Creating Design Knowledge: From Research into Practice." Presented at the IDATER 2000 Conference, Loughborough University.

Friedman, K. 2012. "Models of Design: Envisioning a Future Design Education." www.swinburne.edu.au/health-arts-design/resources/design/Friedman-Models-of-Design-Envisioning-a-Future-Design-Education.pdf.

Gwilt, I. D., and J. Williams. 2011. "Framing Futures for Visual Communication Design Research." *Design Principles and Practices: An International Journal* 5 (5): 81–98.

Haslem, N. 2011. "Not an Academic Type: What Do Communication Designers Know About Research?" *Iridescent* 1 (1): 178–191.

Holsanova, J. 2014. "14 in the Eye of the Beholder: Visual Communication from a Recipient Perspective." In *Visual Communication*, edited by David Machin. De Gruyter.

Kellehear, A. 1993. *The Unobtrusive Researcher: A Guide to Methods*. Allen & Unwin.

Kelly, V. 2014. "Metaphors of Resonance for Visual Communication Design." *Visual Communication* 13 (2): 211–230.

Kress, G., and T. Van Leeuwen. 2020. *Reading Images: The Grammar of Visual Design*. Routledge.

Lawson, B. 2004. *What Designers Know*. Architectural Press.

Lawson, B. 2012. *What Designers Know*. Routledge.

Lotz, Katrine. 2008. "Architectors: Specific Architectural Competencies." PhD diss., Royal Danish Academy of Fine Arts, School of Architecture.

Louridas, P. 1999. "Design as Bricolage: Anthropology Meets Design Thinking." *Design Studies* 20 (6): 517–535.

McIntyre, P. 2007. "Rethinking Creative Practice in the Light of Mihaly Csikszentmihalyi's Systems Model of Creativity." Presented at the 3rd Global Conference on Creative Engagements — Thinking with Children, Sidney, February 9–11, 2007.

McIntyre, P., and S. Coffee. 2016. "The Arts and Design: From Romantic Doxa to Rational Systems of Creative Practice." In *The Creative System in Action: Understanding Cultural Production and Practice*, edited by P. McIntyre, J. Fulton, and E. Paton. Palgrave Macmillan.

Medley, S. 2012. *The Picture in Design: What Graphic Designers, Art Directors and Illustrators Should Know About Communicating with Pictures*. Common Ground Publishing.

Napier, P., and T. Wada. 2015. "Co-Designing for Healthcare: Visual Designers as Researchers and Facilitators." *Visible Language* 49 (1): 129–143.

Noble, Ian, and Russell Bestley. 2005. *Visual Research: An Introduction to Research Methodologies in Graphic Design*. AVA Publishing.

Norman, J. 2000. "Design as a Framework for Innovative Thinking and Learning: How Can Design Thinking Reform Education?" In *Proceedings of the IDATER Design and Technology Educational Research and Curriculum Development: The Emerging International Research Agenda*, edited by E. W. L. Norman and P. H. Roberts. Department of Design and Technology, Loughborough University.

Nusem, E., K. Straker, and C. Wrigley. 2020. *Design Innovation for Health and Medicine*. Palgrave Macmillan.

Oxman, R. 2001. "The Mind in Design: A Conceptual Framework for Cognition in Design Education." In *Design Knowing and Learning: Cognition in*

Design Education, edited by C. Eastman, M. McCracken, and W. Newstetter. Elsevier.

Phillips, Barbara J., Edward F. McQuarrie, and W. Glenn Griffin. 2014. "The Face of the Brand: How Art Directors Understand Visual Brand Identity." *Journal of Advertising* 43 (4): 318–332.

Roxburgh, M. 2013. "The Images of the Artificial or Why Everything Looks the Same." *International Journal of the Image* 3 (3): 1–16.

Roxburgh, M., and E. Caratti. 2014. "The Experience and Design of Stereotype." In *What's on: Cumulus Spring Conference, Aveiro 2014, 8–10 May, Portugal, On-Line Proceedings*, edited by Teresa Franqueira and João Sampaio. University of Aveiro.

Roxburgh, M., and J. Irvin. 2018. "The Future of Visual Communication Design Is Almost Invisible or Why Skills in Visual Aesthetics Are Important to Service Design." Presented at the Proceedings of the Service Design Proof of Concept Conference (ServDes2018), Milano, Italy, June 18–20, 2018.

Sadokierski, Z. 2020. "Developing Critical Documentation Practices for Design Researchers." *Design Studies* 69: 100940.

Schon, D. A. 1983. *The Reflective Practitioner: How Professionals Think in Action*. Basic Books.

Simon, Herbert A. 1969. *The Sciences of the Artificial*. MIT Press.

CHAPTER 13

A Transformative Journey: Exploring Rhythmic Acknowledgment and Collaboration in the Sydney Symphony Orchestra at the Sydney Opera House

Adam Manning and Ray Kelly

Abstract

This chapter delves into the transformative journey undertaken by musician and researcher Adam Manning in collaboration with the Sydney Symphony Orchestra (SSO) at the Sydney Opera House. The focus is on the creation of the inaugural SSO Rhythmic Acknowledgment, a unique musical and cultural endeavor that bridges diverse voices and celebrates Australia's First Nations heritage. Manning's introspective reflections, coupled with the insights of First Nations cultural leader Uncle Ray Kelly, highlight the profound impact of rhythm in fostering cross-cultural understanding. The chapter chronicles the rehearsal process, detailing collaborative discussions that led to adjustments in the musical arrangement. The culmination of this journey is showcased through successful performances, resonating with audiences and reviewers alike. The significance of this event lies in its role as a blueprint for future endeavors promoting diversity, cultural heritage, and meaningful dialogue. Ultimately, this chapter underscores the transformative potential of art, particularly music, in promoting unity, empathy, and the appreciation of cultural richness.

Introduction

In this chapter, we delve into the experiential journey of Adam Manning, a musician and researcher, as he embarks on a brand-new endeavor with the renowned

Sydney Symphony Orchestra (SSO). Together, they set out to create the inaugural Rhythmic Acknowledgment—at the iconic Sydney Opera House. Through Manning's introspective reflections on rehearsals and performances, the reader will gain insights into the harmonious fusion of music, culture, and collaboration.

Woven into the narrative are the invaluable perspectives of First Nations cultural leader Uncle Ray Kelly, whose profound wisdom, and guidance have played a pivotal role in the SSO Rhythmic Acknowledgment. The chapter also provides a glimpse into the experiences and contributions of SSO percussionists, who have been instrumental in shaping this transformational journey.

Further, this chapter witnesses the remarkable power of rhythm. Its inherent ability to bridge divides, harmonize diverse voices, and reverently celebrate the profound cultural heritage of Australia's First Nations peoples unfolds before us. This musical odyssey stands as a testament to the enduring potential of art in fostering intercultural understanding.

Figure 1: A Collection of Clapsticks That Manning Made for SSO Percussionists and Brass Players to Use During the Rhythmic Acknowledgment at the Opera House

Source: Authors

Understanding Acknowledgment of Country

Before exploring the concept of rhythmic acknowledgment, it is essential to grasp the significance of an Acknowledgment of Country. This act, at the beginning of a gathering involves recognizing and honoring the traditional custodians and their enduring connection to the land through deep listening. By doing so, it pays respect to Indigenous cultures that have thrived on these lands for thousands of years, acknowledging their wisdom, resilience, and ongoing contributions to society (Manning 2023). The Acknowledgment of Country invites us to embrace the rich cultural heritage and deepen our understanding of the history and traditions of First Nations peoples (Reconciliation Australia website, as of July 20, 2023).

Expanding on this perspective, we argue that a Rhythmic Acknowledgment emerges as a powerful means of honoring the cultural significance of rhythm. In music, rhythm serves as a fundamental element through changing durations (Arom 1991). Further, contemporary rhythmic authors (Cheyne et al. 2019) suggest rhythm is based on movement; yet it provides structure and coherence to musical compositions, enabling listeners to perceive the underlying pulse and fostering a sense of musical togetherness (Doffman 2013). Interestingly, through the Rhythmic Acknowledgment, the listener either discovers or infers rhythmic patterns forging connections beyond words and cultural boundaries.

At the Opera House, for the first-ever performed Rhythmic Acknowledgment, the SSO incorporated the Sydney Basin rhythm titled "Harry's Song" or the "Gumberry Jah Song" (The University of Sydney 2022). Such rhythms, combined with personal ancestral rhythmic reflections from both Indigenous and non-Indigenous performers, create a shared experience of empathy and collaboration, becoming a catalyst for reconciliation. This nonverbal, inclusive platform allows individuals from all backgrounds and identities to connect, communicate, and find common ground.

Hence, a rhythmic recognition stands as a sonic acknowledgment. In this process, a cultural figure like Manning or Uncle Ray gathers a collective of Indigenous or non-Indigenous musicians. Their purpose is to rediscover the cadences of First Nations while blending them with personal ancestral contemplations, all conveyed through the language of rhythm, or as Bourdieu suggests, the sharing of one's cultural capital (Bourdieu 1993). Further, it is important to underline that a rhythmic Acknowledgment does not seek to supplant a verbal acknowledgment. Rather, it extends a chance, especially to musicians in this context, to forge a sonic bond with the land.

This moment holds significant importance for the SSO, as it marks their in-augural performance of a sonic acknowledgment that is based on rhythm. The SSO, renowned for its classical repertoire and orchestral prowess, ventures into a realm that embraces the cultural mosaic of First Nations rhythms and personal reflections. This step not only showcases their openness to diverse musical ex-pressions but also signifies a meaningful connection with the Indigenous heritage of the land they perform on.

The following on action reflective journal entries shed light on the creative process (Schön 1983). These reflective journal entries give insight into the meaningful interactions between performers, and the rhythmic connections in fostering understanding and unity among diverse communities. As readers delve into the accounts, they will gain a deeper appreciation for the importance of acknowledging and celebrating Indigenous cultures, their knowledge systems, and the vital role of rhythm in this reconciliation journey.

Figure 2: Day 1 Rehearsal Discussions with Manning and Kelly, and SSO Percussionists Regarding the Various Tonal Considerations of Manning Clapsticks

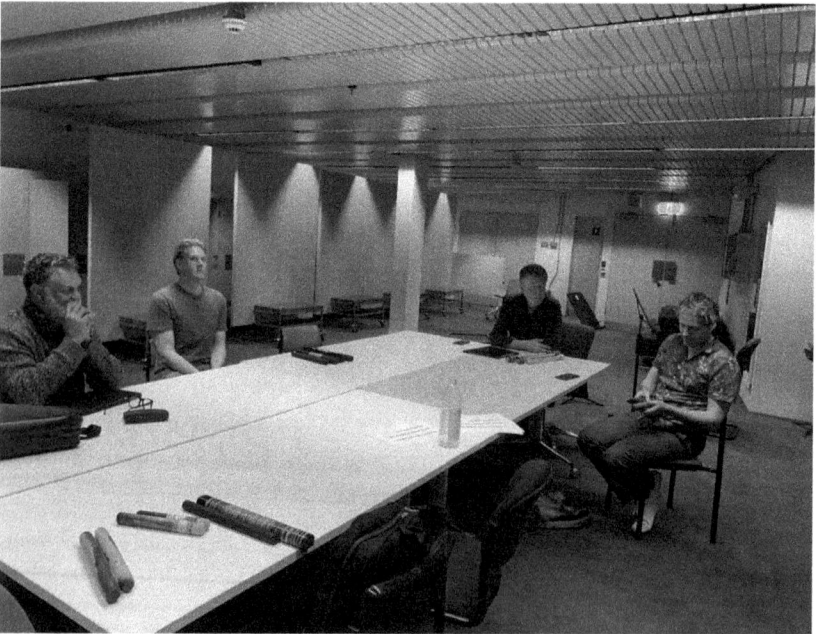

Source: Authors

Day 1 Rehearsal: *Anticipation and Collaboration*

The first day of rehearsals was characterized by anticipation and excitement. Adam Manning, Uncle Ray Kelly, and the Sydney Symphony Percussion Section assembled to explore the Rhythmic Acknowledgment concept. In the rehearsal room, participants engaged in lively discussions, sharing perspectives on how best to honor the traditional custodians of the land through music and storytelling with reference to Manning's draft Rhythmic Acknowledgment document, which was a collection of thoughts and notation.

Throughout the rehearsal discussions, a spirit of collaboration permeated the participants' interactions, as they exchanged ideas and refined the structure and execution of the Rhythmic Acknowledgment. Uncle Ray's wisdom and guidance served as a beacon, illuminating the cultural significance of the rhythms and the transformative power of storytelling. Witnessing Uncle Ray's profound engagement with the group left a lasting impact, with his words resonating deeply and inspiring collective commitment.

Adam Manning: "I felt a sense of unity and purpose in the room as we discussed the Rhythmic Acknowledgment concept, and personally felt in a state of flow (Csikszentmihalyi 1991). Uncle Ray's presence and guidance were invaluable in helping us understand the deeper cultural significance of the rhythms we were working with."

Timothy Constable (SSO Percussionist): "It was a privilege to hear and play the various clapsticks that accompanied Manning to the Opera House." Discussion with the author, July 5, 2023

Day 2 Reflection: *Clarity and Exploration*

The second day of rehearsals brought further clarity and refinement to the Rhythmic Acknowledgment concept, largely due to the notation documentation and Uncle Ray's presence. For example, Uncle Ray Kelly provided invaluable feedback that influenced adjustments to the musical arrangement. His insight and guidance led to a collective decision to eliminate the use of a snare drum, as it conveyed a militaristic quality that contradicted the intended spirit of the performance.

Beyond the musical aspects, the rehearsal provided fertile ground for profound conversations with Uncle Ray. One particularly intriguing topic centered around his ability to express language in a profoundly musical manner. Inspired by this concept, Adam Manning proposed capturing Uncle Ray's language stories through recordings. This exploration of language and rhythm opened new possibilities, envisioning symphonies composed around these recorded words — a harmonious fusion of Indigenous language and Western orchestral traditions. This exploration exemplifies the potential for cultural exchange and cross-pollination, enriching the artistic landscape with diverse influences.

> *Uncle Ray: "Through this collaboration, we are exploring new ways to preserve and share our traditions." Discussion with the author, July 5, 2023*
>
> *July 6, 2023*

Days 3 and 4: Culmination and Fulfillment

The final rehearsals and performances marked the pinnacle of the collaborative journey. The general rehearsal flowed smoothly, enabling participants to refine their performance and deepen their connection with the music and storytelling elements. Marked by focus, dedication, and a profound appreciation for the transformative potential of their collective efforts, these rehearsals were a testament to their unwavering commitment.

> *Melissa King (SSO Artistic Director): "The Rhythmic Acknowledgment was so tight this would not have happened without a clear performance opportunity." Discussion with the author, July 9, 2023*

The concert performances at the Sydney Opera House garnered enthusiastic responses from the audience. The performers felt a deep sense of satisfaction and fulfillment, recognizing the significance of their collaboration and the profound impact it had on both them and the audience. Further, the *Sydney Morning Herald* reviews states, "the Rhythmic Acknowledgement of Country starting with a free, evocative section on sticks, hand-played drums and timpani with the Sydney Symphony percussion section, which then erupted into a faster passage in which SSO brass players (as percussionists) joined in rhythmic exchange" (Herborn et al. 2023).

Performing the first-ever Rhythmic Acknowledgment at the Sydney Opera House holds cultural significance. This historic milestone represents a pivotal step in recognizing and honoring the deep-rooted cultural heritage of Australia's First Nations peoples and their rhythms, breathing life into their ancient traditions on a global stage.

Throughout this transformative journey, the fusion of music, culture, and collaboration with the Sydney Symphony Orchestra has been a testament to the

Figure 3: Manning and Kelly in the Opera House Foyer

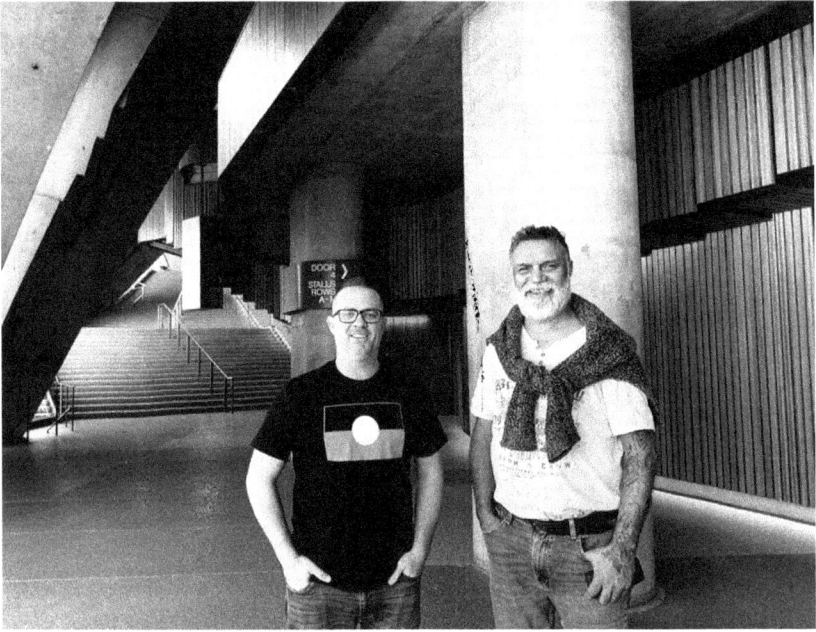

Source: Authors

power of art in fostering reconciliation and cross-cultural understanding. Under the expert guidance of First Nations cultural leader Uncle Ray Kelly, the orchestra and Manning embarked on a profound exploration of rhythm's transformative potential, transcending linguistic barriers.

The Sydney Symphony Orchestra, known for its technical virtuosity, merged its expertise with the ancient rhythms of the Sydney Basin, creating a harmonious tapestry that honored and celebrated the land's traditional custodians. Further, in this creative process, collaboration became an instrument, as the diverse voices of performers from different backgrounds and identities found resonance and common ground through rhythm.

Moving forward, this milestone event serves as an inspiring blueprint for future endeavors that embrace diversity, acknowledge cultural heritage, and facilitate meaningful cross-cultural dialogue (Manning 2019). By continuing to explore and celebrate the significance of rhythm, music, and art in acknowledging and honoring the First Nations peoples, we pave the way for a more inclusive and united society.

Figure 4: Manning and the SSO Percussion and Brass Players Performing a Rhythmic Acknowledgment at the Opera House on the July 9, 2023

Source: SSO

In conclusion, the journey of Rhythmic Acknowledgment and collaboration at the Sydney Opera House will be remembered not only for its musical excellence but also for its profound impact on cultural understanding and reconciliation. It stands as a testament to the transformative power of art in bridging divides and uniting humanity under the universal language of rhythm and respect. As the echoes of this historic event continue to reverberate, they carry with them a resounding message of unity, empathy, and the celebration of the rich tapestry of Australia's cultural heritage.

REFERENCES

Arom, Simha. 1991. *African Polyphony and Polyrhythm*. Translated by M. Thom, B. Tuckett, and R. Boyd. Cambridge University Press.

Bourdieu, Pierre. 1993. *Field of Cultural Production*, edited by R. Johnson. Columbia University Press.

Cheyne, Peter, Andrew Hamilton, and Martin Paddison, eds. 2019. *The Philosophy of Rhythm: Aesthetics, Music, Poetics*. Oxford University Press.

Csikszentmihalyi, Mihaly. 1991. *Flow: The Psychology of Optimal Experience*. Harper Perennial.

Doffman, Mark. 2013. "Groove: Temporality, Awareness and the Feeling of Entrainment in Jazz Performance." In *Experience and Meaning in Music Performance*, edited by Martin Clayton, Byron Dueck, and Laura Leante. Oxford University Press.

Herborn, Daniel, Peter McCallum, and Joyce Morgan. 2023. "Musical Follows in Footsteps of Hamilton and Six, with Modern Take on History." *Sydney Morning Herald*, July 7. https://www.smh.com.au/culture/theatre/this-madcap-sketch-show-has-smash-mouth-cyclists-and-a-mario-moustache-20230705-p5dlvb.html.

Manning, Adam. 2019. "Yarning: A Musical Example." Filmed May 2019 at Lock Up Newcastle. Video, 0:00–0:48. https://www.youtube.com/watch?v=WCGmH6JR9JM.

Manning, Adam. 2023. "A Rhythmic Acknowledgment for Walking Experiences." *Design Principles and Practices: An International Journal—Annual Review* 16 (1): 75–79. https://doi.org/10.18848/1833-1874/CGP/v16i01/75-79.

Reconciliation Australia. n.d. "Acknowledgement of Country and Welcome to Country." Accessed July 20, 2023. https://www.reconciliation.org.au/acknowledgement-of-country-and-welcome-to-country/.

Schön, Donald. 1983. *The Reflective Practitioner: How Professionals Think in Action*. Basic Books.

The Australian Institute of Aboriginal and Torres Strait Islanders. n.d. "Explore." Accessed May 1, 2023. https://aiatsis.gov.au.

The University of Sydney. 2022. "Australharmony." https://www.sydney.edu.au/paradisec/australharmony/.

CHAPTER 14

Navigating the Realm of Online Music Creation: Insights from Collaborative Music Contests

Martin K. Koszolko and Paul Egglestone

Abstract

The proliferation of online music production tools has transformed the landscape of collaborative music-making, enabling artists to transcend geographical boundaries. The Collaborative Music Contest, an international competition, investigates the creative potential of remote collaboration through digital platforms. This chapter presents insights and findings from two contest iterations in 2021 and 2022, which engaged musicians from across the globe. The contest encouraged collaborative music creation using various software platforms, revealing how musicians utilize the Internet for remote co-creation.

This study explores key questions surrounding the impact of geographical separation on creative partnerships, the types of software employed, musicians' openness to working with new collaborators, and the role of community-building in online creative processes. While collaborative Digital Audio Workstations (DAWs) were commonly used, many participants opted for mainstream DAWs without built-in collaborative features, relying on external tools for communication and file sharing. The choice of software significantly influenced both the mix quality and stylistic outcomes of the projects. An important finding is that geographical separation did not hinder effective collaboration, with many musicians willing to work with unfamiliar partners. The contest also highlighted the crucial role of virtual communities in fostering creativity, providing participants with feedback, support, and a sense of belonging. These communities are essential for online music creation, especially in times of social isolation.

The authors—one the contest founder and chair of the judging panel, and the other a judge for the second edition—present findings that emphasize the significance of collaborative software solutions in enabling remote songwriting and production. As the music technology landscape continues to evolve, these platforms are becoming essential tools for contemporary musicians, shaping how music is created and shared in the digital age.

Introduction

The proliferation of diverse online music production tools has created new opportunities for artists to collaborate in the creation of music, transcending physical limitations (Biasutti and Concina 2020). This technological shift has gained significant attention and recognition in recent years, as advances in digital technologies have revolutionized the music industry and expanded opportunities for musicians to create and collaborate on a global scale, particularly during the COVID-19 pandemic (Fallowfield and Gomez 2022). The Collaborative Music Contest (Koszolko 2024), established by one of the authors of this study in Australia in 2021, is an international event designed to explore the impact of remote music collaboration software (RMCS) platforms on the process of musical co-creation. The aims of the contest include stimulating the creation of new collaborative material created with online music software platforms and uncovering how contemporary musicians use the Internet to develop and produce original music with remotely located participants. Initially organized by the School of Music Collaboration, the contest expanded its reach a year later with the inclusion of FASTLab, a research translation hub operating at the University of Newcastle.

The project presented in this paper is an extension of ongoing research on remote music collaboration software and services (Koszolko 2015, 2017, 2022; Koszolko and Montano 2016) which can be grouped into three main categories based on their focus on creative crowdsourcing in online music collaboration activities: Virtual Studio Platforms, Telematic Platforms, and Social Networking Platforms (Koszolko 2024). These platforms serve different purposes in the music industry, with the first type being software that enables virtual studio collaboration, the second being software that facilitates live performances over the Internet, and the third being platforms that enable social and marketplace networking for remotely located musicians. The participants in the Collaborative Music Contest used all three types of software to produce music for the contest.

During the 2021/2022 iterations, the contest received entries from over two hundred musicians, representing diverse regions such as Australia, Asia, Europe, the Middle East, and North America. The 2021 contest edition[1] featured a single submission category, while the 2022 edition[2] expanded to include two categories: Online Studio Collaboration and Online Live Jamming, focused on the theme of "New Meets Old". Artists in both editions were encouraged to explore the creative possibilities of using the Internet for the communication, production, and presentation of their musical ideas. The entry to the contest was free and artists retained all the ownership of the music that they submitted. Submissions were evaluated by a panel of judges, consisting of established artists, academics, and music industry professionals. The contest was not for profit and all the prizes went directly to the winners. The prizes included music software, hardware, and services sponsored by several international music technology companies and creative industry practitioners.

The Collaborative Music Contest stipulated several rules in the call for entries. Anyone over the age of 16, living anywhere in the world could enter; however, only one track could be submitted per group. All tracks needed to be original, and all musical genres were permitted. Groups were required to demonstrate the use of remote music collaboration technologies of their choice. Contest organizers did not match artists as the contest was for teams formed independently. In 2021, judges assessed the scope of collaboration as well as songwriting and music production qualities. In 2022, the additional judgment criterion was the alignment of the submitted music with the contest theme.

Virtual Community

In 2021, Barrett et al. produced a systematic review of creative collaboration concluding that it is an essential component of online music creation and a vital factor for the success of online music collaboration platforms, which, in turn, can facilitate the emergence of new musical scenes and subcultures that reflect

---

1. More information about the 2021 edition of the contest, including audio examples, can be found at: https://musiccollaboration.online/collaborative-music-contest-2021/

2. More information about the 2022 edition of the contest, including audio examples, can be found at: https://musiccollaboration.online/collaborative-music-contest-2022/.

the diversity and creativity of contemporary music makers. Consequently, community-building is an essential component of online music creation—supported through competitions like this.

New media and online community research pioneer Howard Rheingold highlighted the importance of creating online spaces in which musicians can collaborate and learn from each other. He coined the term "virtual community" to describe the online groups that emerge from the exploration and expression of their members on the Internet, which he called the "virtual frontier" (Rheingold 1993, 1). According to Rheingold, the most precious resource on the Internet is information, which he likened to a "gift economy." He argued that freely exchanging information online is essential for building and sustaining successful web communities (Rheingold 1993). In online music-making communities, musicians and fans share their expertise, talents, and works with others. This generosity not only establishes the basis of these communities but also enhances their interactions, making the experience more rewarding for all participants (Jenkins et al. 2013). Therefore, the development of such communities can transform the way music is produced and enjoyed.

The quality of interpersonal relationships is crucial for determining the strategies, goals, and phases of a collaborative composition. The interactions among the composers focus on the organization, task management (Biasutti and Frate 2018), and discussion of the compositional process and products. Group characteristics (Hewitt 2008), the leadership model (Burnard and Younker 2008), and interpersonal relationships level (Burland and Davidson 2004) are some of the social factors that influence collaborative composition. Two main communication styles have been identified (Biasutti 2015; Partti and Westerlund 2013): one based on verbal interactions and the other on the musical manipulation of the compositional product. While musical interventions involve the direct application of compositional strategies (and feedback from other members), verbal interactions aim to share and negotiate the different stages of a musical task (Biasutti and Frate 2018). It is important to explore how the absence of personal acquaintances may affect the management of a collaborative compositional task in a virtual environment where communication may only occur through multimedia devices.

Discussion and Findings

In analyzing the results of the two contests, we considered a variety of factors. First, we investigated the impact of physical distance on music collaborators to determine whether geographical separation affected creative relationships and final musical outcomes. Second, our findings helped identify the common software types used by musicians involved in remote collaboration. Third, our study delved into musicians' willingness to collaborate with new partners they had not met before. Finally, we compared the collaborative methods employed by musicians who were already acquainted before working together with those who partnered with entirely new musical collaborators.

It became evident that many submissions employed a multisoftware approach, utilizing various Digital Audio Workstations (DAWs). This included both collaborative and noncollaborative platforms. The DAWs used by the contestants included collaborative software such as Audiotool, Ohm Studio, SonoBus, and Endlesss as well as a range of mainstream DAWs without dedicated collaborative features such as Ableton Live, Bitwig, Nuendo, Pro Tools, Logic Pro, and FL Studio. The latter were aided by additional applications, such as cloud-based storage, online messaging, and video conferencing tools. Interestingly, the choice of DAW software appeared to influence the mix quality of the final compositions, with noticeable differences between tracks that used different software types. Moreover, stylistic variations among the submitted materials can often be attributed to the specific software platform selected by collaborating musicians. Another noteworthy finding from the contest submissions was the presence of tracks driven by individual songwriters who invited other collaborators, such as session musicians or mix engineers, to contribute to their work. This demonstrates the diverse ways in which collaborative efforts were initiated and conducted during the contest.

The results highlight the importance of considering software compatibility for groups using different RMCS platforms and how the choice of software impacts musical outcomes. Additionally, this study confirmed that geographical separation does not hinder musicians from working together effectively. The willingness of musicians to collaborate with new and unfamiliar partners also demonstrates the capacity of RMCS platforms to facilitate the expansion of creative networks within the online music community. The contrasting collaborative methods used by musicians with existing relationships and those with new connections offer an avenue for further investigation in collaborative music production. Collaborative methods ranged from projects driven by a single producer and/or songwriter to groups in which these leadership roles could be shared across multiple members. Some groups knew each other from past projects, and some were formed exclusively for the purpose of creating a contest submission.

While many collaborators had preexisting nonvirtual creative relationships before embarking on their projects, most creative partnerships were initiated and maintained through online interactions, highlighting the significance of these platforms in fostering global collaborations. For example, in 2021, the winners of the first and runner-up prizes were active members of the communities associated with the Audiotool and Ohm Studio platforms, engaging in ongoing music production projects that transcended geographical boundaries. The winning track of the 2021 contest was a result of collaboration among three individuals located in Singapore and Malaysia ("Back To You" by Icebox, SIREN & dcln) utilizing the Audiotool platform. On the other hand, the runner-up track ("Changer le Monde" by Nikaule) involved four collaborators from France, Norway, Germany, and Australia, who connected through the Ohm Studio platform. The nature of the collaboration varied based on whether the collaborators knew each other previously or met for the first time to work on new material. In cases where prior relationships existed, there tended to be a predetermined division of roles based on experiences from previous projects. Conversely, collaborations among new acquaintances displayed more fluidity, with roles such as composition, arrangement, mixing, and instrumental performance open for discussion.

Responses to the 2022 contest theme of "New Meets Old" provided a greater stylistic variety of submitted entries in comparison to the previous edition of the event. For example, in 2022, the second prize was awarded to a large, multigenerational, communal project called The Continuity and their composition titled "They Kept Going, Going" influenced by Polish ethnic music. The song included vocals, violin, fretless bass guitar, midi instruments, as well as electronic music sounds.

This track embraced the ethos of online music collaboration by reimagining a traditional Polish melody through an intergenerational series of performances that combined traditional and digital instruments. Recordings were shared across multiple platforms and processed using a diverse range of software, including the DAWs Ableton Live, BandLab, Studio One, and Cubase Elements, as well as communication tools such as Dropbox, Facebook Messenger, BandLab chat, and e-mail. Its greatest strength lay in its deeply emotive expression, drawing on the past while being propelled into the present through the artistry that harnessed the technologies enabling this creative exchange.

Some contestants opted not to use DAWs specifically designed for collaboration, which can be attributed to two main reasons. First, awareness about the RMCS remains relatively limited, indicating the need for greater education in this area. Second, musicians often prefer to work with familiar software and may prefer to export audio stems for collaborators using different DAWs. Stems would limit the flexibility of how the material can be manipulated, which would also impact the compositional and production processes. The final musical and production outcomes were influenced by a combination of factors, including composition techniques, production methods, and collaboration approaches. The choice of RMCS platforms also played a role, with demographic considerations, genre preferences among online communities, and the availability of digital instruments and sound processing tools contributing to variations in submissions.

A selection of the winning tracks from both editions of the contest demonstrated that although collaboration-oriented DAWs may not be as established as some major names in the music production software industry, they are, nonetheless, developed to a high standard, offering advanced collaborative features that encompass not only music production tools but also communication and creative crowdsourcing capabilities. Overall, the Collaborative Music Contest underscores the significance of online music collaboration tools in enabling creative crowdsourcing, remote songwriting, and music production. Collaborative software platforms represent a growing segment of the music technology market and are increasingly forming a critical toolset for contemporary music makers (Koszolko 2024). The findings emphasize the tangible impact of these platforms in breaking the barriers of geographical isolation, expanding creative networks, facilitating creative partnerships across borders, and, more broadly, enriching the landscape of music production in the digital age.

Conclusion

Online music collaboration has become an essential mechanism by which musicians can connect, create, and build communities. It provides numerous opportunities for creativity, support, and professional development (Biasutti 2015). These virtual communities not only offer musicians feedback, inspiration, and learning opportunities but also help build resilience and enhance their sense of belonging and identity, particularly in times of isolation, such as during the COVID-19 pandemic (Fallowfield and Gomez 2022).

We observed how the contest highlighted the vast potential of online music collaboration. Participants adopted a wide range of approaches, from cutting-edge DAWs to traditional instruments, demonstrating how contemporary musicians blend new technologies with established practices to innovate and expand their craft (Koszolko 2022). This contest illustrated the accessibility of online music platforms, with both experienced and emerging musicians able to participate, a reflection of the increasingly affordable and democratized nature of these tools (Ingham 2023).

One of the critical insights is the capacity of virtual collaboration to foster meaningful artistic connections, even in the absence of physical proximity. Many participants displayed a remarkable level of cohesion in their work, despite working remotely. This speaks to the growing sophistication of remote music collaboration tools, which allow not only technical production but also facilitate the building of supportive creative communities (Koszolko and Montano 2016).

In addition to technical and creative evaluation, it was clear that the contest inspired participants to explore new creative directions and collaborate across borders. Cross-cultural collaboration frequently resulted in stylistic innovation, often blending genres and techniques from different traditions, as exemplified by the diverse submissions. Such exchanges are crucial in enriching creative outcomes and fostering the emergence of hybrid musical forms.

Remote collaboration introduces opportunities for skill development beyond music composition and production, including project management, communication, and leadership within a digital environment. The asynchronous nature of many collaborations encourages deeper reflection and refinement, which enhances the overall quality of the creative outputs (Biasutti and Frate 2018). This aligns with previous studies suggesting that remote collaboration cultivates essential professional skills, particularly in globalized creative industries.

Another important dimension is the environmental sustainability of remote collaboration. By reducing the need for travel and physical studio sessions, musicians can contribute to lower carbon emissions, positioning online collaboration as an eco-conscious approach to music creation. This shift not only benefits the environment but also enhances the inclusivity of collaboration, as geographical barriers are minimized.

The creative outputs of the contest demonstrate that both synchronous and asynchronous connections can foster a sense of collective creative engagement. As observed by Schlagowski et al. (2023), virtual collaboration tools are crucial for creating a sense of togetherness in creative projects, even without face-to-face interaction. This was evident in the way participants used communication tools both within and outside RMCS platforms, facilitating seamless collaboration and music production.

The contest also underscored the versatility of the platforms used, with participants utilizing dedicated collaborative DAWs such as Audiotool, BandLab, Endlesss, Ohm Studio, and Soundtrap. It was noteworthy that many participants opted for mainstream DAWs without specific collaboration features, instead relying on third-party file-sharing services. This reflects the broad range of software platforms available today, enabling musicians to share ideas and collaborate effectively.

The Collaborative Music Contest highlighted the expanding role of online music collaboration tools in contemporary music production, providing valuable insights into how these platforms foster creativity, innovation, and collaboration across geographic and cultural boundaries. It further demonstrated their capacity to democratise music-making by enabling wider participation, facilitating skill development, and supporting sustainable creative practices. Crucially, the event underscored the significance of not only showcasing artistic talent but also nurturing global artistic communities that flourish through collaboration and cross-cultural exchange.

REFERENCES

Barrett, M. S., A. Creech, and K. Zhukov. 2021. "Creative Collaboration and Collaborative Creativity: A Systematic Literature Review." *Frontiers in Psychology* 12: 1–15. https://www.frontiersin.org/articles/10.3389/fpsyg.2021.713445.

Biasutti, M. 2015. "Creativity in Virtual Spaces: Communication Modes Employed During Collaborative Online Music Composition." *Thinking Skills and Creativity* 17: 117–129.

Biasutti, M., and E. Concina. 2020. "Online Composition: Strategies and Processes During Collaborative Electroacoustic Composition." *British Journal of Music Education* 38 (1): 58–73.

Biasutti, M., and S. Frate. 2018. "Group Metacognition in Online Collaborative Learning: Validity and Reliability of the Group Metacognition Scale (GMS)." *Educational Technology Research and Development* 66: 1321–1338. https://doi.org/10.1007/s11423-018-9583-0.

Burland, K., and J. Davidson. 2004. *The Music Practitioner: Exploring Practices and Research in the Development of the Expert Music Performer, Teacher and Listener*. Ashgate Publishing.

Burnard, P., and B. Younker. 2008. "Investigating Children's Musical Interactions Within the Activities Systems of Group Composing and Arranging: An Application of Engestrom's Activity Theory." *International Journal of Educational Research* 47 (1): 60–74.

Fallowfield, E., and P. Gomez. 2022. "An Etude for Post-Pandemic Practice: The Impact of the COVID-19 Pandemic on Practice Methods and Instrumental Technique." *Frontiers in Psychology* 13: 1–12.

Hewitt, D. 2008. *Understanding Effective Learning Strategies for the Classroom: Strategies for the Classroom*. McGraw-Hill Education

Ingham, T. 2023. "Spotify Wants 50 Million Creators on Its Platform by 2030: Bandlab Already Has 60 Million." https://www.musicbusinessworldwide.com/spotify-wants-50-million-creators-bandlab-already-has-60-million/.

Jenkins, H., S. Ford, and J. Green. 2013. *Spreadable Media: Creating Value and Meaning in a Networked Culture*. New York University Press.

Koszolko, M. K. 2015. "Crowdsourcing, Jamming and Remixing: A Qualitative Study of Contemporary Music Production Practices in the Cloud." *Journal on the Art of Record Production* 10.

Koszolko, M. K. 2017. "The Giver: A Case Study of the Impact of Remote Music Collaboration Software on Music Production Process." *IASPM Journal* 7 (2): 32–40.

Koszolko, M. K. 2022. "The Virtual Studio." In *The Bloomsbury Handbook of Popular Music, Space and Place*, edited by G. Stahl and J. M. Percival. Bloomsbury Academic.

Koszolko, M. K. 2024. "Connecting Across Borders: Communication Tools and Group Practices of Remote Music Collaborators." In *Innovation in Music: Cultures and Contexts*, edited by J.-O. Gullö, R. Hepworth-Sawyer, J. Paterson, R. Toulson, and M. Marrington. Focal Press.

Koszolko, M. K., and E. Montano. 2016. "Cloud Connectivity and Contemporary Electronic Dance Music Production." *Kinephanos, Journal of Media Studies and Popular Culture* 6 (1): 60–86.

Partti, H., and H. Westerlund. 2013. "Envisioning Collaborative Composing in Music Education: Learning and Negotiation of Meaning in operabyyou.com." *British Journal of Music Education* 30 (2): 207–222.

Rheingold, H. 1993. *The Virtual Community: Homesteading on the Electronic Frontier*. MIT Press.

Schlagowski, R., D. Nazarenko, Y. Can, et al. 2023. "Wish You Were Here: Mental and Physiological Effects of Remote Music Collaboration in Mixed Reality." Presented at the Proceedings of the 2023 CHI Conference on Human Factors in Computing Systems (CHI '23), Hamburg, Germany, April 23–28, 2023. Association for Computing Machinery.

Wenger-Trayner, E., and B. Wenger-Trayner. 2015. "Introduction to Communities of Practice: A Brief Overview of the Concept and Its Uses." http://wenger-trayner.com/introduction-to-communities-of-practice/.

CHAPTER 15

Exploring the Evolution of Traditional Afro-Cuban Ritual in Contemporary Neo-Santeria Electronic Music

Vincent Sebastian Labra

Abstract

Santeria is an Afro-Cuban religion that descends from West Africa and uses music performance to facilitate healing, create altered states, and induce psychological transformations (Brandon 1997; Castellanos and Castellanos 1992; Mason 2002; Murphy 1981; Schweitzer 2013). This Phd research project from 2017-2024 aimed to explore the development of Santeria music into the global music marketplace. This development consists of a fusion with contemporary electronic music, and the use of new performance technologies, communication mediums, and the translation of its ritual symbols into new secular settings, both in Australia and around the world.

This study explores this development from a musical perspective, investigating how musical traditions evolve and what it means to translate sacred music into a secular setting. Fieldwork in Cuba is used to explore traditional cultural music of Santeria, its religious rituals and initiations, and its development. This study coins the term *neo-Santeria* to describe the fusion of traditional Santeria music with nontraditional sounds, approaches, and symbols, and its development into new settings. These new artforms produce cross-cultural interpretations of Santeria traditions, using innovative technologies, digital formats, and aimed at new global audiences.

This study helps us to understand how the Santeria musical tradition is evolving and explores the significance of this development in the global arena. Using a mixed-method approach to explore the musical culture, it investigates its subjective effects, musical artifacts, and cross-cultural evolution. Results suggest that neo-Santeria continues the transformation and healing themes of its predecessor, reflected through new technologies and multimedia formats in its music, videos, album artworks, and performances.

Introduction

It is a hot day in Havana, Cuba and I am entering a ritual room to partici-pate in an initiation called the Mano de Orula in the Afro-Cuban religion of Santeria. The first stage is where I will receive the orishas (Santeria deities) Elegua, Ogun, and Ochosi, known collectively as the guerreros (warriors). The ritual establishes a relationship with these orishas, and kinship with the religious community.

The second stage is three-day rest period, where I am asked to fulfill purifi-cations consisting of bathing with omiero, a sacred herbal liquid consecrated during the ritual through chanting and prayers.

The third stage is a divination ceremony which aims to uncover my destiny and guardian orisha. In Santeria it is believed that every individual has a guardian orisha that oversees his or her life and which is important to understanding one's life path and destiny.

(Labra, V.S., Journal Excerpt, June 2017)

This experience marks the beginning of a PhD project exploring the music and rituals of Santeria and their evolution into contemporary music artforms. The study explores how musical traditions evolve and what it means to translate sacred music into a secular context. This study coins the term neo-Santeria to describe the music and its development, which consists of a fusion of traditional Santeria music with Western electronic elements and technologies. Neo-Santeria emerges from Cuba but develops into new global contexts, created by a diverse range of music creators of both Cuban and non-Cuban origin. It is indicative of the globalization of music, of a burgeoning ritual tourism in Cuba, and the exoticization of Afro-Cuban music practices worldwide.

Development of Neo-Santeria

Santeria descended from West African origins during the transatlantic slave trade and is further developed within Cuba (Brown 2003). Its religious practices consist of a series of rituals, one type being the *tambor*, which is a celebratory event containing music and dance. Its musical repertoire consists of a large corpus of songs and rhythms used during religious rituals and celebrations that uses a sacred liturgical language known as *Lucumi* (Schweitzer 2013; Wirtz 2005). The rituals use complex drumming performed by three drummers playing polyrhythmic patterns on hourglass-shaped *batá* drums. These rhythms are accompanied by communal singing in a call-and-response style by a lead singer (*akpwon*) and the congregation (Schweitzer 2013). The music and performances aim to evoke heightened communal atmospheres, sometimes culminating in spirit possessions (Schweitzer 2013). *Tambor* rituals are contrasted from initiation rituals, such as the *Mano de Orula*, which are private events used to introduce devotees into deeper knowledge of the religion, its rituals, worship, and beliefs (Mason 2002).

Spread and Development of Santeria Music

Santeria music spread beyond Cuban borders during the 1950s with the migration of Cubans to New York (Amira 2015). While within Cuba, innovations to the Santeria repertoire during the 1970s further developed the music and performance, disseminated through international touring and recordings that influenced musicians globally (Bodenheimer 2010; Frias 2019; Hagedorn 2001; Manuel 1987). The 1990s era saw a new fusion of neo-Santeria music with hip-hop (Baker 2017) and house music (Hucks 2012), and its further popularization into the global marketplace, with the commodification of Cuban music often presenting a static and exotic view of Cuban culture (Ramsdell 2012). International development was fueled by the Cuban ritual tourism market, developed during the 1990s, and characterized by a commercial market for spiritual experiences (Beliso-De Jesus 2015).

Contemporary trends in neo-Santeria music extend these previous developments, augmenting traditional music with contemporary electronic sounds and hardware technologies (Monasterio 2018), making neo-Santeria accessible to Western audiences due to its fusion with Western popular styles and genres. Often, the music is accompanied by album artworks and music videos that feature Santeria ritual symbols and cultural themes, exhibiting a multifaceted approach to portraying cultural information. These contemporary artists include Daymé Arocena, Okonkolo, Afrosideral, Osunlade, Ibeyi, IFÉ, and MC Oskaro.

Mixed-Method Design

Ethnomusicologist John Blacking (1971) suggests that music needs to be analyzed and understood in relation to its cultural context, a sentiment that has influenced the modern practice of musicology. This idea is echoed in the work of Mihaly Csikszentmihalyi (2014), who provides an analytical method for approaching the study of music as an interaction between *individual*, *field*, and *domain*. Judith Lochhead (2016) adds that subjective experience is also core to the musical experience, alongside cultural, social, and historical markers. This study incorporates these various perspectives, using a mixed-method design to explore the facets of neo-Santeria music, including its subjective, cultural, social, and historical dimensions.

Method 1

The first method consists of analysis of Santeria and neo-Santeria musical artifacts, using musical analysis, content analysis, and thematic analysis. These analytical tools explore traditional Santeria music and its neo-Santeria variants to enable comparison between sacred and secular forms and to establish developmental trends.

Method 2

The second method is *autoethnography*, which addresses the subjective dimension of ritual. Subjective experience is integral to Santeria rituals that aim for an ontological transformation during initiations or possessions (Mason 2002; Schweitzer 2013) and thus is an important part of the assessment of music within rituals. Autoethnography enables a reflection on *self* within a cultural network and entails an ethnography of events, in addition to a reflection on subjective experience of sensory, emotive, and cognitive quality (Adams and Herrmann 2023; Kara 2020). This approach rejects the idea that humans exist in isolation as separate entities, but rather, within networks where subjective experience is core to understanding cultural experience (Barz and Cooley 2008). In conjunction with other methods, autoethnography provides an extra perspective from which to explore music and its effects. Autoethnographic reflections were detailed in a journal during fieldwork, and used to inspire new music compositions, album artworks, and music videos.

Method 3

The third method was practice-led creative research, which consisted of an exploration of the neo-Santeria phenomenon using music composition, live performance, and music distribution. This was achieved using my band Oyobi, which is a four-piece band that consists of the musicians: Adam Ventoura, Daniel Pliner, Quetzal Guerrero, and myself. The band uses electronic technologies augmented by acoustic instrumentation. Figure 1 shows the integration of electronic hardware, percussion pads, bass, and synthesizers, augmented by vocals and violin.

Figure 1: Oyobi Performance, Sweethearts Rooftop, Kings Cross, Sydney – 2022

The creative research produced compositions in the neo-Santeria style, facilitated by previous knowledge of the genre and using insights developed during the research. Compositions were analyzed and reflections noted in a journal. These insights were used to develop a neo-Santeria framework to understand the musical style and its development from traditional Santeria ritual.

Developed within a four-year period between 2018 and 2022, the works produced two extended plays (EPs) of ten songs, a set of audiovisual recordings of
live performances, two album cover artworks, and a music video. These works
were developed through three stages, with each phase expanding the scope and
direction of the research.

Practice-Led Creative Research

Stage 1

Stage 1 of the creative research resulted in a set of live performances and a
four-song EP called "Translations" (Oyobi 2019). The EP was distributed into
the international music market resulting in feedback from industry peers, with
reactions to the music also assessed during live performances. This process was
based on the approach of Csikszentmihalyi (1999) that states that the impact,
originality, and strength of a creative work is judged by its relationship to *field*
and *domain,* with originality defined as the novelty produced to extend the domain. The *field* is the community of musicians, promoters, critics, gatekeepers,
and industry executives that comprise the scene. The *domain* is the musical
tradition or culture, which includes the sanctioned parameters of the genre and
musical practices, which in this case is the neo-Santeria musical style. The
domain is responsible for continuing the tradition by passing works, practices,
and genre parameters from generation to generation in the production of culture.

The creative works blended electronic technologies and instruments in novel
ways. For example, Oyobi used the Elektron Octatrack sampler alongside an
Arturia drum machine[1] and various acoustic and electronic instruments, blending styles of house music, jazz, funk, and Latin, in addition to interpretations
of traditional Santeria chants and the use of Spanish and English lyrics. This
combination sought to retain the band's unique musical voice and style, while
incorporating insights from the fieldwork into its music, artworks, and videos,
thus expanding the genre and creating a unique style.

The final works were distributed in the international music marketplace
through Imagenes Recordings, London, and resulted in appearances on various

---

[1.] These are electronic hardware instruments used to sample external sounds and compose new sounds. They are
used during live performance to trigger sound loops, create new sounds during improvisation, or trigger other
machines through midi-synchronization.

music charts and reviews from artists in the field. The feedback from this process influenced future works and was incorporated into the development of the neo-Santeria framework.

Stage 2

Stage 2 increased the sophistication of works by developing the knowledge and insights developed from stage 1 into new works, resulting in a second EP of six songs called "Transcendence" (Oyobi 2021) released by Atjazz Record Company, London. The process of composition, performance, and distribution developed the understanding of the neo-Santeria style. The process of composition, performance, and distribution developed the understanding of the neo-Santeria style and its place within the international market. These explorations facilitated the expansion of the neo-Santeria framework through various iterations during the research phases.

Extra-musical Elements of Neo-Santeria

The study of neo-Santeria was expanded to include extra-musical elements, such as music videos and album artworks. These elements were found to be critical aspects of the style, used to communicate cultural knowledge and expand the meaning of the music. These artifacts typically contained themes of transcendence and psychological transformation which focused on alterations of consciousness, such as heightened communal states or spiritual possessions. This was related to the Santeria performance ethos, used in traditional ritual settings to produce altered states for healing purposes. This insight was critical to the neo-Santeria style and its development from traditional Santeria, showing a musical and cultural development of the Santeria performance ethos that consisted of elements core to traditional rituals such as the embodiment of aural, kinesthetic, conceptual, symbolic, and psychological dimensions. These appeared to develop from knowledge and experience of traditional rituals and developed into neo-Santeria contemporary forms. The exploration of these themes was the subject of stage 3.

Stage 3: Music Video

Stage 3 included the creation of a music video (Figure 2) in the style of other neo-Santeria videos. The aim was to explore the symbols and narratives of neo-Santeria music videos, while also including my own personal reflections of

Figure 2: Oyobi Videoclip for "Transcendence" (Oyobi 2021c)

Santeria ritual. The music video, "Transcendence" (Oyobi 2021c), was directed by Maia Dal Berger, and consists of an integration of Santeria archetypes within a story that reflects the psychological experience of ritual encountered during the fieldwork. It uses symbols and narratives consistent with neo-Santeria's focus on transcendence but contains a personal interpretation that fuses my personal experience of Santeria ritual and its aftereffects.

The music video narrative describes a boy that gets lost in a labyrinth of underground tunnels (Figure 3) and encounters a mystical deity and musicians within a rocky moonlike underground lair. This emphasizes the altered state experienced during Santeria rituals, a representation of subjective psychological experience. The boy endures an ordeal, struggling to find the tunnel's exit and is shown frustrated and dejected, before eventually emerging as a spiritually transformed orb of light. This highlights the difficult personal journey experienced during the ritual and through the research project, where the integration of an alternate worldview during ritual produced psychological resistance, eventually resulting in a transpersonal transformation. Like other neo-Santeria videos, the narrative uses a transformation theme but includes new combinations of symbols based on personal reflections and my own cultural context as a Latino living in Australia.

Figure 3: Music Video "Transcendence" (Oyobi 2021c)

Tripartite Symbols in Ritual, Music, and Other Formats

Important to the study was the insight that music and ritual structure uses a tripartite form that is used symbolically to depict the transformation of states of consciousness across various communication formats. This form was initially outlined by van Gennep ([1960] 2013) and later developed by Turner (1966) and is a feature of many Santeria rituals (Mason 2002). The tripartite ritual form includes a separation from a previous identity, a middle liminal stage of ambiguity, and a final state of incorporation where one emerges with a new identity. The music video uses this form to portray a transformation and is reinforced through transformation symbols observed during ritual. Similarly, the music uses a three-part musical form to accompany the visual which results in a musical transformation.

An example of the tripartite form is when the musicians are pictured in an underground rocky cavern to highlight the liminal aspect of the boy's transformation.

This image is a symbolic repesentation of a personal refection, developed from experience within Santeria liminal ritual space. The music in the video depicts this state of ambiguity by using delays and reverbs and otherworldly sounds to show a transformation, eventually converging into a new musical landscape[2] which depicts a transformation of consciousness.

The Transcendence Theme in Neo-Santeria

Transformation was found to be a core theme in traditional Santeria performance, an important part of its cultural ethos for creating transformation through altered states and possessions. This theme is translated through the neo-Santeria style, exemplified in its music, artworks, lyrics, and music videos. This suggests a development of the traditional Santeria ethos from sacred to secular contexts, but altered from producing alterations of consciousness in traditional rituals, to the representation of a transformation theme in neo-Santeria through symbolic depictions, typically without ontological consequence.

This cross-cultural evolution may reflect a shared desire for transformation, common to both Santeria and Western audiences that seeks transcendent and trance encounters. This idea is found in the work of Becker (2004), Sylvan (2002), and Tacey (2013), who suggest a desire for transcendence is common among Western audiences, often appearing as states of trance. Judith Becker (2004) suggests that, in a Western secular context, trance is divorced from religious but displays feelings of transcendence or of power beyond oneself. Robin Sylvan (2002) suggests that these trance states are found in Electronic Dance Music cultures, resulting from musical techniques comparable to those of West African possession practices. On the other hand, David Tacey (2013) proposes that the cross-cultural desire for transformation experience is exhibited in rebirth symbols, where a killing of the old identity is represented. Rebirth symbols are frequently employed in Santeria rituals to facilitate a transformation of identity, consisting of symbols of death and regeneration (Mason 2002). These themes are also reflected in neo-Santeria through narratives of purification, ordeal, and transformation. The implications of translating rebirth motifs from sacred to secular contexts is that, unlike a traditional context, neo-Santeria forms do not

---

[2] Oyobi 2021c, "Transcendence," song, Transcendence album, Atjazz Record Company London, UK. Available at: https://open.spotify.com/track/4G3p4eqaw026rt5L7VcHVc. This middle section in the music occurs from 2:24 to 3:01 and develops into a new musical landscape by 4:01.

advocate for ontological transformation but suggest the evocation of spiritual feeling through artistic representations. This idea is explained by Katherine Hagedorn (2006), a Santeria priestess and scholar, who suggests that secular performances of Santeria music results in listeners connecting their musical experience with spiritual transcendence due to the music's effects on listeners' awareness. She argues that musical devices such as repetition, variation, tempo, density, and dynamics as primary to the evocation of religious feeling, suggesting the importance of music and cultural context to the creation of transcendent feeling. Even though Santeria music emerges from a distinct cultural framework, its musical devices and themes may resonate with secular audiences due to the evocation of transcendant feeling, giving credence to the idea that neo-Santeria provides a type of spiritual reflection to a dispersed secular global audience.

Conclusion: The Neo-Santeria Framework

This PhD work resulted in a framework which helps to explain the neo-Santeria style and its development from traditional Santeria ritual. The framework suggests that cultural knowledge is acquired through Santeria rituals and applied to new neo-Santeria works in various degrees, depending on the level of initiation and experience. Integral to this knowledge is the experience of ritual and its transformation themes, which forms the Santeria ethos-a way of performing particular to Santeria—a way of performing specific to Santeria. This ethos consists of knowledge of ritual performance, and its application in various sensory modes including aural, kinesthetic, conceptual, symbolic, and psycho logical dimensions.

This study proposes that neo-Santeria reflects the development of the Santeria ethos into new settings and its representation within new artistic forms. This is represented as a hierarchy of elements in the neo-Santeria style, as shown in Figure 4. These outline the core components of the neo-Santeria style, and their position within the hierarchy highlights their importance to the overall style.

A core factor is the Santeria ethos, which is the approach to music performance determined by representation of transformation themes. Following this are the Santeria songs, rhythms, symbols, and transformation motifs, which are critical elements of the aesthetic style. These are often accompanied by the communication of cultural beliefs in its song lyrics, in either English or Spanish, or as defined by the cultural context. They are augmented with nontraditional elements, such as electronic sounds, performance techniques, and acoustic instrumentation to create a fusion of traditional and Western sonic elements

Figure 4: Hierarchy of Neo-Santeria Elements

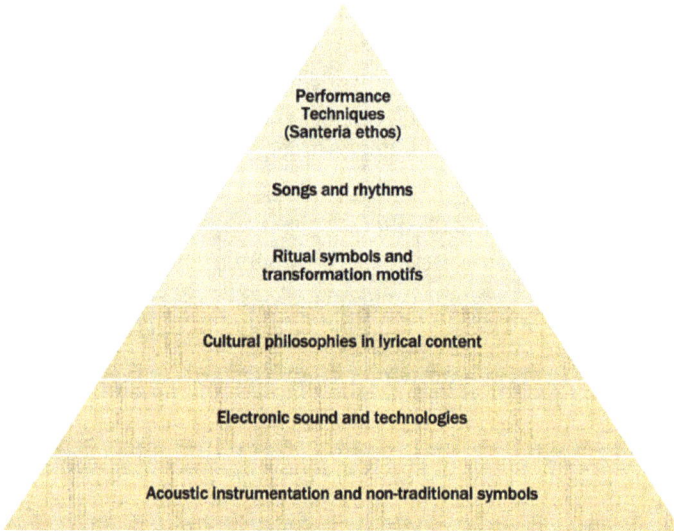

These combined elements make up the neo-Santeria style and highlight the development and hybridisation of traditional and non-traditional elements and themes. In conclusion, this study helps us understand how the neo-Santeria style is evolving, taking on new aesthetic designs and formats that appeal to new audiences within cross-cultural settings.

REFERENCES

Adams, T. E., and F. Herrmann. 2023. "Good Autoethnography." *Journal of Autoethnography* 4 (1): 1–9. https://doi.org/10.1525/joae.2023.4.1.1.

Baron, R. 2003. "Amalgams and Mosaics, Syncretisms and Reinterpretations: Reading Herskovits and Contemporary Creolists for Metaphors of Creolization." *Journal of American Folklore* 116 (459): 88–115.

Barz, G. F., and T. J. Cooley, eds. 2008. *Shadows in the Field: New Perspectives for Fieldwork in Ethnomusicology*. Oxford University Press.

Becker, J. 2004. *Deep Listeners: Music, Emotion, and Trancing*, vol. 2. Indiana University Press.

Blacking, J. 1971. "Deep and Surface Structures in Venda Music." *Yearbook of the International Folk Music Council* 3: 91–108.

Brandon, G. 1997. *Santeria from Africa to the New World: The Dead Sell Memories*. Indiana University Press.

Brown, D. H. 2003. *Santería Enthroned: Art, Ritual, and Innovation in an Afro-Cuban Religion*. Routledge.

Castellanos, J., and I. Castellanos. 1992. *Cultura Afrocubana: Las religiones y las lenguas*. Ediciones Universal.

Csikszentmihalyi, M. 1999. "Implications of a Systems Perspective for the Study of Creativity." In *Handbook of Creativity*, edited by R. Sternberg. Cambridge University Press.

Csikszentmihalyi, M. 2014. *The Systems Model of Creativity: The Collected Works of Mihaly Csikszentmihalyi*. Springer.

Daniel, Y. 2005. *Dancing Wisdom: Embodied Knowledge in Haitian Vodou, Cuban Yoruba, and Bahian Candomblé*. University of Illinois Press.

Hagedorn, K. J. 2001. *Divine Utterances: The Performance of Afro-Cuban Santería*. Smithsonian Institution Press.

Hearn, A. H. 2003. "Transformation: Transcendence or Transculturation? The Many Faces of Cuban Santeria." *Humanities Research* 10 (1): 56–62.

Kara, H. 2020. *Creative Research Methods: A Practical Guide*. Bristol University Press.

Lochhead, J. 2016. *Reconceiving Structure in Contemporary Music: New Tools in Music.* Routledge.

Manuel, P., and O. Fiol. 2007. "Mode, Melody, and Harmony in Traditional Afro-Cuban Music: From Africa to Cuba." *Black Music Research Journal* 27 (1): 45–75.

Mason, M. A. 2002. *Living Santería: Rituals and Experiences in an Afro-Cuban Religion*. Smithsonian Institution.

Murphy, J. M. 1981. *Ritual Systems in Cuban Santeria.* Temple University.

Navarro, V. M. 2013. "Aché, Music, and Spiritual Experience: The Concept of Aché and the Function of Music in Orisha Spirit Possession." [Doctoral diss.], Florida State University.

Schweitzer, K. 2013. *The Artistry of Afro-Cuban Batá Drumming: Aesthetics, Transmission, Bonding and Creativity*. University Press of Mississippi.

Skoog, D., and A. C. Guerra. 2010. "Batá Drumming (the oru seco): The Instruments, the Rhythms, and the People Who Play Them." Contemporary Music Project.

Sylvan, R. 2002. *Traces of the Spirit: The Religious Dimensions of Popular Music*. NYU Press.

Tacey, D. 2013. *Gods and Diseases: Making Sense of Our Physical and Mental Wellbeing: Theory and Analysis*. Taylor & Francis.

Turner, V. W. 1966. *The Ritual Process: Structure and Anti-Structure*. Cornell Paperbacks.

van Gennep, A. (1960) 2013. *The Rites of Passage*. Routledge.

Windress, K., 2011. "The Outsider Going in: Research and Participation in 'Bata' Drumming and 'Santeria' Ritual." *Journal of Music Research* 35/36: 153–165.

Creative works

Oyobi. 2019a. *Translations*, EP, Imagenes Recordings. https://imagenes. bandcamp.com/album/translations.

Oyobi. 2019b. *Translations (Album Cover)*, [Digital Artwork], April 77 (Designer), Sydney, Australia. https://www.oyobi.com.au/music.

Oyobi. 2021a. *Transcendence*, EP, Atjazz Record. https://oyobi.bandcamp. com/album/transcendence.

Oyobi. 2021b. *Transcendence (Album Cover)*, [Digital Artwork], April 77 (Designer), Sydney, Australia. https://www.oyobi.com.au/music.

Oyobi. 2021c. "Transcendence," Song, *Transcendence* Album, Atjazz Record. https://open.spotify.com/track/4G3p4eqaw026rt5L7VcHVc.

Oyobi. 2021d. *Transcendence*, Online Video Recording, Atjazz Record, Maia Dal Berger (Director). https://www.youtube.com/watch?v=ui_UTcUebtM.

Glossary

Batá: sacred drums of Santeria; a set of three batá drums of different pitches is used for performances.

Guerreros: means "warriors," and pertains to the name of the first group of orishas received in the religion: Elegua, Ogun, Ochosi.

Igbodu: sacred room where the most important ritual functions are performed. Only attended by those who have undergone the same ceremony.

Mano de Orula: an initiation ceremony in Santeria where orishas are received and destiny is revealed.

Omiero: a sacred herbal mixture consecrated during the ritual.

Orisha: deities of the Afro-Cuban religion with origins in West Africa.

Santeria: an Afro-Cuban religion of Yoruba origins.

Tablero de Ifá: a divination board used for Santeria divination by *babalawo* priests in Santeria—a specific order of priests trained in the secrets of the orisha Ọrunmila.

Tambor: a celebratory religious event to worship orishas using music and dance.

SECTION IV:

Experimental Practices

Introduction

This section collates perspectives from more experimental and/or blue-sky practices. These stand in for a range of forms of research practices which demonstrate the continual churn of open-ended creative exploration and quest for new knowledge which characterizes (academic) research. In part, these chapters suggest a broader collective of creative practitioners exploring possibilities with technologies, although "technology" can be defined very broadly here. This is creativity in action without necessarily a predefined end goal, looking instead to extend and test creative practices and refine research methodologies.

This is an open field of possibilities but might involve exploring technologies for specific purposes, such as for architectural work (Dierikx et al. 2022) or building 3D environments (Schmid et al. 2022), or exploring the storytelling potential of virtual reality (VR) (Gidney et al. 2022; Weaving et al. 2022) or augmented reality (AR) (Seengal et al. 2022). Or it might deploy visualization techniques within archaeological projects, such in the recovery of inscriptions on a 2,600-year-old faded timber sarcophagus of Mer-Neith-it-es (Drabsch et al. 2022). Or this might entail responding to the challenges of curating and presenting multiple forms of creative research during the COVID-19 (coronavirus disease 2019) lockdowns, through online exhibition (Chand et al. 2022).

In the first chapter (Chapter 16), Louisa Magrics and Nicole Schild provide an overview of a transdisciplinary project intersecting textiles-based and choreographic practices, bringing their established creative workflows together through a focus on improvisation. In this project textiles are the material (or medium?) of choice (Neilson 2021), but these are put into play using structures originally generated from architecture and musical rhythm. As Magrics and Schild illustrate, progress in creative research can be usefully documented

260

through photography and other means to provide a basis for reflection and future iterations of their practice.

Then, Marilia Lyra Bergamo and Giselle Penn, in the second chapter (Chapter 17), outline an experimental art installation practice engaged in understanding the distinctive nature of robotics. The small-scale project outlined here is part of a broader research program focused on both theorizing and working through practice to investigate how robotic systems emerge and evolve. This involves considering the interplay between coding, the technical challenges of the robotic body, and (in this case) how these interact with humans as part of an interactive installation.

Finally, Stuart McBratney reports on the most recent iteration of a long-standing research strategy focused on democratizing high-end cinematic production—i.e., creating feature films on a micro-budget. His project represents experimentation with an established real-world endpoint. This involves a highly deliberate and evolved practice of project management and experienced hustling for resources, designed to maintain an efficient and effective workflow which leverages some of the advantages of filmmaking in the academy. McBratney's creative works build upon decades of experimentation within constrained budgets but are "tested" in real-world film distribution and exhibition.

REFERENCES

Chand, Ari, Andrew Howells, Alan Male, et al. 2022. "Illustration Research: Exploring the Role of Non-Traditional Research Outcomes and Exhibition." Presented at the Peer Review Proceedings of the 16th International Conference of Design Principles and Practices, Newcastle, January 19–21, 2022.

Dierikx, Kaitlyn, Zi Siang See, Luis Alexander Rojas Bonilla, and Erin Conley. 2022. "Development of a Virtual Reality Prototype for Architectural Visualisation with the Integration of Dynamic Electroencephalogram in the Creative Thinking Process." Presented at the Peer Review Proceedings of the 16th International Conference of Design Principles and Practices, Newcastle, January 19–21, 2022.

Drabsch, B., A. Howells, and L. O'Donnell. 2022. "A Colourful Past: Digitally Recoloring the Sarcophagus of Mer-Neith-it-es." Presented at the Peer Review Proceedings of the 16th International Conference of Design Principles and Practices, Newcastle, January 19–21, 2022.

Gidney, Matt, Jack McGrath, and Zi Siang See. 2022. "The Dining Car: Experiments with Retinal Rivalry in Virtual Reality." Presented at the Peer

Review Proceedings of the 16th International Conference of Design Principles and Practices, Newcastle, January 19–21, 2022.

Neilson, Faye. 2021. "Making Matters: Concept, Process and Context." In *The Elephant's Leg: Adventures in the Creative Industries*, edited by Craig Hight and Mario Minichiello. Common Ground Research Networks.

Schmid, Jean-Luc, Zi Siang See, and Simone O'Callaghan. 2022. "3D Scanned Nature-Based Virtual Environment Design: A Hunter Valley (NSW, Australia) Case Study." Presented at the Peer Review Proceedings of the 16th International Conference of Design Principles and Practices, Newcastle, January 19–21, 2022.

Seengal, Divya, Simone O'Callaghan, and Zi Siang See. 2022. "Design Beyond Screen: A Primer for Designing Mobile Augmented Reality Storytelling Application." Presented at the Peer Review Proceedings of the 16th International Conference of Design Principles and Practices, Newcastle, January 19–21, 2022.

Weaving, Simon, Benjamin Matthews, and Zi Siang See. 2022. "We'd Like to Give You Some Presence: Cinematic VR Narration and the Sense of 'Being There.'" Presented at the Peer Review Proceedings of the 16th International Conference of Design Principles and Practices, Newcastle, January 19–21, 2022.

CHAPTER 16

TIMMY (Threads in Motion: Moving Yarns)

Louisa Magrics and Nicole Schild

Abstract

TIMMY (Threads in Motion: Moving Yarns) explores possibilities for a generative synthesis of body movement with sculptural crochet. Emerging from the 2023 Regional Action Research Project at choreographic center Critical Path, the project is a practice-based research inquiry rooted in the combined tacit knowledge of the two participating artists. The inquiry has an experimental systems orientation, in terms of methodically creating space to explore different combinations of variables to produce fluid epistemic outcomes, which are subsequently metabolized by TIMMY as the basis of further experimentation.

Over the course of the research process, wearable crocheted structures have come to define the contours of the landscape being explored, revealing themselves as modular spaces or dwellings for an individual body. This can take the ongoing process in a number of directions both creatively and conceptually, including looking at modular systems, topologies of the body, and multisensory bodily holding.

Introduction

TIMMY (Threads in Motion: Moving Yarns) is a creative inquiry that explores possibilities for interweaving body movement with sculptural crochet. It is a synthesis of the two participating artists' respective practices: Dr. Louisa Magrics as a fine artist who uses crochet to construct large-scale installations, sculptures and wearables, and Niki (Nicole) Schild as a dancer/choreographer. Both artists have additional skill sets from their work in arts-adjacent fields: Magrics as a lecturer in the School of Humanities, Creative Industries, and Social Sciences at the University of Newcastle, and Schild as a creative arts therapist specialized in dance movement therapy.

The development of TIMMY has been cultivated within the Regional Action Research Project, a fellowship facilitated by the choreographic center Critical Path throughout 2023. For much of this process, each artist operated from their respective studio locations in Newcastle and the Dandenong Ranges, with interaction happening remotely via Zoom meetings, as well as through sharing materials

Figure 1: Street Shot by Lee Illfield

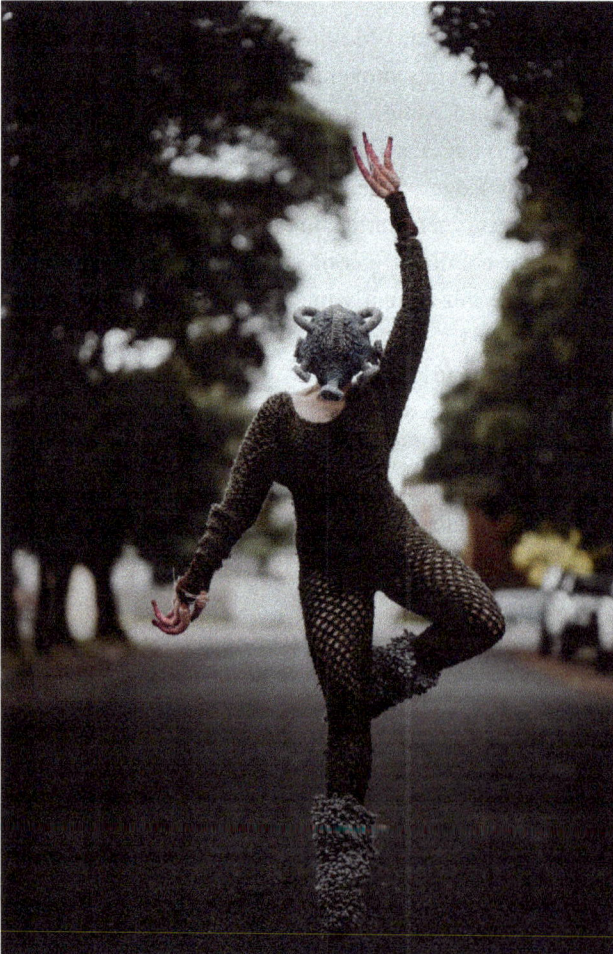

on private and public channels (e.g., Instagram) with a focus on visual content. These remote interactions were paired with a number of face-to-face sessions throughout the year, including a studio intensive in Newcastle in July 2023.

In the course of this intensive, the project came to focus on the dimension of Magrics' practice concerned with designing and making wearable crocheted structures. Approached through a sensory–motor lens (integrating tactile, kinesthetic, visual, vestibular and other sensorial factors), these revealed themselves as info-rich modular spaces or dwellings for an individual body, posing strong creative parameters for Schild's choreographic investigation.

Project Origins

The two artists have similar approaches to instigating and engaging with collaborative opportunities, shaped by a shared practice of performing live music with bands.[1] Each has developed a collaborative approach grounded in the dynamic interplay of distinct yet complementary musical parts, and characterized by active play, listening, and improvisation. This has laid the foundation for an intuitive understanding of how to work together, which has translated readily into the TIMMY project.

In a live music setting, collaboration may be conceptualized in terms of division of labor. This is often based on individual specialization with the roles allocated based on expertise, such as the ability to play a specific instrument. This approach is echoed across the creative industries — for example, in the structure and operations of a film production crew, in which roles and responsibilities are typically clearly defined and often coordinated with a top-down or hierarchical approach. In the live music context, however, rigid organizational structures are often not necessitated.

While some music projects will work with a hierarchical structure (e.g., one person at the center of a project, assigning technical tasks to other players), there is opportunity for a collectively driven approach, which increases the potential for symmetrical collaboration and shared ownership of outcomes. Songs may arise

---

[1] Louisa has almost twenty years of experience playing drums for live music projects. This has been foundational to the development of her crochet research and body of work. Niki has performed over the past decade with Ungus Ungus Ungus, a festival-focused performing and recording band project, which has significantly shaped her approach to dance making. Max, the bandleader of this project, played with Louisa in a two-piece project called Spine (2009–2013), and it is through this musical connection that Louisa and Niki originally met.

Figure 2: TIMMY In-Person Studio Intensive, July 2023

Figure 2: TIMMY In-Person Studio Intensive, July 2023

Source: Lee Illfield

from a process of organic collaborative play without a predetermined composition being required or expected. In many cases, the process of playing and trying out individual impulses within the sonic whole is critical to the songwriting process. This applies as well to elements of other performing disciplines that can be worked into the live music performance context—for example, Schild's role in the band is centered on dance conceptualized as a layer in the construction of the band's music.

This broader context of creative practice, heavily informed by the artists' live music experience, has shaped the emergence of TIMMY. From the open-ended, playful nature of the collaborative approach to the rhythm, repetition, and composition embedded in the conceptual architecture of both crochet pattern design and choreography, the project seeks a landscape for collaborative art-making grounded in shared experience.

Previous Collaborations

The artists were originally inspired to pursue an interdisciplinary collaboration by the complementary properties of their individual practices, as well

Figure 3: Left – Louisa Magrics with Dan Huish Playing as Banjo Beats at the Butcher Shop, 2018. Mural Art by Ben Graham. Photo by Louisa Magrics. Right – Niki Schild Performing with Ungus Ungus Ungus at Port Fairy Folk Festival, 2020

Sources: Louisa Magrics and Ungus Ungus Ungus

as the potential for generative synthesis observed in previous moves toward collaborating. In 2017, Schild incorporated Magrics' crocheted structure "Honeycomb v3" into the set design of a physical theater work, "Of Giants," devised with Sophia Constantine and staged at La Mama Theatre in Naarm/ Melbourne as part of its annual Explorations program. The structure was installed on anchor points mounted above the performance space, and served to create unique spatial parameters that informed the choreographic arrange- ment of the work.

In late 2022, Schild again sought the use of a crocheted structure from Magrics as part of a live action artwork, "BIOME," commissioned for the 2023 Burrinja Climate Change Biennale and staged amid raised beds filled with late summer produce at a community garden in the Dandenong Ranges (the Belgrave Food Garden). A different (untitled) crocheted structure was used for this, and was chosen partly for being smaller, lighter and less reliant on solid mounts and struc- tures to support it. This enabled it to be distributed and dynamically supported across the moving bodies of four dancers, providing a loose choreographic and improvisational anchor, as well as biomorphically evoking the networked nature of healthy soil ecosystems.

Figure 4: Twyla Wulantuya and Hadassah Wallis with Crocheted
Structure by Louisa Magrics in "BIOME" (2023), Part of the Burrinja
Climate Change Biennale

Source: Laki Sideris

Both "Of Giants" and "BIOME" were developed within very limited budgets
and timeframes, which meant that exploration of how moving bodies interact
with the structures was relatively peripheral. The Critical Path fellowship has
enabled a deeper, more thorough mapping of the landscape of this edge and some
of its potentials for cultivating new dimensions of practice.

External Partnering: Critical Path

Based in Gadigal/Sydney, Critical Path is a national center for artist-led choreographic enquiry, research and development, with stated aims including pushing
the boundaries of contemporary practice and developing new collaborations.
Following an application process, Schild and Magrics were selected as participants
in the organization's Regional Action Research Project, in which five regionally
based choreographic artists and their collaborators from other disciplines were
invited to pursue independent research activities over twelve months in 2023.

The invitation included financial support from Create NSW, along with in-kind support from Critical Path, including facilitation of a research group.

These supports enabled remote and in-person collaboration throughout the year with no predetermined outcome, allowing a considered approach to possibilities emerging from a novel interdisciplinary space. Research group sessions scheduled throughout the year assisted in establishing the openness of the brief and scope of enquiry as a developing understanding shared among the participating artists, as well as mapping out common ground and divergence across the five individual projects. In these discussions, constellations of themes surfaced, contrasted, converged, and multiplied across the projects. Individual project meetings with Critical Path also took place at intervals throughout the year, with a focus on supporting the artists to plan their research process and be responsible for its implementation.

The open, artist-led nature of the brief and its positioning in a research group framework (including a degree of accountability to the host organization) required the artists to devise a series of concrete steps to be flexibly implemented over the twelve-month timeframe. This "action plan" included loosely defined time pockets for activities such as:

- Initial discussion carried out remotely and with a focus on framing the research question and methodology.
- Iterative making in our respective studios using existing material artifacts and creative concepts to develop new prototypes.
- Testing of prototypes in a performance context.
- In-person collaborative practice-based research at Magrics' studio in Newcastle.
- Documentation processes (including photos, video, writing/journaling) and development of emergent presentation outcomes.

As the research period progressed and the action plan was implemented, more specific subplans were identified. For example, as the in-person session in Newcastle approached, it was determined that findings from this segment should be documented by a professional photographer. Funding for this had been allocated in the budget submitted to Critical Path as part of the fellowship application. The process of actualizing this unfolded organically through artist networks in Newcastle, with local photographer Lee Illfield coming onboard at short notice to create a set of images. These provided strong visual feedback from an outside (photographic) eye, which highlighted conceptual and aesthetic features of

Figure 5: Photo by Lee Illfield, Shot in Photographic Studio with Shutter Drag Technique to Capture Motion

collaborative practice that could become a focal point for the remainder of the research process and suggest directions for future creative development.

Research Methodology

In developing the project, a practice-based research (PBR) methodology was implemented. Rooted in the experiential and embodied aspects of creative practice and grounded in the artists' individual bodies of tacit knowledge, this approach proved advantageous for exploring the novel landscape of interplay between body movement and sculptural crochet. The addition of an experimental systems orientation contributed to defining a dynamic inquiry space, which fostered an exploratory approach to combining variables and the emergence of fluid epistemic outcomes.[2]

As a framework for conceptualizing a PBR inquiry, the experimental systems approach provides a lens for finding out "what is out there" (locating tangible and intangible presences, impacts, and outcomes) in the constantly changing and unpredictable landscape of an artistic collaboration. In the context of the Regional Action Research Project, this methodology was well suited to the initial research question, which was framed loosely: What happens when the practices of crochet and choreography (distinct units of tacit knowledge) come together? TIMMY is an emergent response to that question, having surfaced from the dynamic space of the inquiry before becoming central to that space.

Numerous variables were involved in the experimental process, including channels of communication between the artists and with other participants (e.g., online, in person, a/synchronous, visual, verbal), the form and presence of material elements (crocheted structures, artists' bodies), elements of individual practice influencing the parameters of shared creative work (body conditioning, music), environmental factors (locations, daily rhythms, spatial constraints), and physiological elements (how the artists present in the space at a given time—cognitively, physically, socially, etc.).

These variables were worked with tacitly as means to invite the experiential state of "flow," a term coined by psychologist Mihaly Csikszentmihalyi and frequently applied to the experiences of artists, including musicians and dancers. Conceptually, the flow state is recognized as a heightened state of focus and absorption in a given task or activity, which is conducive to optimal engagement, efficiency, motivation, and creativity (Csikszentmihalyi 2014). Csikszentmihalyi's research identifies that artists across disciplines are often able to achieve flow states in the course of creative processes (Csikszentmihalyi 2004), and this is reflected in both Magrics' and Schild's direct experience.

On that experiential basis, the two artists were able to adjust and arrange variables of practice to invite flow into the PBR process as a means to enhance creative performance and foster innovation. The psychological reward inherently derived

---

[2] The notion of experimental systems within the context of PBR in the creative arts is set out in Schwab (2013) with reference to its origins in the work of molecular biologist and scientific historian Hans-Jörg Rheinberger. In contrast to conventional scientific approaches that focus on proving or disproving predetermined hypotheses, experimental systems frame scientific processes as potential drivers of epistemological discovery.

from accessing the flow state could then power the search for new possibilities, affirming play and artistic impulse as values driving the artists' combined practice. In this way, flow was experienced as an aspect of the research process in both individual and in-person collaborative settings. Fostering a considered approach to unifying site-specific, physical, and ephemeral variables, this methodological framework unpins PBR experimentation in the project.

While the collaborative process faced certain constraints in the separation of the artists' physical locations across two states, the geographic distance enabled an autonomy of pacing that caters to asynchronous styles of working. This allowed for individual immersion and reflection, which was then brought forward in shared creative practice carried out face-to-face at convenient intervals. As such, flow was accessed both individually through prolonged periods of rhythmic movement in either crochet construction or dance-based experimentation, and collaboratively, in the discovery of new territories for these individual activities to occupy.

The process demonstrates both advantages and challenges inherent in collaborative PBR, particularly for regional artists, emphasizing the richness of the tacit knowledge space while recognizing the need for innovative solutions in overcoming geographic barriers to sharing and combining that knowledge with other practitioners. In particular, asynchronous working and working at distance/in

Figure 6: Photo in Magrics' Studio by Lee Illfield

geographically distinct locations may be understood as variables in the landscape of collaborative practice, rather than merely as hindrances to the process. This approach aligns with the position (implicit in Critical Path's establishment of the Regional Action Research Project) that creative practice and research are intimately intertwined, co-dependent processes that can be carried out collaboratively regardless of participants' proximity to a common working location.

Outcomes

Tangible outcomes of the process include original material artifacts arising from the research inquiry, which concerns the bringing together of crochet with the moving body. A key example of this is the "Fingers," a set of anatomically-influenced structures developed and made by Magrics in 2023. The design of these was informed by the physical properties of the human hand, and by the opportunity for the crocheted structures to be activated kinesthetically. Recognizing the movement of hands as a key aspect of Schild's movement compositions, Magrics developed the Fingers to be activated by body movement focused in the hands, with the fingers being a natural point of wearability, as well as of kinesthetic amplification for both wearer and viewer.

The first iteration of the Fingers set was trialled by Schild in a live show with band Ungus Ungus Ungus, whose performances characteristically feature a strong visual presence in the form of choreographed and improvised dance, physical theater, design elements, and sometimes puppetry or circus. This was critical in testing the viability of the Fingers as having applications in performance contexts—particularly those of the type already present in Schild's performing arts practice.

The Fingers design was iteratively refined through individualized customizations for Schild as the primary wearer in the research context, and for the logistics of performance—for example, adjusting sizing for a more secure fit, and a color scheme that blended with Schild's skin tone to visually emphasize continuity with the moving body. The effects produced, both in the studio and in performance, were highly arresting and rich in artistic potential on both sides of the collaboration; as a result, the Fingers have come to play a central role in shaping and characterizing TIMMY as both an artistic process and research space.[3]

---

[3] This is an instance of experientially locating a zone of practice conducive to flow states, and prioritizing this in shaping subsequent phases of the research process.

Figure 7: Experimentation with Fingers Prototype During Ungus Ungus Ungus Set at Bulga Beats Festival, 2023

Source: Sheri Court-Kriesch

The development of the Fingers and their activation by a moving body sparked a process of recontextualizing and remixing existing crocheted works as TIMMY artifacts, and in turn a surfacing of various "characters" or habitable sites of bodied expression. This has given rise to the beginnings of a modular system of spatial design, defined by both the topology of the body and environmental influences on body movement. This system relies on discovering individual artifacts — whether existing or purpose-made — as elements of a choreographic architecture.

From the choreographic perspective, Schild has begun to conceptualize the crocheted artifacts as (a) instigators of action-based knowledge that manifests as a boundary-occupying thinking tool, and (b) data-rich structures that can be processed through the perceptual mechanisms of the body — particularly through kinesthetic sensing, as well as tactile, visual, proprioceptive, and vestibular pathways.[4] These epistemic outcomes have potentials for application in creative

---

[4.] Theoretical influences on conceptualizing TIMMY choreographically have included William Forsythe's notion of choreographic objects and Improvisational Technologies, Rudolf Laban's Space Harmony, and the Vulcan Tech Gospel created by Noel Yee and David Cantor.

Figure 8: An Example of Schild's Initial Mapping of Artifacts as Modules, for Use in a Bodily, Kinetic System of Habitation and Movement, 2023[5]

Source: Lee Illfield

practice, as well as in Schild's adjacent practice as a dance movement therapist and Magrics' in arts pedagogy. At the same time, they are fluid in the sense of being in-process foundations of further inquiry.

In experimental systems, we see the generation of knowledge that does not reflect a fixed state of affairs but rather can develop and transform responsively as the practice proceeds. This type of fluid epistemic outcome may inform the creation of new variables (e.g., through the making of new crocheted objects or choreographic languages), and thus set conditions for furthering the research in new, innovative directions. This process supported the surfacing of ideas and images throughout the twelve-month fellowship period. At times, lo-fi, transient approaches were used to iterate ideas—for example, new crocheted objects or related movement sketches were captured on phones, and shared and stored digitally as a means of asynchronous collaboration at distance.

[5.] "Surround" refers to structures not worn on the body, but adjacent to wearables in terms of defining space occupied by a wearer—e.g., the rug pictured. It could also refer to a larger-scale installation as in "Of Giants," 2017, or a dynamic nonwearable object as in "BIOME," 2023.

A counterpoint to this freeform approach was the subsequent incorporation of a more intentionally structured photographic approach to produce higher-quality visual images. This had two stages: an initial DIY shoot using Magrics' DSLR camera, which allowed for visual ideas to be tested and iterated with the use of studio lighting, and a shoot with professional photographer Lee Illfield. Initially intended to serve as documentation of the research process, and input for the project's next stage of development, the images made with Illfield (as seen throughout this chapter) emerged as a fertile landscape for consolidating the progress of the collaborative inquiry while furthering its ground, and communicating findings with stakeholders.

Conclusion

As a project and a process, TIMMY demonstrates the value of bringing together distinct and complementary domains of tacit art-making knowledge to produce novel outcomes. Central to this has been the opportunity to develop the creative interaction without an expected performance or exhibition outcome—a need that has been recognized and encouraged by Critical Path in its facilitation of interdisciplinary collaborations around its primary disciplinary focus area (choreography).

From the outset, creative practice and research were regarded as interlinked processes, both by the participating artists and by Critical Path. This stacking of functions has served to generate an array of outcomes including physical artifacts, visual documentation (some of which takes the form of creative output capable of standing alone as artwork for exhibition), and a rich bank of conceptual and aesthetic starting points for future work.

Loosely structured time, with opportunities for artists to follow their own emergent patterns of engagement (synchronous, asynchronous, intensive, reflective) was identified as a key factor supporting the creative generativity of the research process. With the twelve-month fellowship facilitated lightly by the host organization and guided significantly by the inputs of participants in the research group, there emerged a collective recognition of a need (particularly among regional artists) to be supported in accessing collaborative time—specifically, time that is not oriented to the linear production of work for performance or exhibition. Without emphasis on the production of predetermined outputs, this time lends itself to more fluid processes of uncovering, settling, discarding, and recycling of elements.

Figure 9: Photo by Lee Illfield, Shot in Photographic Studio

These fluid processes have surfaced structured artistic knowledge such as crochet patterns and movement sequences, alongside (and perhaps more significantly) an increasing, shared familiarity with the constellation of structural, bodied, sensory, and conceptual elements that constitutes TIMMY. In combination, these position the collaborative project as fluid in both form and potentials for activation and engagement.

References

Csikszentmihalyi, Mihaly. 2004. "Flow, the Secret to Happiness." TED, video, 18:43. https://www.ted.com/talks/mihaly_csikszentmihalyi_flow_the_secret_to_happiness.

Csikszentmihalyi, Mihaly. 2014. "Flow: Psychology, Creativity, & Optimal Experience with Mihaly Csikszentmihalyi." 59:45. Kanopy Streaming.

CHAPTER 17

Deceptive Practices

Marilia Lyra Bergamo and Giselle Penn

Abstract

This chapter presents a practice-based research (PBR) design/art small-world system of robotic deceptive flowers and their reproductive behavior. The research methodology implies the development of different generations of outputs named robotic individualizations. The present text also describes the background research and the computational behaviors coded into each robotic body. The key concept is based on the idea that deceptive flowers decoy pollinators by advertising a reward, which is not provided. The genus Aristolochia inspires the system, which uses fly-trapping to spread its pollen. This study seeks aesthetic visual fabrics and sizes to impress people to interact with the robotic structures. Once a person is close enough to the flower, it should trap the person for a few seconds. The project is also a feasible design experiment intending to study individuals' reactions to the trap conditions. The research also aims to sensitize individuals to the high cost of the mind and body's reproductive circumstances.

Introduction

This chapter will describe a practice-based research (PBR) design/art small-world system of generations of robotic deceptive flowers and their computational behavior. Within this practice, we understand technology as an evolutive process, and we will contextualize this argument by employing Gilbert Simondon's concept of individualization. *Individualization* is a process that all technical beings undergo. As such, the chapter presents the background research that motivated this individualization and how the generations of this artefact had taken its forms and behaviors.

Our methodology implies that these structures are about reproduction as a transductive act within individualization, a process that escapes the individual body where it takes place. This study is motivated by this topic because reproduction is so essential for the continuity of life. Evolution itself is a concept described by an immensurable time of recursive reproductions and adaptations (in opposition to the idea of creation). We want to emphasize the importance of this argument in both life and technology development.

Using a small-world as a solution also highlights that individualization does not happen just within isolated individuals but due to their relationships with others. Although each robotic flower has autonomy within its own body, the other also feels what happens with the one.

Two goals are pursued with this endeavor: the perception of flowers connected and behaving separately and humans as part of another species' reproduction process. As all reproductions have a cost, we intend to securely trap humans within the robotic flowers to mark this conceptual condition.

Background Research

Living organisms can be perceived as more and less individualized where the difference is not necessarily related to superiority in their vital organization (Simondon et al. 2020). Through *individuation* theory it is possible to understand robotic plants as small-world systems that challenge the concept of the individual. A plant, a living being, is in an excellent position to question robotics' biological mimicry because the biological definition of a plant can flow from colony to rhizome to individual. *Individuation* can be a philosophical response to understanding the process of being in time, including robots, in many levels of integrated systems. The orders of magnitudes of interchange information transfer the notion of the individual to the individuation process, in other words no individuation exists without being in transformation: "the living being retains within itself an activity of permanent individuation" (Simondon et al. 2020, 21). The metastability of the process is perceived as individual, and metastability is viewed in orders of magnitude or domains.

Within the individuation process, transduction is the mechanism by which systems exchange. According to Simondon, transduction corresponds to the existence of a nexus. It is an operation, either physical, biological, mental, or social, where an activity propagates from each part to another part within a domain and between domains. O'Sullivan and Igoe (2004) in the field of physical computing consider transduction through a limited definition of transforming analogue to digital information and vice versa. It is essential to establish that although it is also a transductive event, the only transformation between analogue to digital and vice versa precludes a broader understanding of transduction as the process of propagation that enables living structures to exist in a metastability state.

Simondon's individuation theory also comprehends evolution as an essential process of both technological and living beings. Within evolution, while individuations are limited in time and space, the specific *reproduction capacity* creates the absence of this limit. Simondon argues "Adding a living being is a specific transductive act permanent and localised, without analogy in physics: a particular individuation added to a specific one" (Simondon et al. 2020, 235).

In the case of technical beings, in which this study understands robots as a particular example, evolution results from an internal condition within the being (Simondon 2007). Caused by the imperfection of abstract thinking to reflect conditions of existence, the technical being faces obstacles in its interior functioning. That incapacity is born from the saturation of the system of subsystems to resist the limits of individuation (Simondon 2007). A new technical being is assembled and becomes possible through abstract thinking and technologic relaxation, and here, Simondon explicitly changes the individuation process and renames this *individualization*. As such, reproduction is a very particular form of transduction, which requires further investigation as outlined below.

Research Methodology and the Robotic Outputs

The Aristolochia species of plant uses a reproductive behavior characterized by deception deployed through a variety of hairs and appendages; a decaying protein scent, and anthers and stigmas hidden in the bottom of the flower, mimicking decaying matter. It also has a kettle-like structure to lock the pollinator for twenty-four hours until the female flower becomes male and liberates the fly carrying potential pollen to other female flowers. This reproductive behavior sounds fascinating, and while not trying to mimic or understand the plant itself, the design outlined here searches for a way of recreating the attraction/trapping structure to entice people to interact with its robotic structure.

Would people feel deceived by translating this behavior in plants to a social situation, trapped inside something for a few seconds? Would people spending some time inside the robotic structure feel concerned or alarmed? Can this experience raise questions about the reproductive body? These are all research questions in art/design.

Another challenge of this research is to describe how things become what they become appropriate for the artist/designer within the individualization process, which is co-dependent on the specific design/art concepts, technologies, and practices of assembling.

While answering these questions requires building the structure, letting it interact with people, and conducting data gathering with direct and indirect agents within this process, the description of the individualization itself is the main object of this chapter once the system is under construction. Figure 1 presents an *ontology* of the process that forges the first generation of this process of individualization. It is presented as an ontology based on Heidegger's philosophy "to lay down in front of" a metaphysical oblivion of existence (apud Hui et al. 2016, 33). In Figure 1, it is possible to see it becoming a thing, from the initial abstract idea of a robotic flower into an assembled structure capable of behavior and interaction. The prototype is necessarily small in scale. It cannot interact with a person's entire body or trap a person, but only a hand or a small object like the wooden mannequin used to simulate a person's presence. Within the Ontology presented in Figure 1, two things coincide; the robotic rigging and the textile-deceptive manifestation.

Figure 1: Aristolochia Ontology from May 14 to August 11

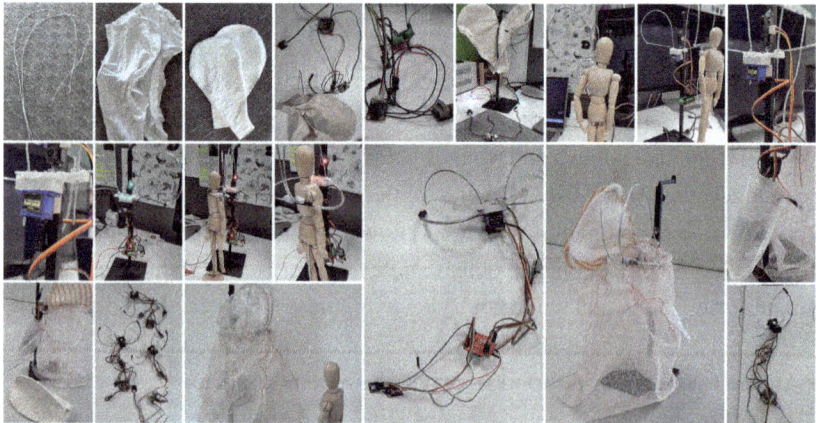

Source: Authors' collection

The robotic riggings (Figure 2), which can be considered a second generation within this individualization process, were sent to an exhibition in the National Museum of the Republic in Brasilia, Brazil, in September 2023. The collective exhibition is called #15.EmMeio, is in its fifteenth edition and is characterized by the presentation of experimental projects in Art and Technology. (Figure 2 shows how the robotic rigging composed of three flowers was exhibited and experimented with by the public.)

Figure 2: Aristolochia Rigging, Exhibit in #15.EmMeio #22Art International Congress: XenoPaisagens (n.d.), September 2023 on National Museum of the Republic – Brasilia, Brazil

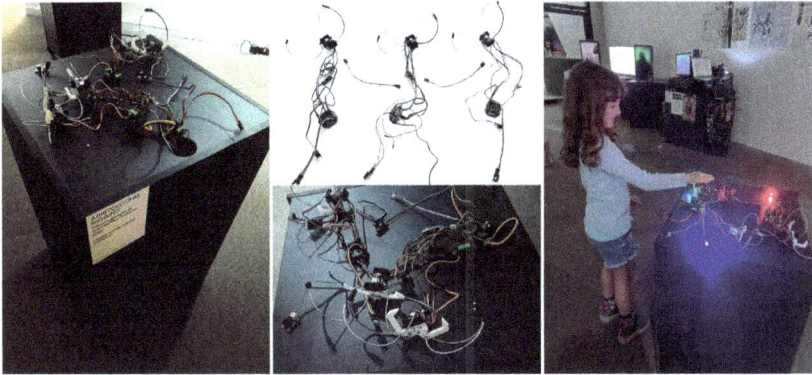

Source: Authors' collection

Within this second generation, the goal was to test the communication between individuals. The electronic board used within this process was prepared for this small-world communication, allowing it to exchange information about its sensors and coordinate interactive reactions accordingly (Bergamo and Benigno 2023). They structure could not trap people — as noted above only a hand could be trapped by it — but the exhibition allowed us to see the potential of this interactive body and of the collective to be perceived as a system.

As of this writing, a third generation of this system has been achieved. It was exhibited in the Chromatic Festival in Newcastle, NSW (Chromatic 2023). Figure 3 shows this individualization process, going through the challenge of using a stronger servo and being able to handle a weightier metal structure produced by Nathan Keogh, a fellow artist. A more significant technical stage was undertaken within this process because the growth of the mechanical challenges

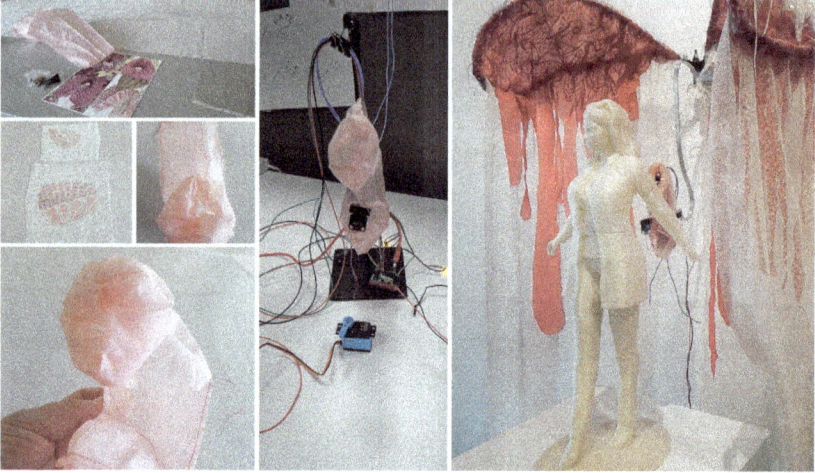

Source: Authors' collection

had created a bottleneck situation where the design needed to be completely rethought to ultimately make the robotic structure human-sized.

Also, a new distance sensor was used due to the necessary distance between the interactive actor and the robotic structure. This also presented challenges because although more precise for longer distances, it was also more sensitive to the broken connections when the piece needed to be turned on and off during exhibition open hours.

Figure 3 presents documentation of the process of building this third generation. The level of complexity has changed significantly, especially regarding the development of the concept of attracting people through the texture and visuality produced by the textile assemblage. There was an extensive effort toward transforming the fabric into a female flower, reflected by the transcription of the flower patterns onto fabric and the development of a sack structure able to receive the electronic circuit. The metal arrangements' curvature also reflected nature's organicity, including appropriate curves and waves.

The challenge of a weightier metal structure determined the size of the piece, and in order to express the concept of trapping people, we printed a 3D figure to represent the goal of interactivity. The public moved the 3D-printed figure into and out of the structure to see the deceptive flower working. The robotic structure could function with public interaction for the three days of the exhibition.

Coding the Robotic Structures

Computation is an essential part of the individualization process of robotic structures. Within Simondon's theory, we could not identify robotic structures as technical beings when his thesis was produced in the 1960s, as robots were at the time only available as products of scientific fiction and in no way as accessible to the public as they are today. Only within the philosophical discussions of Yuk Hui (2018) could we connect the notion of individualization to a digital object and understand this as the necessary computation for the development of robotic structures.

Digital Objects undergo individualization like technological beings, although the conditions of their existence differ from physical to digital environments. However, to exist as a digital object, computation is obviously required. We do not intend to describe here the differences between these existential conditions, as this would require a profound reflection on how digital existence is integrated within robotic physical structures, and to the best of our knowledge we do not have a specific reference to this issue.

The coding process itself evolves in tandem with the existence of each generation of robotic structure within the individualization process. This is intrinsically related to the use of specific sensors. Our coding was based on logics developed within the firmware aligned with our chosen hardware, called Windrose (Bergamo and Benigno 2023). The firmware is based on object-oriented language in C++ and is open source. We create a class called Being, where each robotic structure acts as an autonomous agent. The class receives data from the sensor connected to the board and can receive information through Tx/Rx pins connected to it. This practical transfer of information between the boards allows us to use these as building blocks to create a small-world system. All the generations use the same board with the same pattern of information exchange, which would allow many generations to exchange information between themselves.

Figure 4 represents the abstract thinking behind the concept of autonomous agents. In all generations, the *s* represents the sensors, one for proximity, another for presence and another for magnetic closure sensing. In the image, the *a* represents the actuator, a servo and a buzzer. Last, the *e.s* represents data captured from other beings connected to it, an external agent. The entire Being class is composed of the setting of that sensor, a Decision Layer and a couple of actuators that react accordingly to the internal agent decision process.

Figure 4: Autonomous Agent Organization, the Image Represents the Abstract Logic of Generations 1, 2, and 3

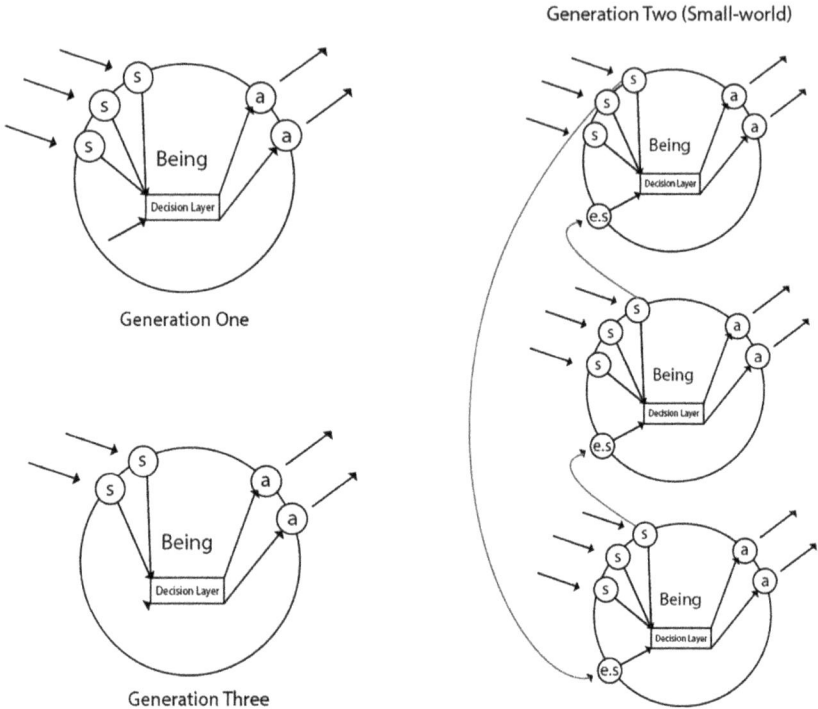

Source: Authors' collection

It is within the Decision Layer that the computational poetics and the concept of behavior mimesis happens. While we do not intend to replicate the Aristolochia behaviour literally, we do need to culturally include behaviors to adapt our robotic structure to its existence within the concept we are trying to achieve. As a mix of both inspiration from the natural world, added to computational creative coding, we have developed the following decision-making layer expressed in pseudocode for generation 1.

1. If I sense someone close, I open myself mapping the distance accordingly using also sound and green lights as indication of the distance from me;
2. If someone is inside me, I will close complete for three seconds, and will change my color lights to red;
3. If I detect I am closed, I will open for more three seconds before returning to step 1 and change my color lights to green;

For generation 2, the code was modified as follows to use data from *e.s*:

1. If I sense someone close, I open myself mapping the distance accordingly using also sound and green lights as indication of the distance from me;
3. If someone is inside me, I will close complete for three seconds, and will change my color lights;
4. If someone is inside my neighbor, I will change my color lights to blue;
5. If I detect I am closed, I will open for more three seconds before returning to step 1;

In Generation 3, the robotic structure lost its magnetic sensor, and the code was modified as follows for use in the exhibition:

1. If I sense someone close, I open myself mapping the distance accordingly using also sound and yellow lights as indication of the distance from me;
2. If someone is inside me, I will turn my lights down, and close entirely otherwise I will return to step 1;

There is a simplification of rules from generations 1 and 2 in generation 3 due to the loss of the magnetic sensor. Although the behaviour was more straightforward in generation 3, it was designed to be more efficient for the more considerable robotic body. The body here relies on one sensor to define two different states. The result was a more stable behaviour within the individual. (This new coding is still to be tested when communicating with other individuals within a small-world network.)

Discussion

Exhibiting parts of the individualization process is a fundamental action of this research, which contributes directly to the evolution of each step. In an exhibition, the robotic structure must reach a material existence and be able to interact with the public, which coordinates and changes the process of individuation itself.

A "generation" is a metastable individual—contrived into existence and destined to die in favor of another generation. The individual in this experiment can only be understood within its order of magnitude, for example, being able to encapsulate a hand or a 3D-printed figure. The collection of those individuals represents an ontology capable of indicating the individualization process which can be perceived externally.

The reproductive discussion intended with this research praxis will still be addressed when the individualization process delivers a metastable individual capable of encapsulating an actual full-size human for a few seconds, where some of our original research questions can be addressed.

Future Research

We have applied for funding for this project and intend to create a fourth-generation of five human-sized flowers. However, if funding is unavailable, we will develop at least one fourth-generation human-sized flower and connect all the generations in a small-world network. This connection will allow the establishment of a network, and its existence will depend on another exhibition space for us to more meaningfully address the necessary research question this project proposes.

Acknowledgments

We thank Sandro Benigno for constant support and help with the hardware design that this installation depends on. To Nathan Keogh for his contribution to the development of metal structures and servo motor adaptions to create the third generation of this project. To #EmMeio and Chromatic Festival for allowing the exhibition of this artwork and the University of Newcastle and FASTlab for creating the conditions for this study to exist.

References

#22Art International Congress: XenoPaisagens. n.d. "Programação Completa." Accessed November 21, 2023. http://www.medialab.unb.br/index.php/component/sppagebuilder/?view=page&id=19.

Ballif, Edmée. 2023. "Anticipatory Regimes in Pregnancy: Cross-Fertilising Reproduction and Parenting Culture Studies." *Sociology* 57 (3): 476–492. https://doi.org/10.1177/00380385221107492.

Bergamo, Marilia Lyra, and Sandro Benigno. 2023. "Hardware Speculation for Robotic Plants Through Cellular Automata Principle." Presented at the Proceedings of the ALIFE 2023: Ghost in the Machine: Proceedings of the 2023

Artificial Life Conference. ALIFE 2023: Ghost in the Machine: Proceedings of the 2023 Artificial Life Conference, Online, July 24–28, 2023. ASME. https://doi.org/10.1162/isal_a_00565.

Blackstone Gallery: Art-Science Exhibition. 2023. Accessed November 21, 2023. https://www.chromaticfestival.com/blackstone.

Hui, Yuk. 2018. "On the Soul of Technical Objects: Commentary on Simondon's 'Technics and Eschatology.'" *Theory, Culture and Society* 35 (6): 97–111.

Hui, Y., N. K. Hayles, P. Krapp, R. Raley, and S. Weber. 2016. *On the Existence of Digital Objects*. University of Minnesota Press.

O'Sullivan, Dan, and Tom Igoe. 2004. *Physical Computing: Sensing and Controlling the Physical World with Computers*. 1st ed. Thomson.

Simondon, Gilbert. 2007. *El modo de existencia de los objetos técnicos*. 1ª edição. Prometeo Libros.

Simondon, Gilbert, Luís Eduardo Ponciano Aragon, and Guilherme Figueiredo dos Santos Ivo. 2020. *A individuação à luz das noções de forma e de informação*. 1ª edição. Editora 34.

CHAPTER 18

Strangers in a Car Park: A Case Study in Microbudget Feature Filmmaking

Stuart McBratney

Abstract

This chapter outlines a practical model for microbudget feature film production, drawing from historical examples and personal experience, focusing on the production of *Strangers in a Car Park* (2025, 85 minutes). It explores my experience as the writer and director of five major microbudget productions — four movies and a TV series — and details strategies for script development, casting, locations, cinematography, and post-production. The study illustrates how filmmakers can create high-quality cinematic productions and secure international distribution, even with limited budgets. It highlights how using nonstandard technology, such as affordable Chinese cameras and lenses, combined with student collaborations, can significantly reduce production costs.

Achieving the "Film Look"

As a teenager desperate to make movies, I had no money and very little equipment. I wanted my home movies to look like *Star Wars*. But how could I make something so cinematic without millions of dollars? To answer that, we must first interrogate the word itself, "cinematic."

While most people can instinctively differentiate between an amateur skateboarding video on YouTube and a masterpiece like *Apocalypse Now*, they may struggle to articulate the technical and aesthetic elements that create this distinction. We know that one looks more "cinematic," but what does that really mean? To answer, let us go back a century or so. When motion picture film was invented in the late nineteenth century, various frame rates abounded. By 1909, twenty-four frames per second became the industry standard; it struck the perfect balance between smooth motion and manageable production costs.

The 35 mm frame, which became synonymous with cinema, did not achieve its status through technical superiority. Instead, it was inventor Thomas Edison's business acumen that cemented his 35 mm projectors as the standard (Nowell-Smith 1996).

Figure 1: Location Photo, *Strangers in a Car Park*

Source: Kamis (2023)

For a hundred or so years, films were almost exclusively exhibited using this technology until digital projectors replaced them in the early twenty-first century. The absence of competing systems meant that 35 mm celluloid projected at 24 frames per second became the de facto look of cinema. Our perception of what constitutes a "film look" is a product of standardization and conditioning.

So then, how can a filmmaker make something cinematic without millions of dollars? I have spent the last few decades attempting to answer that question, and my answers have taken the form of four indie feature films (and counting), one TV series, and hundreds of commercials. Collectively these form a practice-based research agenda into the possibilities for more democratic cinematic filmmaking.

Collectively these form a practice-based research agenda into the possibilities for more democratic cinematic filmmaking. Making something cinematic is about more than matching the 35 mm film aesthetic, though that's part of it. It involves numerous factors including locations, performance, composition, lighting, and lens blur. It is impossible to cover everything in a single book chapter, but below I provide a brief overview using my 2025 film *Strangers in a Car Park*.

Historical Context

In the 1990s, filmmakers including Richard Linklater (*Slacker*), Kevin Smith (*Clerks*), Robert Rodriguez (*El Mariachi*), and Darren Aronofsky (*Pi*) produced feature films on extremely low budgets which secured international distribution and launched their careers.

Smith's *Clerks* (1994) was made for $27,000, primarily funded by maxing out credit cards. Rodriguez's *El Mariachi* (1992) was made for $7,000; this figure itself being part of the film's marketing campaign. Aronofsky's *Pi* (1998) was produced on a $60,000 budget, with much of the funding coming from private investors. These films demonstrated that compelling stories and creative problem-solving could overcome financial constraints.

The landscape of microbudget filmmaking has evolved significantly since the days of *Clerks* and *El Mariachi*. Advances in technology have lowered the barriers to entry, allowing filmmakers to create high-quality content with relatively inexpensive equipment. Steven Soderberg has made several films on iPhones including *Unsane* (2018) and *High Flying Bird* (2019). Director Sean Baker shot *Tangerine* (2015), on an iPhone 5s, and went on to win the Palme D'Or at Cannes in 2024 with *Anora*.

In addition to lowering the cost of production hardware, technology has also expanded consumers' access to movies. The primary challenge for contemporary microbudget filmmakers is no longer access to gear, or even to attain distribution, but rather their ability to secure viewers' attention. Streaming may allow filmmakers access to living rooms around the world, though their work may be a needle in a haystack among higher profile films with significant marketing budgets. Unlike in the 1990s, simply making a movie is no longer newsworthy.

Figure 2: Poster of *Pop-Up* (2015)

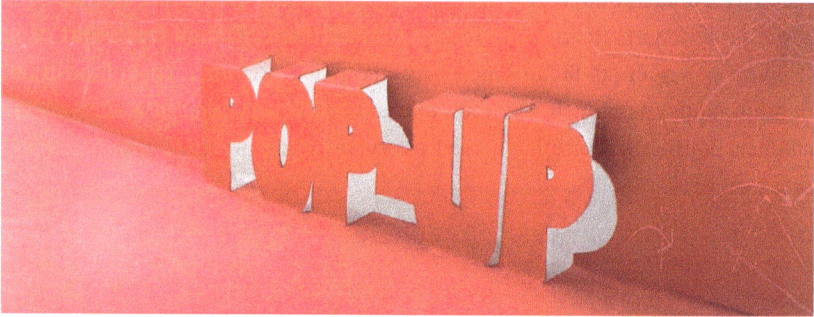

Antecedents

I produced my first microbudget feature film *Spudmonkey* in 2000 on a budget of $50,000. Shot on Super 16 mm and edited on an Avid suite, the film was a learning experience in pragmatism and bricolage—writing my available resources into the script and scaling back the scope to accommodate limited means. The film did not secure distribution and literally sat on a shelf until YouTube was invented. It would be over a decade before I started another feature film, though in the meantime I secured work in advertising and subsequently made around five hundred TV commercials with clients including Honda, Nike, and McDonalds.

In 2010 I made *Back in the Soviet Bloc*, a factual TV series shot in Russia and Ukraine comprising of 7×26 minute episodes, which was later acquired by SBS Australia, and is currently available on the documentary streaming platform iWonder.[1] With a budget of $30,000, the series utilized a Canon 5D Mark II and crew of two people—myself and presenter Julia Nalivaiko. SBS reported that the series was viewed approximately 800,000 times via their broadcast platforms and SBS On Demand. This experience taught me that I did not need a big crew to make a movie, nor "permission" from a gatekeeper such as a studio or funding body. I could just do it myself, like the trailblazers Smith and Linklater. And thanks to this new DSLR technology, the "film look" was finally within my reach.

Pop-Up (2016), my third major project, was a pivotal moment in my career, as it led to my representation in Los Angeles as a director, and subsequently more opportunities as a filmmaker. The film, which served as the creative component

---

[1] https://iwonder.com/.

of my PhD thesis, explored the interconnected stories of three individuals in Australia and Romania. With a budget of $50,000, it was shot over two years on the RED Scarlet-X and received recognition at numerous international film festivals. It subsequently secured distribution in China, the US, and Canada via streaming platforms and Blu-ray/DVD.

My third feature, *Don't Read This on a Plane* (2020), marked a step up in terms of budget and scope. With a budget of $125,000, the film was shot in nine countries using the 8K RED EPIC-W. It showcased the potential of microbudget productions to achieve a high level of visual polish and technical sophistication, in which I pushed the concept of "bricolage"[2] to an extreme level—filming all over Europe. It has subsequently secured distribution via streaming, broadcast, and Blu-ray/DVD in sixteen countries spanning North America, Europe, and Asia, and has been translated into several languages.

Strangers in a Car Park (2025)

Budget constraints, minimal resources, and accessible locations were all considerations during the creation of *Strangers in a Car Park*. The film's primary setting, the multilevel concrete car park of The University of Newcastle's Callaghan campus, was chosen for its brutalist yet cinematic quality, twenty-four-hour availability to staff such as myself, and minimal need for set dressing. This approach mirrors the strategies outlined in my PhD thesis, "Shoestring Theory: Pragmatism and Bricolage in Microbudget Feature Filmmaking" (McBratney 2017), which emphasized the importance of adapting the narrative to fit the production's logistical and financial limitations. Knowing I could access the car park, I wrote the script around it.

Screenplay

With financial constraints limiting the scope of the production, the script must employ bricolage—writing with the available resources in mind. Additionally, pragmatism must be practiced to ensure that scenes are filmable without set construction or complex visual effects. By oscillating between pragmatism and bricolage, the film can make the transition from script to screen without the reliance on major financing.

---

[2] Merriam-Webster: https://www.merriam-webster.com/dictionary/bricolage

Figure 3: Streaming Service, *Don't Read This on a Plane* (Movie Generation TV, Croatia)

Prior to my commencement of the scripting process, I contacted actors I already knew, and whose talent and screen presence belied their relative obscurity. I asked if they would be interested in playing a lead role in a movie for deferred payment, (otherwise known as profit share). Those who responded enthusiastically were written into the story. Here is a synopsis which resulted from this approach:

> *In a single, intense night in a concrete car park, four lives collide, each unravelling secrets of tragedy, triumph, compulsion, and connection.*
>
> *Renee, a hardworking cleaner, works the late shift at an auditorium during the prestigious Newcastle Bravery Awards. Peering through a door at the ceremony, she is horrified to recognize local surfer Damien—a hero being honored—as the man who once assaulted her.*

Figure 4: Still from *Strangers in a Car Park*

> *Overwhelmed, she flees and bumps into Aleki, a gentle but imposing Samoan courier. In a moment of vulnerability, Renee confides in him, inspiring him to*

bravely and publicly accuse Damien of assault. Aleki is quickly silenced by security and booed away.

Later, in the venue's car park, Damien and his fiancée Lana are approached by Aleki and Renee. They want Lana to know the truth—that her heroic husband-to-be is dangerous.

As the tense confrontation unfolds, the film divides into four backstories, revealing the intertwined lives of Renee, Aleki, Damien, and Lana. Each character's journey paints a surprising, poignant, vivid picture of their struggles and triumphs, culminating in a chaotic and revelatory finale.

Casting

Casting is a critical component of microbudget filmmaking, where the success often hinges on the performances of unknown actors. Selecting those willing to work within the microbudget framework is essential. The focus must be on actors' talent and ability to bring characters to life, rather than their star power. Actors must be flexible and committed, understanding that they may need to work without the amenities typically available on higher-budget sets. No one gets their own trailer. Catering is more French fries than foie gras. Makeup is often do-it-yourself or eschewed altogether.

The cast are often found online rather than through agencies. Platforms such as StarNow provide access to reels, and actors can register their interest in casting calls posted on the site. My casting call for *Strangers in a Car Park* yielded 1,555 applications from actors, some of whom were ultimately cast.

Figure 5: Still from *Strangers in a Car Park*

A key to creating a cinematic film is cinematic locations. An apartment is convenient, but white walls are boring, and they are the hallmark of an amateur production. Before I wrote a word of *Strangers in a Car Park*, I listed the most visually interesting locations I could access.

The car park at the University of Newcastle's Callaghan campus provided a controlled environment that allowed for efficient filming, reducing the need for costly permits. Other University of Newcastle locations included the Q Building's TV studio, Newcastle Conservatorium of Music's Harold Lobb Concert Hall, various streets within Callaghan campus for driving scenes, various buildings as establishing shots, the nursing and midwifery training ward as a hospital stand-in, and several generic foyers and offices.

By utilizing these locations I was able to obtain cinematic production values with minimal set dressing. Around half of the film was shot at a University of Newcastle venue. The remaining scenes were spread across public or private locations including Newcastle Beach, Nobbys Beach, Horseshoe Beach, Bar Beach, King Edward Park, Shepherds Corner Church in Woodville, Hotel Kerwick in Ipswich, Newcastle Winter Fun Fest, Maitland Showground, and two private residences. Location fees totaled $319.

The production phase of *Strangers in a Car Park* involved the use of affordable digital cinema cameras and anamorphic lenses to attain a highly cinematic look. Traditionally, anamorphic cinematography has been beyond the reach of micro-budget filmmakers due to the prohibitive costs, with lenses typically ranging from $40,000 to $140,000. More affordable anamorphic lenses from Chinese manufacturers such as Vazen, Sirui, Laowa, and Great Joy made their debut in 2019, retailing between $2,000 and $5,000.

Additionally, the advent of new digital cinema cameras like the Chinese-made Z CAM E2-S6, which retails for approximately $4,000, offers a cost-effective alternative to traditional industry-standard digital cameras from the US (RED), Japan (Sony), or Germany (ARRI), which cost between $50,000 and $200,000. I purchased my cameras and lenses on eBay in used condition. The total cost of my two Vazen anamorphic lenses plus one Z CAM digital cinema camera was approximately $10,000. (See the camera and lens setup in Figure 7) By

Figure 6: Location Photo, *Strangers in a Car Park*

Source: Kamis (2023)

Figure 7: Location Photo, *Strangers in a Car Park*

Source: Kamis (2023)

comparison, an ARRI Alexa LF and two Cooke Anamorphic lenses would cost approximately $250,000.

Additional production tools, such as stabilizers and LED lights, were also manufactured in China, including the DJI Mavic Air 2 drone, Zhiyun Crane 2 gimbal, Aputure lighting, and Ledgo LEDs. This cost-effective yet high-quality gear allowed us portability and flexibility at a considerable price reduction.

The total budget of *Strangers in a Car Park* was approximately AUD 25,000. The primary expenses were catering, flights, accommodation, transport, external hard drives, additional equipment rental, and petrol. Three of the actors would only agree to perform in the film if they were paid union minimum rates up front, though their days on set were minimal. Note that this figure does not include the cost of purchasing the camera equipment which I already owned. Other accessories such as lighting, dollies, and tripods were hired at no cost through the University of Newcastle.

Crew

The crew consisted primarily of undergraduate media production students who wished to receive experience on a feature film in major production roles. This approach not only kept costs down but also provided valuable training opportunities for aspiring filmmakers. Students were offered course credit for their work on set.

I took on the dual role of director and cinematographer, allowing for greater creative control and ensuring that the visual and narrative aspects of the film were closely aligned. My experience working as a cinematographer is considerable, having shot most of the five hundred TV commercials I have directed, plus *Back in the Soviet Bloc*, and *Don't Read This on a Plane* (uncredited). My knowledge of parts of lighting, camera operation, and image composition allowed me to work with a relatively inexperienced team; their tenacity and dedication was more valuable than previous credits on a film set.

On average, the crew size was around seven people per day. On some days it was just the director/cinematographer alone capturing the sunrise, or waves breaking at Newcastle Beach. On other days there was a crew of two, such as the "jail" scenes shot at Hotel Kerwick.

Post-Production

Footage was 5.9K ProRes Raw 12bit recorded via a Ninja V+ external recorder/ monitor. Each day of principal photography resulted in approximately one tera-byte of data, which was backed up onto two separate external hard drives, then transcoded using Adobe Media Encoder into ProRes Proxy video with 1/30th of

Figure 8: Location Photo, *Strangers in a Car Park*

Source: Kamis (2023)

Figure 9: Location Photo, *Strangers in a Car Park*

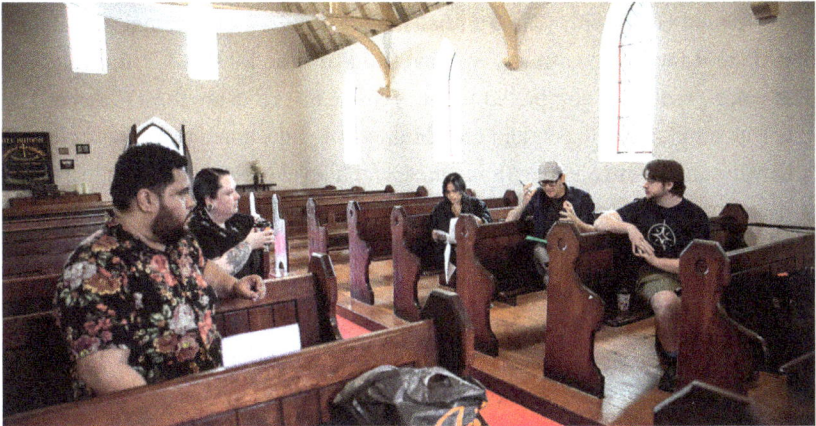

Source: Roxburgh (2023)

the file size. The proxy footage of the entire film totaled less than 1 TB, allowing for ease of editing.

Upon the proxy edit being completed using Final Cut Pro X, a shot list was generated, and the uncompressed Raw footage was transferred onto 3 × 4 TB

Figure 10: Location Photo, *Strangers in a Car Park*

Figure 10: Location Photo, *Strangers in a Car Park*

Source: Kamis (2023)

Samsung T9 SSD drives. Using an Apple MacBook Pro 16.2in M3 Max (16-core CPU/40-core GPU) with 48 GB unified memory and a 2 TB internal SSD, I then edited the Raw footage directly in Final Cut Pro X in 4,096 × 1,716 resolution. The color grade was completed within Final Cut Pro using the Dehancer Pro Lite film emulation plug-in and the "Maffei" LUT designed by Lukas Eriksen.

Downscaling from 5.9K to 4K ensured a high level of detail and image quality, while allowing shots to be cropped without a loss of resolution. The Z CAM E2-S6 has sensor dimensions of 6,244 × 4,168 pixels. With the Vazen anamorphic lenses having a 1.8X squeeze factor, this equates to desqueezed acquisition footage measuring 11,239 × 4,168 pixels. This subsequently allowed for significant horizontal reframing, and partial vertical reframing to fit into the master resolution of 4,096 × 1,716 pixels at a 2.39:1 aspect ratio.

Artificial Intelligence Tools

The AI tools within Descript, Adobe Podcast, Topaz Video AI, Photoshop, and ChatGPT were utilized in *Strangers in a Car Park*. They were primarily used to polish and augment various elements of the sound and image, addressing shortcomings inherent to microbudget productions.

Figure 11: Location Photo, *Strangers in a Car Park*

Source: Kamis (2024)

ChatGPT was utilized to generate an image of a dog eating chocolate while wearing a raincoat at the beach which was used in a text chat between characters, plus logos for apps seen briefly on screen.

Initial poster designs were generated using ChatGPT based on prompts detailing the film's four key characters, the car park setting, and an "indie movie" tone. While the majority of these AI-generated designs were not viable, a few provided conceptual frameworks. These preliminary designs informed on-location photoshoots with the actors, which were then refined in Photoshop to create the final posters. Notably the final poster designs bore little resemblance to the AI-generated ideas.

To transform a cramped, run-down hotel room in Ipswich into a jail cell, Photoshop's "Generative Fill" feature was employed to extend the scenery. This feature leverages Adobe's Firefly Generative AI model to manipulate images based on textual prompts. After shrinking the original footage within the frame, Generative Fill was used to expand the walls and ceiling, helping to transform a hotel room into a jail cell.

Topaz Video AI proved indispensable in post-production, particularly in mitigating the high noise levels of footage shot in low-light conditions. Conventional noise reduction software within Final Cut Pro or DaVinci Resolve was insufficient for the task, whereas Topaz Video AI generated a clean image barely distinguishable from one exposed correctly. While occasionally introducing strange artifacts

Figure 12: Still from *Strangers in a Car Park*

such as rippled skin, I was able to achieve satisfactory results by experimenting with its output settings.

Audio quality presented another challenge, as it was often compromised by the use of poorly maintained student equipment. Descript's Studio Sound feature and Adobe's Podcast Enhance each allowed substandard audio to be regenerated to an acceptable quality with an exceptionally low signal-to-noise ratio and minimal digital artifacts. The process involved initial cleanup of the dialogue using iZotope RX 7's "Dialogue Isolate" function. In some instances, the audio quality was too poor to be salvaged, in which cases I dubbed the actors' voices.

Conclusion

Strangers in a Car Park was completed on a budget that would have purchased eight frames—or a third of a second—of *Avengers Endgame* (2019). This was possible due to the writer-director-cinematographer practicing pragmatism and bricolage, and working with a crew of hardworking students eager to learn. Through strategic planning and resourcefulness, filmmakers such as myself with extremely limited budgets can generate high production values, cinematic imagery, and polished sound design, allowing $25,000 and $250,000,000 movies to sit side-by-side on streaming platforms. At the time of writing, the film has secured distribution in the United States and Canada. It will be available through Amazon, Fandango at Home, Hoopla, Verizon, Rogers & Shaw, YouTube Movies & TV, local cable providers, and Tubi.

However, this expanded access also introduces challenges. The vast quantity of content available on Netflix, Amazon, Stan, and other major streaming platforms necessitates rigorous promotion to ensure visibility and engagement. When microbudget films do find an audience however, they have the potential for tremendous cultural impact, and to launch careers, such as in the cases of Smith, Aronofsky, and Linklater.

As AI technologies evolve at a startling pace, their applications in scriptwriting, editing, sound design, and visual effects are poised to become more sophisticated. When used strategically — to augment production values and correct errors — this can be a tremendous benefit to filmmakers working at all budget levels.

Filmmakers who strive to create work that is moving, inventive, and cinematic now have additional tools to overcome budgetary restraints. And while AI-generated content is fast becoming ubiquitous, it is my hope that artists have an intrinsic desire to express the human experience and that audiences will seek and reward such authenticity.

For filmmaking to retain its place in culture as a valuable art form, AI must remain an augmentative tool rather than a replacement for human expression and ingenuity.

The future of the "film look" will likely be shaped by market demand. With the rise of smartphone content, vertical video formats, and higher frame rates, these trends may redefine what audiences perceive as "cinematic." However, just as photography's invention spurred new forms of painting, emerging technologies may lead to new interpretations of cinematic aesthetics. Regardless of the technological changes ahead, the power of motion pictures as a storytelling medium remains strong. The next century holds countless possibilities for how this art form will evolve.

References

McBratney, S. 2017. "Shoestring Theory: Pragmatism and Bricolage in Microbudget Feature Filmmaking." PhD diss., Australian Government Research Training Program.

Nowell-Smith, Geoffrey, ed. 1996. *The Oxford history of world cinema.* Oxford University Press.

SECTION V:

Future Tools, Future Research Workflows

Introduction

This final section touches on the transformative potential of artificial intelligence. There is no doubt we are already deep into a new era in which all forms of creative research will evolve in tandem with a host of still-emerging AI agents and tools (Esling and Devis 2020). We are very aware that all the previous chapters in this volume cover projects which could be achievable with variations of AI-centered workflows (Anantrasirichai and Bull 2022). The capabilities and implications of these technologies will take time to realize, as well as required new critical literacies toward each new tool and competencies such as prompt engineering. There are obvious advantages, for example, in being able to simulate, accelerate, and scale forms of rapid prototyping outlined earlier in this volume (see Section II). Despite the very real anxieties prompted by these technologies, there is also excitement over the potential of human–AI collaborative workflows (Cropley et al. 2023; Korteling et al. 2021; Peeters et al. 2021; Vinchon et al. 2023). The two chapters in this section suggest these poles in current debates within a rapidly shifting field of possibilities (Maslej et al. 2024).

First, Jon Drummond, in Chapter 19, outlines a case study in the potential for human–AI collaboration, discussing the deployment of AI in developing an innovative robotic percussion instrument that has featured within high-profile musical performances. Drummond's research points to the tremendous potential for transforming musical composition and performance, effectively extending the nature and scale of these forms of human creativity.

In contrast, Mario Minichiello and Andrew Selby, in the second chapter (Chapter 20), consider a less optimistic future for the art and design sectors in the wake of the release of AI image synthesis tools. Their assessment of the value and utility of these AI tools is tempered by a deep understanding of what is potentially at stake for existing human creative practices in accommodating these technologies.

REFERENCES

Anantrasirichai, Nantheera, and David Bull. 2022. "Artificial Intelligence in the Creative Industries: A Review." *Artificial Intelligence Review* 55 (1): 589–656.

Cropley, David H., Kelsey E. Medeiros, and Adam Damadzic. 2023. "The Intersection of Human and Artificial Creativity." In *Creative Provocations: Speculations on the Future of Creativity, Technology & Learning*, edited by Danah Henriksen and Punya Mishra. Springer International Publishing.

Esling, Philippe, and Ninon Devis. 2020. "Creativity in the Era of Artificial Intelligence." Presented at the JIM Conference 2020, Milan, Italy, February 13, 2020. arXiv preprint arXiv:2008.05959.

Korteling, J. E. (Hans), Gillian C. van de Boer-Visschedijk, Romy A. M. Blankendaal, Rudy C. Boonekamp, and Aletta R. Eikelboom. 2021. "Human-Versus Artificial Intelligence." *Frontiers in Artificial Intelligence* 4: 622364.

Maslej, Nestor, Loredana Fattorini, Raymond Perrault, et al. 2024. *Artificial Intelligence Index Report 2024*. AI Index Steering Committee, Institute for Human-Centered AI, Stanford University, April 2024. https://policycommons.net/artifacts/12089781/hai_ai-index-report-2024/12983534/.

Peeters, Marieke M. M., Jurriaan van Diggelen, Karel Van Den Bosch, et al. 2021. "Hybrid Collective Intelligence in a Human–AI Society." *AI & Society* 36: 217–238.

Vinchon, Florent, Todd Lubart, Sabrina Bartolotta, et al. 2023. "Artificial Intelligence & Creativity: A Manifesto for Collaboration." *Journal of Creative Behavior* 57 (4): 472–484.

CHAPTER 19

Musical Creativity and AI Gesture-Interactive Robotics

Jon Drummond

Introduction

This practice-based study explores creative approaches to AI–human–computer interface (AI-HCI) interactions in music, performance, artificial intelligence, and robotics. Synergizing via gesture-controlled robotics, physical acoustic instrument design, and incorporating novel software/hardware, this new interface for musical expression (NIME) explores new potentials for musical expression and suggests a transformative approach to creative interactive music performance technologies. The novel robot handpan percussion (Moller Instruments 2024) interface described in this chapter explores the potentials and affordances of a physical musical interface design approach, incorporating analog theremin-based gesture interaction to facilitate and create real-time dynamic modulation of musical parameters including pitch, rhythm, intensity, and dynamics with AI facilitated analysis, interpretation and response. I note below the work of other artist-researchers in this field exploring the creative potential of combining robotics with acoustic musical interfaces, including Ajay Kapur's digital tabla controller (2005b) and Eric Singer's League of Electronic Musical Urban Robots (Singer et al. 2004). This interface diverges from previous interactive synthesis and sample-based music installations such as the Reactable (Jordà 2005b), by incorporating physical actuators with analog capacitive captured gesture interactions. This innovative analog gestural approach not only facilitates a "physically mediated" response but also reproduces the subtleties and inaccuracies of "organic" human performance, play, and interaction. This enhancement significantly extends the engagement and interaction of human performers with the musical content, challenging and expanding the conventional paradigms of musical human computer/machine and robot music performance and interaction.

The architecture of the system is designed to support real-time musical expression, offering performers and participants an engaging and intuitive interface to navigate a sonically complex landscape of polyrhythmic and polymelodic possibilities. By allowing intuitive gestural expression through theremin-based gesture interactions, the physical interface provides a unique exploration into the synthesis of music, pulse, and movement, fundamentally questioning and extending traditional notions of musicality, performance, temporality, composition, and interaction. Through this gestural interface, the research explores these new potentials of creative musical expression for both performers and audiences contributing to the broader discourse on the role of AI in changing, enhancing, and transforming our creative capabilities. This exploration not only provides valuable insights into the future of musical performance and interactive design but also explores the integration of AI-enhanced technology and art in creating enriched, immersive experiences.

Background and Related Work

This project has a genealogy of musical interfaces which have evolved from purely acoustic instruments to complex digital interactive systems (new interfaces for musical expression [NIME]). Recent explorations in robotic musicianship have focused on enhancing the interactive capabilities of such systems, enabling more nuanced and expressive performances. Notable works in this domain include the use of robotic interfaces for performing with traditional acoustic instruments (Kapur 2005a). However, the integration of interactive gesture theremin-based controls into a robotic percussion setting remains underexplored, presenting a novel area of research.

Musical automata, which trace their origins back to ancient civilizations including the Greek and Chinese empires, initially featured mechanical figures designed to perform music for religious ceremonies or royal entertainment. By the eighteenth and nineteenth centuries, these devices surged in popularity across Europe with creations like singing birds, automated organs, and piano-playing machines that captivated audiences with their complexity and lifelike performances. Today, these automata have evolved into sophisticated systems within the field of new interfaces for musical expression (NIME), incorporating advanced robotics and digital technologies to enhance interactive experiences and creative potential. Modern musical automata serve not only as autonomous performers but also as dynamic tools that extend musical expression, appearing in forms ranging from robotic instruments capable of executing precise musical sequences to interactive installations that respond actively to audience interaction. As they integrate with emerging technologies like AI, virtual reality (VR), and augmented reality (AR), musical automata continue to push the boundaries of how music is composed, performed, and experienced, offering novel and immersive ways to interact with music.

Creating musical interfaces that cater to both expert and nonexpert musicians involves balancing simplicity with depth, as seen in the field of New Interfaces for Musical Expression (Newton 2004). Interfaces, like the Reactable, use intuitive, tangible interactions that lower the entry barrier for novices while offering complex settings for professional musicians. Customization and flexibility allow users to tailor experiences to their skill levels, and incorporating educational tools and AI can help adapt the interface to enhance learning and creativity. Additionally, collaborative features encourage communal learning and creativity among users with varied skills. Overall, the aim is to democratize music creation by making it accessible and engaging, providing creative and novel responsive feedback that enhances the experience for all users.

The integration of artificial intelligence (AI) into practice-based research in the creative arts is profoundly reshaping artistic creation, collaboration, and consumption. AI enhances creative processes by enabling artists to explore complex ideas quickly and at scale, often acting as a co-creator that brings new dynamics to the creative workflow. This also democratizes art-making, allowing individuals without specialized training to produce sophisticated artworks and contribute diverse perspectives. AI also introduces novel forms and aesthetics, such as interactive installations that evolve in response to audience input, and it fosters ethical debates about authorship and the nature of creativity. The integration of AI with practice-based research not only expands the tools available to artists but also challenges traditional notions of artistry, enhancing cultural discourse and broadening the scope of artistic expression.

System Design

The robotic handpan interface was iteratively designed as an integrated system, incorporating physical robotics and digital sensor technologies to create a unique musical instrument that facilitates real-time artistic expression. The design incorporates several key components, each playing a critical role in the functionality and performance of the interface.

Acoustic Handpan

The acoustic handpan crafted by Charles Moller, an Australian instrument maker and mathematician (Moller Instruments 2024), often referred to as a hang drum, is a musical instrument made from two steel half-shells welded together to form a resonant hollow chamber. Originating in Switzerland in the early 2000s, it produces ethereal, melodic sounds that are created by striking the tuned indentations on the top shell. The handpan is typically played with the hands and fingers, and its sound is akin to a mix of a steelpan, harp, and bells. Its unique tonal qualities make it popular for solo performances, meditation music, and ensemble pieces that require a soothing, melodic instrument. The handpan was chosen for its rich harmonic and resonant qualities, which offer a wide range of tonal possibilities. The unique timbre of the handpan makes it an ideal candidate for robotic augmentation, as its sound is both distinct and melodically and rhythmically versatile (Figure 1).

Figure 1: The Robot Handpan and Theremin Interface

Source: Author

Robotic Actuation System

The robotic actuation system and frame was designed to interact physically with the handpan. This system consists of an array of precision robotic arms equipped with mallets engineered to strike the handpan (Polyend 2024). Each robotic actuator is capable of controlled, nuanced movements via MIDI (Musical Instrument Digital Interface) that can vary the intensity, angle, and speed of each strike. This allows the system to produce everything from gentle, ambient tones to complex, rhythmic patterns, mimicking the nuanced performances of human musicians while achieving consistency and precision that extends beyond human capability.

Theremin-Based Gesture Detection Module

Incorporating a theremin-based gesture detection module provides a nontactile interaction framework for the performer. This module uses the theremin's capacitive sensing technology to detect the proximity and movement of the performer's hands in relation to the antenna. By translating these movements into control signals, the system dynamically adjusts musical parameters such as pitch, rhythm, and dynamics in real time. This gestural interface allows performers to intuitively manipulate the music output with physical gestures, enhancing the expressivity and immersive quality of the performance.

Music AI Software

The integration of music AI software is pivotal to the system's design. This software component serves as the brain of the operation, processing input from the gesture detection module to interpret and predict the performer's intentions. It utilizes advanced algorithms and machine learning techniques to manage data from the theremin module, synthesizing this information to control the robotic actuators effectively. The AI can learn from each interaction, adapting its responses to fit the musical context and the performer's style, thereby supporting a wide range of expressive capabilities and ensuring a seamless, responsive interface.

System Integration and Communication

The effective communication between these components is facilitated through a custom-built digital interface that ensures synchronization and real-time data exchange. This integration is crucial for maintaining the fluidity and responsiveness of the musical expression, ensuring that each component operates harmoniously to produce a cohesive musical performance.

System Design Conclusion

The design of the robotic handpan interface represents a significant leap in musical instrument technology, blending traditional musical artistry with cutting-edge robotics and AI. By harnessing the unique sounds of the handpan with robotic precision/imprecision and intuitive gesture-based controls, this system not only enhances musical performances but also pushes the boundaries of what is possible in the realm of digital musical interactions.

Implementation Evaluation and Engagement

The implementation of this project has involved a range of public engagements that showcase the integration of robotic and AI-driven musical systems in diverse cultural and performance settings. Key activities include high-profile collaborations, installations, and recordings that demonstrate both the creative and technical capabilities of the system.

SSO and Sydney Opera House Collaboration

One of the highlights of public engagement was the collaboration with the Sydney Symphony Orchestra SSO (Mendes, n.d.) at the iconic Sydney Opera House. This event brought together music and robotics, featuring innovative applications of the robotic handpan percussion interface. The integration of such a cutting-edge system into the realm of classical and contemporary orchestral music offered audiences a unique auditory and visual experience. This collaboration has been documented in LinkedIn articles by Ysobel Sims[1] and Alexandre Mendes,[2] which detail the project's innovative approach and its reception.

---

[1] https://www.linkedin.com/posts/ysobel-sims-719528151_music-and-robotics-at-the-sydney-opera-house-activity-6989024902842372096-ggjI.

[2] https://www.linkedin.com/pulse/music-robotics-sydney-opera-house-alexandre-mendes?trk=public_post_reshare_feed-article-content.

Figure 2: Public Interacting with Robot Handpan and Theremin Interface

Source: Author

Parramatta Laneways Library Installation

The installation at the PHIVE, 5 Parramatta Square library was another signifi-cant engagement. As part of the Australasian Computer Music Conference 2023, the robotic percussion system was presented as a site-specific installation. This event aligned with PHIVE's mission to merge community engagement with cutting-edge innovation, providing visitors with an interactive, musical, and educational experience. The installation was a focal point for discussion about the role of robotic systems in public art and education, as noted in reports from the University of New England[3] and City of Parramatta.[4]

ABC Fine Music Commission and Recording with Adam Manning

The project also extended its impact into the public Australian (ABC) recording industry through a commission and collaboration with musician Adam Manning. The result, a recording titled "Guparr," was broadcast by ABC Fine Music, combining traditional musical artistry with robotic precision. The recording exemplifies how robotic systems can enrich conventional music practices, as discussed in ABC Classic[5] and distributed through Guparr's streaming platforms.[6] This collaboration highlights the project's ability to bridge the gap between experimental and mainstream music, fostering accessibility and appreciation for advanced music technology.

Discussion

The integration of a gestural analog theremin-based gesture control system into a robotic percussion real-time composition system proposes an innovative step forward in the field of new interfaces for musical expression (Jordà 2005a). This system enhances musical interaction by facilitating performers with a gestural, intuitive, and expressive way to modulate musical parameters such as pitch, rhythm, and dynamics. The fluidity of the gesture-controlled theremin interface mimics human expressivity, enabling nuanced, real-time control over the robotic percussion system.

This installation suggests new possibilities for performers and composers, to explore creative dimensions that are not easily achieved with traditional acoustic or digital instruments. This interactive gesture control system adds a performative layer, creating an engaging physical and visual element for audiences and

[3] https://www.une.edu.au/about-une/faculty-of-humanities-arts-social-sciences-and-education/hass/news-and-events/australasian-computer-music-conference-2023.

[4] https://www.cityofparramatta.nsw.gov.au/phive/about-phive.

[5] https://www.abc.net.au/listen/classic/shop/adam-manning-guparr-men-s-shed/102993022.

[6] https://snd.click/Guparr?pid=NIg97ph1tJV4.

broadening the system's potential applications in live performances, educational contexts, and multimedia art installations.

Practice-based research in this project allows for a hands-on, iterative approach to developing the robotic handpan interface. By continuously creating, testing, and refining the system, researchers directly engage with the material and technological aspects of the instrument, gaining insights into both its creative capabilities and limitations. This approach bridges artistic sensibility and technical expertise, enabling the development team to craft an interface that is not only functionally effective but also emotionally and aesthetically resonant. The feedback from actual musical practice helps inform adjustments and enhancements, ensuring the technology aligns with artistic goals. This research also emphasizes understanding the user's experience—in this case, the musicians, composers, and audience. The research methodology helps designers tailor the interface to better meet the needs of artists and participants, making the technology more accessible and fulfilling for both experts and novices in music.

AI has proved crucial for enabling real-time musical interaction that mimics the nuances of human play. In this project, AI analyses input from the theremin-based gesture control to determine how the robotic arms should move to produce the desired sound on the handpan. This allows the system to respond dynamically to the performer's gestures, facilitating a fluid and expressive musical experience. The AI component can learn from each interaction, adapting its algorithms based on the performer's style and preferences. This capability makes the system increasingly responsive and personalized over time, enhancing its ability to support creative musical expression.

AI handles the complex decision-making processes required to operate the robotic actuators and manage the musical output. It interprets the performer's gestures, translates them into mechanical actions, and ensures that these actions are musically meaningful. This includes adjustments to pitch, rhythm, intensity, and dynamics, which are all critical for the artistic integrity of the performance. By integrating AI, the project adds further to explorations into how technology can not only replicate human musical interactions but also extend them. AI will likely open up new dimensions of creative expression, enabling performances that would be difficult or impossible for humans to achieve alone, such as playing at superhuman speeds or with perfect rhythmic precision.

However, the project also faces technical and practical challenges:

- Calibration of Gesture Sensitivity: Ensuring precise and reliable recognition of performer gestures is critical to maintaining the fluidity and accuracy of musical responses. Current limitations may hinder the system's ability to respond uniformly to variations in performer input.

- Mechanical Reliability: The actuators and robotic components must maintain high reliability under extended use. Ongoing refinement is needed to ensure durability and consistency, particularly for live performances and installations.
- Scalability and Accessibility: Expanding the system's use in diverse musical genres and settings requires consideration of cost and accessibility, particularly for educational and community engagement purposes.

By addressing these challenges, the system has the potential to redefine human-robot interactions in music, contributing significantly to the NIME community and beyond.

Conclusion and Future Work

This chapter discusses the impact of integrating practice-based research and artificial intelligence in developing a new musical instrument, advancing the boundaries of music creation and performance in the digital AI age. The novel robotic handpan interface, which utilizes theremin-based gesture control for dynamic musical expression, illustrates a deeper exploration at the intersection of human creativity and robotic AI precision/imprecision. This integration not only potentially indicates a future where technology and creativity are seamlessly integrated but also significantly broadens our conceptualization of musical instrument design and performance.

As we look to the future, efforts will concentrate on refining AI algorithms to better support complex musical interpolations and enhance the robustness of the physical system for use in various musical performance environments. Additionally, the project plans to explore the integration of more sophisticated sensing interfaces to capture a wider range of gestures, potentially increasing the musical versatility and expressiveness of the interface. By merging human artistry with robotic accuracy/inaccuracy, this initiative paves the way for a continuing fusion/diffusion of technology and creativity. This ongoing development is committed to pushing the boundaries of what can be achieved at the intersection of technology and the arts, suggesting a vibrant future for interactive musical performance innovations.

Combining practice-based research and AI in this way offers more than just the creation of a novel musical instrument; it transforms our understanding of music production and performance in the digital era. Future efforts will focus on refining AI algorithms to support more intricate polyrhythmic interpolations and improving the robustness of the physical system for diverse performance environments. Additionally, the project will explore the integration of more sophisticated sensors to broaden the range of detectable gestures, thereby enhancing the musical versatility of the interface. By examining the interplay between human creativity and robotic precision, this research moves us toward a future where technology and artistic creativity are seamlessly integrated, broadening our concept of musical instrument design and enabling a deeper, more interactive performance experience.

REFERENCES

Adkins, M. 2010. *The Mechanical Music Box Handbook*. Mechanical Music Press.

Bowers, Q. D. 2019. "Musical Automata." In *Encyclopedia of Musical Instruments*, edited by A. P. Jenkins. ABC-CLIO.

Dahl, L., and J. Herrera. 2014. "Interactive Software Technology at the Intersection of Computer Music, Human–Computer Interaction and Music Psychology." *Journal of New Music Research* 43 (4): 390–409.

Fels, S., A. Gadd, and A. Mulder. 2002. "Mapping Transparency Through Metaphor: Towards More Expressive Musical Instruments." *Organised Sound* 7 (2): 109–126.

Groce, S. B. 2018. "Musical Automata." In *The Oxford Handbook of Musical Automata*. Oxford University Press.

Jordà, S. 2005a. *Digital Lutherie: Crafting Musical Computers for New Musics' Performance and Improvisation*. University of Pompeu Fabra.

Jordà, S. 2005b. "Reactable: A Tangible Tabletop Synthesizer." http://reactable.com/experience/.

Kapur, A. 2005a. "A History of Robotic Musical Instruments." *International Computer Music Conference* 10 (88): 4599.

Kapur, A. 2005b. "A Digital Tabla Controller: A New Interface for Musical Expression." Unpublished master's thesis. University of Victoria.

Kassler, J. C. 2016. *The Mechanical Muse: The Piano, Pianism, and Piano Music, C.1760–1850.* Cambridge University Press.

Leech-Wilkinson, D. 2016. *Performances of Ancient Greek Music: An Introduction.* Cambridge University Press.

Mendes, A. n.d. *"Music and Robotics at the Sydney Opera House. "* LinkedIn. https://www.linkedin.com/pulse/music-robotics-sydney-opera-house-alexandre-mendes?trk=public_post_reshare_feed-article-content.

Miranda, E. R., and M. M. Wanderley. 2006. *New Digital Instruments: Control and Interaction Beyond the Keyboard.* A-R Publications.

Moller Instruments. 2024. "Handpan." https://mollerinstruments.com/handpan.

Newton, D. 2004. "The International Conference on New Interfaces for Musical Expression (NIME)." *Organised Sound* 9 (2): 203–204. https://doi.org/10.1017/S1355771804000346.

Polyend. 2024. *"Polyend Perc: Drumming Machine. "* https://polyend.com/legacy/polyend-perc/.

Schivelbusch, W. 1988. *Disenchanted Night: The Industrialization of Light in the Nineteenth Century.* University of California Press.

Singer, E., J. Feddersen, C. Redmon, and B. Bowen. 2004. "LEMUR's Guitar-Bot: MIDI Robotic String Instrument." In *Proceedings of the 2004 Conference on New Interfaces for Musical Expression (NIME04),* edited by Michael J. Lyons. Shizuoka University of Art and Culture.

Singer, E., K. Larke, and D. Bianciardi. 2003. "LEMUR GuitarBot: MIDI Robotic String Instrument." In *Proceedings of the 2004 Conference on New Interfaces for Musical Expression (NIME04),* edited by Michael J. Lyons. Shizuoka University of Art and Culture.

CHAPTER 20

Making Human-Generated Art and Design in an AI-Dominated Future

Mario Minichiello and Andrew Selby

Abstract

In his celebrated book and TV series, Nigel Spivey delivered an exciting rethinking of the history of art. Using a contemporary documentary style illustrating how the world's most moving and enduring works of art have been used in mass persuasion, even to start and end wars, empires and dethrone rulers, Spivey speculates that art is essential in social, cultural, and political hierarchies. The arts have been used throughout history to promote social cohesion, new modes of thinking and as a tool of mass behavior modification including limiting the appeal of radicalization in the UK. In essence, *How Art Made the World* (2005) was about how humans made art that ultimately enhanced or even defined our characteristics as humans. "Throughout history, people have used art to communicate without relying on words."[1] Art can express political ideas, reinforce religion, or convey deeply personal thoughts' (Carey 2006). Good art and design in all its forms helps the viewer and user to discover things and experiences that they did not know about themselves and, by extension, can be used to understand and even experience the lives of others.

Introduction

Numerous academic and practising psychologists have theorised that art has a relationship to culture similar to the ways that dreams affect humans' mental

---

[1] Art as Communication—Overview & Examples—Lesson—Study.com.

stability. Perhaps then, in the same way that a dream does not have to be about anything, it just is, so art just is. "The aim of art is to represent not the outward appearance of things, but their inward significance." (Aristotle)

This chapter considers what actions human artists can take in the wake of the spread of AI technology. It aims to do so by finding strategies in an era where they are no longer exclusively the ones who create art, design, music, writing, and other forms of culturally expressive outputs. These creative products have a primacy to all cultures and have defined humans from our very beginning as a species. If artificial humans can imitate us so well that they outperform us in many of the existing creative roles, how do we find our uniqueness and recast AI in a way that complements and advances humanity? How do we overcome our historically proven instincts to create slaves, as well as other unsettling aspects of colonization inherent in this process?

At an Open Culture conference on AI versus human songwriting on November 24, 2023, two of the delegates employed AI to write the lyrics to songs "to save time," using the large language model to assess the most likely combinations of rhymes, and poetic imagery. In reply, the British novelist and broadcaster Stephen Fry, who was one of the other conference speakers, read a letter from singer-songwriter Nick Cave to the AI collaborators. He stated, as quoted in Open Culture website:

> 'ChatGPT rejects any notions of creative struggle, that our endeavours animate and nurture our lives giving them depth and meaning,' Cave writes. 'It rejects that there is a collective, essential and unconscious human spirit underpinning our existence, connecting us all through our mutual striving.' In 'fast-tracking the commodification of the human spirit by mechanizing the imagination,' it works toward eliminating 'the process of creation and its attendant challenges, viewing it as nothing more than a time-wasting inconvenience that stands in the way of the commodity itself.' But the creative impulse 'must be defended at all costs, and just as we would fight any existential evil,' we should fight the forces set against it 'tooth and nail, for we are fighting for the very soul of the world.'[2]

The battle lines seem to have been drawn around the dehumanization of a key creative process. The ability of AI to go beyond imitating and originating

---

[2] https://www.openculture.com/2023/11/stephen-fry-reads-nick-caves-stirring-letter-about-chatgpt-and-human-creativity-we-are-fighting-for-the-very-soul-of-the-world.html.

Figure 1: The Other Her, Waiting for God. Reportage; Care Homes

Source: M. Minichiello

art in all its forms as we have experienced it in the past is in dispute. However, it is increasingly clear that AI can do well in fact-based areas where a factual appraisal within logic-driven processes or the scanning of things is required, such as radiology in the treatment of cancer, or the calculation of stress in built environments. It is supremely fast and accurate in the areas frequently referred to as STEM (science, technology, engineering, and mathematics). It also performs exceptionally well where there are stringent rules, such as human language models. It appears to apply the same methods used in these first two models to the arts. It looks for recognizable patterns and rule-defined parameters. A good example of this is music where there are 2,197 three-note combinations by using a set of seven notes, and a total of 4,096 possible combinations using a set of twelve notes. This is not accounting for the variations in rhythm, and other musical elements which can increase the number of possible melodies. This gives AI great opportunities to create variations on themes, a method used by many composers in the history of classical music. It may also curate popular motifs, but would it create something as original as David Bowie's song "Heroes," a song which only reached 23rd place in the popular music charts? As ever, the success of a product is about what measures you apply to the process that governs its production and dissemination.

AI's efficiency in finding mathematical patterns and sorting big data sets will enable companies to replace humans with AI systems in many traditional STEM jobs. AI seems less convincing when dealing with the origination of creative and novel things. AI replacing human creativity will inevitably be the concern of many academic papers and speculative articles. This chapter looks at the problem from a human practitioner perspective—and considers how we might think about our human intelligence and creativity in ways that could allow us to make the best use of AI in the future.

> *If you can have a conversation with a simulated person presented by an AI*
> *program, can you tell how far you've let your sense of personhood degrade in*
> *order to make the illusion work for you? (Lanier 2011)*

The march of AI into every aspect of our lives can feel like being invaded by an alien superpower threatening our future existence. The speed of change has seldom been seen before in human history. For example, the Roman Empire's invasion of Britain in 43 AD took forty-five years to establish. AI appears to have become a dominant worldwide force in a few years, even absorbing the entire canon of human literature in a matter of months. This is particularly significant

Figure 2: South Africa's New Dawn (More Colonialism) Geographic Front Cover

Source: M. Minichiello

to universities because literature and libraries have been the core of knowledge storage and retrieval by humans for generations. This was reflected in the term "reading for a degree," as being part and parcel of university studies. Knowledge, in all its forms, helps humans to be able to think freely, share ideas collaboratively, and create and innovate into the future.

Rule-based knowledge applications are both AI's advantage and its Achilles' heel when compared to human creativity; conversely, artists and designers in every discipline have a history of rule-breaking. Breaking rules to create something original has been the driver of art, music, and design in every discipline; it is how creatives are trained. There is no evidence that AI can do this; this ability to break and make is uniquely human and should not be overlooked in the future of AI.

> *People degrade themselves in order to make machines seem smart all the time.*
> *(Lanier 2011)*

Jaron Lanier's views particularly pertain to this chapter because of the diversity of his roles as a computer scientist, composer, visual artist, and author. He is credited with a key role in developing as well as coining the term virtual reality in the early 1980s and founded VPL Research, the first company to sell VR products. In the late 1980s, he led the team that developed the first implementations of multiperson virtual worlds (Lanier 2011).

While the principal appeal of AI rule-based systems is commercial and STEM-based in that they are well suited to, "carrying out many routine diagnostic decisions made by professionals such as doctors or engineers." However, human doctors are more than merely reasoning diagnostic tools. They have human empathy and are inventive in finding new ways to carry out medical interventions. Doctors share with artists the understanding of what it means to be human and the value of life, to be loved and cared for, to have and know meaning. The realization of the meaning of existence and its implications came to the seventeenth-century French philosopher René Descartes whose statement "I think; therefore, I am" has been the baseline of our understanding of human conscious thought.

Even if our knowledge of self is a figment of imagination, self-deception, or error, the very act of doubting one's existence, serves as proof of the reality of one's mind; there must be a thinking entity (or self) for there to be thought. Unlike AI, we have biological consciousness and thinking processes including the ability to imagine something that does not exist and create it through our will and own physical efforts. To act creatively we have to overcome the fear of failure; in fact, overcoming failure is part of the creative mentality. The designer Ken Robinson's observation, "You cannot be creative or do anything original if you are not prepared to fail,"[3] is especially pertinent in this debate. AI draws on existing models of successful materials but needs core, original content to feed from.

---

[3] https://www.ted.com/talks/sir_ken_robinson_do_schools_kill_creativity?.

Figure 3: "Obituary: Shinzo Abe," *The Japan Times*, January 2023

Source: Andrew Selby

Spivey contends that human creative expression has made the world. It also allows us to communicate with each other through a range of senses so that we can interact and influence each other to create meaningful cultures. People are subjected to subtle forms of influence and behavior modification. An example of our inherent influence on each other on the subconscious is demonstrated through "yawning" in public, which results in most people yawning as an auto-response. We are influenced by what we see and this can be exploited by a technology designer, as Lanier observes,

> *The Most Important Thing About technology Is How It Changes People When I work with experimental digital gadgets, like new variations on virtual reality, in a lab environment, I am always reminded of how small changes in the details of a digital design can have profound unforeseen effects on the experiences of the humans who are playing with it. The slightest change in something as seemingly trivial as the ease of use of a button can sometimes completely alter behaviour patterns. (2011)*

This is largely due to how our brain is formed and this may be a factor in the way we adapt AI to us or we to AI.

> *The brain is heavily influenced by genes. But from birth through young adult-hood, the part of the human brain that most defines us (frontal cortex) is less a product of the genes with which you started life than of what life has thrown at you. Because it is the last to mature, by definition the frontal cortex is the brain region least constrained by genes and most sculpted by experience. This must be so, to be the supremely complex social species that we are. Ironically, it seems that the genetic program of human brain development has evolved to, as much as possible, free the frontal cortex from genes. (Sapolsky 2018)*

Our frontal cortex, which forms as we interact with things and situations in the world, is still evolving. Recent research in this area has led to the development of the "theory of mind." This is the branch of cognitive science that investigates how we ascribe mental states to other persons and how we use the states to explain and predict the actions of those other persons. The theory of mind tries to predict as well as influence behavior providing insights into other people's intentions, understanding the underlying rules for interactions, and reading implicit body language (Apperly and Butterfill 2009).

The practical application of this can be seen in acting classes, in animation, and in narrative arts. This all sounds like the kind of brief that any artist might get as a filmmaking, writer, animator or a range of visual artists and designers. While science discovers, it is the arts that provide the social license for discoveries to

Figure 4: "Blitz: Stories of London" (2018), London Transport Museum

Source: Andrew Selby

be socialized and become culturally pervasive. Another part of designing AI has been to use what science understands about human creativity—this has been greatly enhanced by the work being done in neurasthenics. "This is a field within cognitive neuroscience investigating the neural underpinnings of aesthetic experience, particularly in visual arts. Neuroscience has investigated this area using brain imaging and neurophysiological techniques" (Baron-Cohen 1991).

A great deal of work in this area was organized by a small group of scientists with a deep interest in creativity, including Professor Ramachandran. In his 1993 Reith Lecture for the BBC, he examined the meaning of *art* from a neurological perspective. His Reith lectures and book *The Artful Brain* provided new insights into the human creative process but also what is "hardwired into us from how we evolved. Further research published in Turner's *The Artful Mind: Cognitive Science and the Riddle of Human Creativity* found that

> *cognitively modern minds produced a staggering list of behavioural singulari-*
> *ties — science, religion, mathematics, language, advanced tool use, decorative*
> *dress, dance, culture, art — that seems to indicate a mysterious and unexplained*
> *discontinuity between us and all other living things. (2006)*

This gives rise to the question of how we operate. Understanding how the human brain operates and functions is key to the imitation game of AI. How we perform in the creation of art and its social significance has been largely investigated through the creative-making process or psychology, including the work of Professor Mihaly Csikszentmihalyi, whose seminal book *Flow: The Psychology of Optimal Experience* (1990) was a highly influential book in which he created simple, generative models of flow, creativity, and aesthetic experience. This sheds light on how we operate as creatives. His work focused on motivation that contributed to individual success. These higher experiences of the world can also be traced to sociology, and in particular "habitus" a concept posited by Pierre Bourdieu. His work is concerned with norms, values, attitudes, and behaviors of a particular type of group, including artists and how they perceive and respond to the social world they inhabit, by way of their personal habits, skills, and disposition of character — to Bourdieu, art and the creative mind are important as he was seeking to develop a comprehensive "theory of society" and saw power as culturally and symbolically created, and "constantly re-legitimised through an interplay of agency and structure. The main way this happens is through what he calls habitus or socialized norms or tendencies that guide behavior and thinking. Habitus is "the way society becomes deposited in persons in the form of lasting dispositions, or trained capacities and structured propensities to think, feel and act in determinant ways, which then guide them" (Wacquant 2005, 316, cited in Navarro 2006, 16). For the practitioner the practice-based research of artists such as such as Betty Edwards' *Drawing on the Right Side of the Brain* (1979) and *Ways of Seeing* (1990) by John Berger as well as peer-reviewed papers and emerging doctoral thesis publications, many of which have been championed by Bloomsbury Publishing and Common Ground Research Networks have helped to develop their own best practices.

The cutting edge often comes through the practitioner's tacit knowledge of their particular creative methodologies. One discipline where AI's ability to work to formulas is making a strong impact is Architecture. Architects have for many years worked in the style of Le Corbusier's Modernism. In 1920 it was a new revolution, an "Esprit Nouveau," has been applied to many city building projects. With the zeal of true acolytes, every city has had this style imposed on its urban environment, resulting in a new variation known as "Block Design." It turns out that AI can do this very efficiently and cut out the need for any human input. For many, this has dehumanized and impoverished the experience of living in urban environments. People look to the arts for authentic human experiences and interpretation of the world—artists absorb the world and its ideas and remediate their experiences through their work.

> Remediation did not begin with the introduction of digital media. We can identify the same process throughout the last several hundred years of Western visual representation. A painting by the seventeenth-century artist Pieter Saenredam, a photograph by Edward Weston, and a computer system for virtual reality are different in many important ways, but they are all attempts to achieve immediacy by ignoring or denying the presence of the medium and the act of mediation. (Bolter and Grusin 1999, 11)

Experience sharing is a form of social learning and marks one of many differences between human creatives and AI:

> The first and most obvious is 'visual language' this is a creative and highly personal way of working where each person develops their visual methods and practical methodologies. AI machines can work in an existing 'style' of a human artist or movement and replicate and develop millions of variations on a theme, the uncanny effect often is the result, and this might in the end be AI's recognisable 'style'. (Downey 2024)

So far, there is little evidence of the kind of origination or forming an original visual language and making method that humans are capable of. AI at its heart is Turing's imitation game but vastly expanded and speeded up. Therefore, the question that arises is, Can AI move from tracking human creativity and copying human innovation to genuinely originating new forms of art and innovation?

Human artists work differently; they may use established styles of art as a platform to develop new ways of working and refresh their means of thinking about the world that they are experiencing as a living organism. Humans are even powered differently; this is an important difference because humans are not plugged into mains power and do not have the limitations of being plugged into an external power supply. Humans are free to roam, think, live, and breathe, and have multiple senses, evolved through millions of interactions and biological development.

> *Probably the most important fact about genetics and culture is the delayed maturation of the frontal cortex—the genetic programming for the young frontal cortex to be freer from genes than other brain regions, to be sculpted instead by the environment, to sop up cultural norms. To hark back to a theme from the first pages of this book, it doesn't take a particularly fancy brain to learn how to motorically, say, throw a punch. But it takes a fancy, environmentally malleable frontal cortex to learn culture-specific rules about when it's okay to throw punches. (Sapolsky 2018)*

These two parts enable us to reason and imagine at the same time, to enhance the perception of new experiences. For example, the understanding of how media transforms human perception occurred in 1895 through the work of the Lumière brothers. A seminal moment, for example, in the understanding of how media transforms human perception occurred in 1895 through the work of the Lumière brothers. In 1895 they first screened

> *the arrival of a train at La Ciotat station, [and] the newspapers reported at the time that the audience in the theatre were so shocked at the stark realism of a train driving towards them that they ran for their lives. (Bolter and Grusin 2000, 38)*

At first, this story seems to illustrate how powerful a medium can be and how it takes time for an audience to accommodate the effect it has on their senses; however, in recent years, there have been some revisions to this tale. Bolter and Grusin remark of Gunning's observation:

> *What astonished the audience, he thinks, was precisely the gap between what they knew to be true and what their eyes told them. They admired the capacity of the film to create so authentic an illusion in the face of what they knew to be true. (2000, 155)*

Figure 5: "Sounds of the City" (2017), London Transport Museum

Source: Andrew Selby

Very quickly, the scenario by which a train entered a station was parodied by other filmmakers, equally demonstrating that images could reintroduce the sense of reassurance to what people knew yet still remain inventive in the act of image-making. This sense of "re-invention" in the image, is a common factor in all forms of visualization but is most naturally determined by the primal and intrinsic nature of mark-making in drawing. What remains significant, though, in the act of image-making is not only how it may innovate formally or technically but how it communicates and makes an audience feel and respond. This suggests, in effect, that is also mediates the same tension between the authenticity of the illusion and how the audience evaluates what they "know to be true."

Figure 6: Australian Landscape Muswellbrook NSW

Source: M. Minichiello – N Tully Art Collection

People's experience of the Lumiere Brothers' film is but one example of how discoveries in the function of "vision" can be exploited to enhance the visual experience of an audience. This includes remediating visual constructions such as perspective, or responses to the compositional placement of information. There is a system of remediation that is inherent in drawing and enables it to be a carrier of visual communication; for many artists, drawing is the practical outcome of seeing. This effectively suggests that drawing acts as a provocateur of memory and significantly "re-mediates" the photorealist nature of recalled imagery into an emotional and sensory image, and thereafter alters perception.

At this time, vision and seeing are unique to humans. Seeing as a process is different from surveillance and scanning which AI machines engage with. Surveillance scanning helps you locate a particular fact in real time. This is more than a form of data collection; through drawing, the practitioner develops a detailed understanding of the meaning of something and not just its appearance. We interpret what we see using our biological brain. The human brain is a massively complex and changing organ — its size makes us unique, taking around 20% of our energy. While the brain is physical, its function generates an invisible world — the mind.

This is our main creative advantage. The mind enables our becoming conscious of existence, enabling us to think philosophically to reflect on what we see and how we are, to question and think philosophically. When we act creatively, we are becoming fully human. Per Maslow's theory of self-actuation, through art and design we are shaping the world and its cultural element that everything exists in. Making art seems to be the integration of mind and body in "flow."

> *We know that it is the right hemisphere of the human brain, which 'reads' and stores our visual experience. This is significant because the areas and centres where this takes place are strictly identical to those in the left hemisphere, which processes our experience of words. The apparatus with which we deal with appearances is identical to that with which we deal with verbal language. Furthermore, appearances in their unmediated state — that is to say before they have been interpreted or perceived — lend themselves to reference systems (so that they may be stored at a certain level in the memory) which are comparable to those used for words. And this again prompts one to conclude that appearances possess some of the qualities of a code. (Berger 1972, 114–115)*

Philosophers have long explored arts' relationship to humans. Kant posited that it is fundamental to human nature to, "achieve a synthesis between the competing traditions of rationalism and empiricism." From "rationalism," he draws the idea that pure reason is capable of significant knowledge but rejects the idea that pure reason can tell us anything about things in themselves. The arts move us beyond reasoning alone. Maslow's hierarchy of human development and physiological needs puts at its base developmental needs such as safety, and love and belonging, esteem, and self-actualization at the top. In 1969, Maslow revised this model by adding a new pinnacle: self-transcendence — placing art at the top of the pyramid. "*Self-transcendence* is a personality trait that involves the expansion or evaporation of personal boundaries. This may potentially include spiritual experiences" (De Fruyt et al. 2000) such as considering oneself an integral part of the universe (Frankl 1966). Self-transcendence is distinctive as the first trait concept of a spiritual nature to be incorporated into a major theory of personality (MacDonald and Holland 2002).

While computer technology requires "vast amounts of precision and detail," Creativity in human hands often relies on the imprecise nature of creative thinking, the very lack of a systematic approach, and prioritizing the judgment of aesthetics over the systemic use of data models that results in the most meaningful leaps forward. Meaning and meaning-making are still essentially a human process. It results in diversity and inventiveness that draws on human memory, and the tacit knowledge that is transmitted with the kinetic learning process, using touch, memory, imagination as well as sight in the drawing process.

> *Drawing does not come out of philosophy, mathematics, linguistics, or scientific method. It is measurable neither by language nor numbers. Thus, in a world that places such a high value on the word and accountability, it appears an imprecise and vaguely defined methodology. Yet, this is also its strength. Drawing — the drawn image — remains resistant to other forms of analysis and its singularity forces the viewer to engage with it on its own terms. (Minichiello and Horton 2019, 266)*
>
> *Much of the confusion about the use of AI comes from our own largely un-conscious beliefs about 'intelligence.' To a great extent, these beliefs reflect notions of general-purpose intellectual power, analogous to concepts like strength or speed. (This is one reason journalistic accounts of AI often cover 'supercomputer' technology as well as AI, even though the two fields have little in common) (Sheil 1987).*

MacKinnon's creativity equates to playfulness which he explains as

> *the facility for mood change, an ability to engage in play, childlike playing with ideas, no purpose but the enjoyment of playing, nothing much to do with IQ much to do with the willingness to be playful. They procrastinate and seem to do no more than doodies of their annoy employers and other staff. (1963)*

The research literature into human creativity and learning is well documented. We aim to develop ourselves and our creative systems (culture) to bring meaningful experiences and things into the world. Psychologist Viktor Frankl, the founder of logotherapy, stated in his 1946 book *Man's Search for Meaning*, where he argued that the primary goal of humans was to lead meaningful lives (1985). Perhaps meaning-making, which seems uniquely a human ability, might be the next goal of AI technologies.

AI seems to represent a new framing of our systematic capitalist culture dispensing with the need for human agency for the Industrial Revolution 0.5. AI can imitate at great speed, but the questions that arise are: Can it originate and elaborate, and investigate? Can it develop the presence of mind to be playful and anarchic? Can it co-create and develop away from merely imitating to become a creative partner to human intelligence? Can it, for example, aid humans to learn faster? Can it become a super teaching classroom assistant? There is great optimism about this possible role: "AI may never in any sense "take over" the role of teacher because how it works and what it does are so profoundly different from human intelligence. However, within the limits that we describe in this chapter, it offers the potential to transform education in ways that—counterintuitively perhaps—make education more human, not less (Cope et al. 2021).

Many educationalists have researched the creative aspects of humans, for example, Professor Ted Wragg, Betty Edwards, Steven Pinker, Sir Ken Robinson, and many others. Rule-breaking is a significant part of the process; you have to be willing to "risk being wrong."[4] Drawing is at this time a uniquely human process, a personal language that is formed and characterized by its imperfections, a kind of fingerprint of the person that made the drawing. Drawing has many rules, but at a certain point, the artist/drawer has to decide which rules to apply or if any rules no longer apply to their way of working. For these reasons, drawing remains a wicked problem for AI systems. For example, for an AI machine to draw an original picture of the world (rather than merely trace its on-screen appearance), it has to be able to see and sense as humans can. It has to have experiential knowledge and formal knowledge of the world and what things mean.

Computer vision works much the same as human vision, except humans have a head start. Human sight has the advantage of lifetimes of context to train how to tell objects apart, how far away they are, whether they are moving or something is wrong with an image.[5]

---

[4] https://www.ted.com/talks/sir_ken_robinson_do_schools_kill_creativity?.

[5] IBM Research: Team https://www.ibm.com/topics/computer-vision (Last accessed October 1, 2024).

IBM's computer vision team is focused on using computer "Vision" for business. Here are a few examples of established computer vision tasks:

- *Image classification* sees an image and can classify it (a dog, an apple, a person's face). More precisely, it is able to accurately predict that a given image belongs to a certain class. For example, a social media company might want to use it to automatically identify and segregate objectionable images uploaded by users.
- *Object detection* can use image classification to identify a certain class of image and then detect and tabulate their appearance in an image or video. Examples include detecting damages on an assembly line or identifying machinery that requires maintenance.
- *Object tracking* follows or tracks an object once it is detected. This task is often executed with images captured in sequence or real-time video feeds. Autonomous vehicles, for example, need to not only classify and detect objects such as pedestrians, cars, and road infrastructure but need to track them in motion to avoid collisions and obey traffic laws.
- *Content-based image retrieval* uses computer vision to browse, search, and retrieve images from large data stores, based on the content of the images rather than metadata tags associated with them. This task can incorporate automatic image annotation that replaces manual image tagging. These tasks can be used for digital asset management systems and can increase the accuracy of search and retrieval.[6]

This looks like surveillance. As Berger noted, "To draw well you have to see well" (2000). To draw like a human, AI has to have a kinesthetic interface of touch, to be able to mark make. So, to translate light, shade, and color into meaningful designs, to interpret using both data-driven thinking (perspective shape etc.) and the left-hand side of the human brain dealing with emotion and empathy to create a meaningful narrative of construct symbolistic meaning, feelings—it has to not only have knowledge but understand the culture and significance of the human stories. In his book *Do Androids Dream of Electric Sheep*, Philip K. Dick wrestles with the problem of differentiating the authentic human being from the reflexive machine, the android (1968). "The android is a metaphor for people who are psychologically human but behaving in a nonhuman

---

[6.] IBM Research: Team https://www.ibm.com/topics/computer-vision (Last accessed October 1, 2024).

way" (cited in Sammon 1996). Humans also learn by imitating and interacting with our environment and culture. Then it is possible that in the future we might assimilate some of the characteristics of AI and the disposition of the android.

Conclusion

There is no doubt that AI represents a real threat to humans as Noam Chomsky argues:

> *The human mind is not, like ChatGPT and its likes, a glutton statistical machine for structure recognition, that swallows hundreds of terabytes of data and snatches the most plausible answer to a conversation the most likely to a scientific question. The other way round…the human mind is a surprisingly efficient and elegant system operating with a limited amount of information. It doesn't try to injure raw corrections from data but tries to create explanations. Let's stop calling it 'Artificial intelligence' and call it what it is: 'plagiarism software.' Don't create anything, copy existing works from existing artists and writers and alter it sufficiently to escape copyright laws. It's the largest theft of property ever since Native American lands by European settlers. (Chomsky et al. 2023)*

More than ever, if humans are to survive and thrive in the future, they have to do so as creatives and not merely economic units in some man-made political economic system — the arts are a means of maintaining healthy humans and the renewal of sociality through individual acts of adding meaning to our cultural life.

> *We need to recognise our symbiotic relationship with each other, our machines, and the natural world. We need to invent new ways to creatively and constructively bridge differences toward common goals and manage rapid technological change.*[7]

Historically a great deal of the goal of human intelligence has focused on how we come to terms with existence; the arts afford us to dream and think beyond the confines of everydayness — ultimately, we have been driven by our creative minds to not only survive but improve our lives.

[7.] https://www.media.mit.edu/posts/the-mit-media-lab-an-idea-worth-growing/.

How we think creatively will be a key means of differentiation. The philosopher Arthur Schopenhauer offers an unparalleled understanding of the human condition above all he understood the primacy and significance of arts and their ability to free us from the boundaries of the material world—as a means of confronting the brutalities of existence and the world. He saw the arts as a superior force, which he applied to ideas of God or the Soul (note that it was illegal to deny the existence of God at that time), and as humanity's desire to reach beyond the cares of everyday existence. Art was the creative act derived from these desires and ideas. He dealt with art and artists in great depth. Seeing music as a super form of art forms. In the end, his work had more influence on art and artists than did the work of Marx, Kant, or even the philosopher-artist Nietzsche, who tried to see the world in new ways that would reveal more about human existence—perhaps AI is a new species that will replace us or simply a different art form, another of humankind's attempts at self-anthropomorphism.

REFERENCES

Apperly, I. A., and S. A. Butterfill. 2009. "Do Humans Have Two Systems to Track Beliefs and Belief-Like States?" *Psychological Review* 116 (4): 953–970.

Baron-Cohen, Simon. 1991. "Precursors to a Theory of Mind: Understanding Attention in Others." *Natural Theories of Mind: Evolution, Development and Simulation of Everyday Mindreading* 1: 233–251.

Berger, John. 1990. *Ways of Seeing*. Reprint ed. British Broadcasting and Penguin Books.

Bolter, Jay David, and Richard Grusin. 1999. *Remediation: Understanding New Media.* MIT Press.

Bolter, D., and G. Grusin. 2000. *Remediation: Understanding New Media.* MIT Press.

Carey, J. 2006. *What Good Are the Arts?* Main edition. Faber & Faber.

Chomsky, Noam, Ian Roberts, and Jeffrey Watumull. 2023. "Noam Chomsky: The False Promise of ChatGPT." *New York Times*, March 8.

Cope, Bill, Mary Kalantzis, and Duane Searsmith. 2021. "Artificial Intelligence for Education: Knowledge and Its Assessment in AI-Enabled Learning Ecologies." *Educational Philosophy and Theory* 53 (12): 1229–1245.

Cziksentmihalyi, M. 1990. *Flow: The Psychology of Optimal Experience*. Harper & Row.

De Fruyt, Filip, L. Van De Wiele, and K. van Heeringen. 2000. "Cloninger's Psychobiological Model of Temperament and Character and the Five-Factor Model of Personality." *Personality and Individual Differences* 29 (3): 441–452.

Dick, Philip K. 1968. *Do Androids Dream of Electric Sheep?* Doubleday.

Downey, A. 2024. "The Return of the Uncanny: Artificial Intelligence and Estranged Futures." *Visual Studies* October 2024: 1–10. https://doi.org/10.108 0/1472586X.2024.2406709.

Edwards, Betty. 1979. *Drawing on the Right Side of the Brain*. Jeremy P. Tarcher/Putnam.

Frankl, Viktor E. 1966a. "Self-Transcendence as a Human Phenomenon." *Journal of Humanistic Psychology* 6 (2): 97–106.

Frankl, Viktor E. 1966b. "Logotherapy and Existential Analysis—A Review." *American Journal of Psychotherapy* 20 (2): 252–260.

Frankl, Viktor E. 1985. *Man's Search for Meaning*. Simon & Schuster.

Horton, C., C. Jenkins, C. Rhodes, and J. Spalding. 2001. *Debating the Line*. European Illustrator Gallery and Collection.

Lanier, Jaron. 2011. *You Are Not a Gadget: A Manifesto*. Vintage.

MacDonald, Douglas A., and Daniel Holland. 2002. "Examination of the Psychometric Properties of the Temperament and Character Inventory Self-Transcendence Dimension." *Personality and Individual Differences* 32 (6): 1013–1027.

MacKinnon, Donald W. 1963. "The Identification of Creativity." *Applied Psychology* 12 (1): 25–46.

Minichiello, M. 2019. "Putting Theory into Practice." In *A Companion to Illustration*, edited by A. Male. John Wiley & Sons.

Sammon, Paul. 1996. *Future Noir: The Making of Blade Runner*. Orion Media.

Sapolsky, Robert M. 2017. *Behave: The Biology of Humans at Our Best and Worst*. Penguin.

Selby, A., and M. Minichiello. 2023. "Artificial Intelligence in Editorial Illustration: An Insight into Proximity and Plausibility; Emotion, Empathy and Ethics." Presented at the Proceedings of the 10th International Conference on Illustration and Animation (CONFIA10), Caldas da Rainha, Portugal, July 6–7, 2023.

Sheil, Beau. 1987. "Thinking About Artificial Intelligence." *Harvard Business Review* 65 (4): 91–97.

Turner, Mark, ed. 2006. *The Artful Mind: Cognitive Science and the Riddle of Human Creativity*. Oxford University Press.

LIST OF CONTRIBUTORS

Marilia Bergamo is a computer artist and lecturer in Design and Digital Art, focusing on digital systems, computer art, artificial life, and interaction design.

Dr. Helena Bezzina is a creative industries professional and academic with over twenty years of experience in museums and galleries across Australia and Southeast Asia, whose current research focuses on museums as sites for health and wellbeing.

A/Prof Tamara Blakemore is a social work practitioner, researcher, and educator. Her work embraces creative methods for trauma-informed responses to violence, abuse, and trauma.

Duncan Burck is the Founder and CEO of MCB Business Partners, dedicated to enhancing education through innovative, place-based learning experiences.

A/Prof Amy Cain is an ARC Future Fellow at Macquarie University, in Sydney Australia, who specialises in using functional genomics to understand how microbes tolerate stresses and evolve resistance to antimicrobials.

Dr. Andrea Cassin is a Lecturer and Professional Placement Lead at the School of Humanities, Creative Industries, and Social Sciences at the University of Newcastle, Australia.

Dr Ari Chand is a Lecturer in Illustration and Animation at UniSA Creative, University of South Australia, specialising in storytelling through animation, illustration, and visual communication.

Justin Dean is a visionary industrial designer, martial artist, and PhD scholar pioneering trust-centered AI avatars while leading multimillion-dollar ventures with discipline, creativity, and purpose.

Associate Professor Jon Drummond is a composer and researcher at the University of Newcastle whose practice-based research investigates interactive music and sonic interfaces, with a focus on how sound can enrich human–computer interaction and enhance creative engagement and wellbeing.

Paul Egglestone is 'Chief Imagineer' and co-founder of FASTlab, an independent innovation studio translating bold, creative research into real-world impact.

Evan Gibbs is a PhD candidate at the University of Newcastle and a founder of Wild Yeast Zoo, leading innovations in sustainable biotechnology.

Karl Hassan is an Associate Professor at the University of Newcastle with expertise in molecular microbiology, functional genomics, synthetic biology and protein biochemistry/biophysics.

Dr Craig Hight is an Associate Professor in Creative Industries at the University of Newcastle, Australia.

Ray Kelly is a Dhanggati/Gumbayngirr man who has been a steadfast advocate for Land Rights in NSW for many years, with significant contributions to the broader Aboriginal community.

Ralph Kenke is a design academic and practitioner whose research and teaching intersect graphic design, interface, and computational photography, with a focus on experimental methods and collaborative outcomes across digital and physical environments.

Dr Martin K. Koszolko is a Polish-Australian composer, electronic music producer, researcher, and audiovisual artist whose work explores mobile music-making, remote collaboration, and experimental sound design.

Vincent Sebastian Labra is a musician and ethnomusicologist whose research explores the role of music and ritual across both non-Western and Western cultural contexts. He specializes in Latin American and Electronic Dance Music styles.

Christopher Lean is a researcher at Macquarie University working on philosophy of the life sciences (biology, ecology, medicine) and ethics (bioethics, environment, technology).

Dr Louisa Magrics is a Newcastle-based artist specialising in large-scale crochet installations and wearable sculptures.

Adam Manning is a Kamilaroi musician, composer, and researcher whose work integrates First Nations rhythms, visual art, and contemporary performance.

Ben Matthews, a Senior Lecturer in Communication and Media at the University of Newcastle and a brand strategist with over 20 years of experience, specialises in emerging technology, entrepreneurship, and bringing creative strategy into STEM innovation.

Dr Stuart McBratney is a filmmaker, composer, and lecturer whose work focuses on character-driven storytelling and resourceful production.

Mario Minichiello is Professor of Design and Creative Arts at Loughborough University, UK.

Dr Kristefan Minski (AU) is an artist, producer, academic, entrepreneur and expert in transdisciplinary (Art-Science) collaboration.

Giselle Penn is a Newcastle based Fibre Artist who utilises her passion for the found and collected item to combine with felted forms in her creative practice.

Niki Schild is a multiform artist and creative arts therapist working in private practice, with specialisation in dance movement therapy.

Andrew Selby is Senior Lecturer in Illustration and Animation at Loughborough University.

Angus Stevens is the CEO and co-founder of Start Beyond, Australia's leading VR & AR immersive learning studio; which was recently awarded by the Australian Financial Review as one of Australia's Top 10 Most Innovative Tech Companies.

Dr Leicha Stewart is a media and communications academic passionate about language and media and how they shape our experience in the world.

Elmar Trefz is a Media Artist & Experience Design Director working and lecturing on the development of novel interactive brand and product experiences.

Dr. Rachael Unicomb is a certified speech-language pathologist, Senior Lecturer, and Program Convenor for the Bachelor of Speech Pathology (Hons) program at the University of Newcastle, with a focus on communication disorders, innovative educational technologies, and bridging research and practice in speech pathology.

Joanne Walters is a certified practicing speech-language pathologist, Lecturer and Practice Education Coordinator for the Speech Pathology program at UON.

www.ingramcontent.com/pod-product-compliance
Lightning Source LLC
Chambersburg PA
CBHW071010140426
42814CB00004BA/178